MODERN ENGLISH PAINTERS
Volume 1: Sickert to Smith

MODERN
ENGLISH PAINTERS

★

SICKERT TO SMITH

by

John Rothenstein

MACDONALD AND JANE'S · LONDON

FOR JASPER RIDLEY
a too late token of gratitude

Copyright © John Rothenstein 1976

First published in 1952

First published in a revised edition
with new preface and biographies
in Great Britain in 1976 by
Macdonald and Jane's Publishers Ltd
Paulton House
8 Shepherdess Walk
London N1 7LW

Printed in Great Britain by
REDWOOD BURN LIMITED
Trowbridge & Esher

ISBN 0 356 08120 6

CONTENTS

LIST OF PLATES

PREFACE TO NEW EDITION

WHEN I was invited by Macdonald and Jane's to prepare for republication the first two volumes of this series of three, namely *Sickert to Smith* and *Lewis to Moore*, I found myself in a dilemma. Should I revise them, bring up to date my accounts of those still living, and embody some of the results of the detailed research subsequently carried out on others? Or should these volumes be left as 'period pieces', as expressions of how, in 1952 and 1956, the painters concerned—with a few exceptions—known, some intimately and others superficially, to me, were regarded by me at the time when they were written?

The former course was tempting. Were I to rewrite the first two volumes of *Modern English Painters*, I would consider excluding one of my subjects and replacing him by several others, such as Lamb and Bomberg. At the risk of causing annoyance to any possible Irish readers, I would include that greatest and most profoundly Irish of painters, Jack Yeats. He was born and educated in England, where for thirty-nine years he mainly worked and made his home, and for more than half a century was a British subject, all of which served however to intensify his response to the particular beauties of Ireland, as well as to her history and her political aspirations. Likewise Kokoschka, who became a British subject in 1947 and for whom the Thames provided the themes for several of his finest works, is an artist I would have liked to have included in my series.

In spite of these temptations I have decided that any introduction of 'hindsight' would destroy such consistency of judgement as these two volumes may express. I have, accordingly, left them in their original form, but have brought up to date the brief biographies with which they conclude, adding brief bibliographies and correcting such errors as I could discover in the text.

A number of pictures have changed hands since I wrote and gone into public collections. I have not the resources to trace them all and must content myself with noting only what has come to my knowledge.

With regard to the original second volume, I have made a few corrections of fact to which correspondents have kindly drawn my attention since publication. There are, however, two substantial changes from the first edition. A paragraph in my chapter on Wyndham Lewis has been rewritten. In this paragraph I had characterized some of the activities of some members of the Bloomsbury circle in terms that now seem to me to be in one respect misleading and in another too categorical in view of the nature of the evidence. Misleading, because in a book in which there were few, if any, moral judgements, such judgements in connection with one set of people took on an obtrusive emphasis, and misleadingly suggested that this group was uniquely or quite especially vindictive. Too categorical, in that the evidence for the view that I then set down is not primarily documentary, but what painters have themselves described to me as being the effect that Bloomsbury activities had on their lives. The evidence, then, is what has been said by men who seriously and consistently believed that their careers were adversely affected by these activities; it is convergent but, of course, its reliability turns largely on the credibility of the witnesses. Since, however, many of these witnesses were reluctant to be quoted or named, it has seemed to me to be more equitable to confine myself to the recording of what these painters were seriously convinced was the case, without any categorical comment of my own about whether it was or was not the case. Secondly, in the chapter on William Roberts, I have taken account of the version of the facts published by the artist in a pamphlet (1957) entitled *A Reply to my Biographer Sir John Rothenstein*.

I had two motives for writing these studies. First, in spite of the fact that there is, almost inevitably, much about his subjects that a contemporary is unlikely to know, as well as facts which it would be, for one reason or another, unkind or imprudent to disclose, it sometimes happens that a friend or an acquaintance—even of friends or acquaintances of his subject—may record something which, however trivial it seems, may prove of some value later on to the author of a fuller study. Secondly, that I am convinced that British painters of the past century and—with one exception sculptors—are undervalued both abroad and even at home. The exception, of course, is Henry Moore. In Los Angeles in 1973 a large exhibition of his work was held, and, happening to be in

California at the time, it was evident to me that the surprise expressed in one of the newspapers that an artist of such eminence 'should come from Britain' seemed to be fairly widely shared.

The succession of French painters of genius from David and Delacroix to Rouault, the emergence, in Rodin, of the greatest sculptor since Michelangelo, has given French critics and officialdom the opportunity, which they have been quick to seize and tenacious to exploit, to maintain that where the visual arts were concerned there was nothing of consequence being created outside France; foreign-born artists such as Van Gogh and Picasso, provided that they settled there, formed part of the galaxy. (Brought up among artists as I was I would be ashamed to confess how old I was before I had heard of Munch or Ensor.)

In the United States until the 'forties the American painters most widely admired were those who had won high reputations in Europe, such as Mary Cassatt, Whistler and Sargent. But as a consequence of the Second World War, which drove American artists and collectors back from Europe, many European artists sought refuge, permanent or temporary, in America. This combined with her emergence as a major world power both to stimulate the arts and to foster an unprecedented pride in the achievements of American artists. American whole-heartedness has led at times to an overestimation of American artistic achievement—considerable as it is— previously ignored or even denigrated. I have related elsewhere how, as an assistant professor in Kentucky in the late 'twenties, having 'discovered' Eakins and Ryder, I proceeded to lecture on them with enthusiasm but was petitioned in writing by my students 'to lecture on *artists*, not *Americans*' and how, when working in Pittsburgh I was offered as a gift (which I declined) one of the outstanding American self-portraits of the time, that of John Kane (now in the Museum of Modern Art, New York) 'because', the artist said, 'nobody else has ever liked it so much'.

From the 'forties the situation was transformed, especially by the formation of the New York School, a group of artists marked by energy and conviction, exhilarated by a sense of 'making a new start'. The group contained several painters of outstanding talent. The work of Jackson Pollock, in the last few years of a life prematurely and tragically cut short, was original and majestic. But that of certain other members, had they not been associated with a group that was for a time the cynosure of the eyes of the art world, not only of the United States but also of Europe, would have been unlikely to have attracted attention and will I believe very shortly be forgotten. Yet Irving Sandler, a responsible scholar, subtitled his book on the New York School, published in 1970, long after its dissolution, *The American Triumph*.

Britain produced during the later nineteenth century nothing comparable to the unbroken succession of masters that made France the unrivalled focus of the world of painting. But Britain was neither the heir to a century and more of achievement, both dazzling and continuous, nor, like the United States, did she enjoy a sudden sense of self-discovery, of pride in the recognition, both at home and abroad, of what American painters were accomplishing—not painters like Whistler, (who worked mostly in London and who had once even denied, on oath, his American birth), Mary Cassatt (who worked mostly in France) or Sargent (who was born in Italy and worked mostly in England)—but painters, even those foreign-born, who wholly identified themselves with the United States. With Britain, the situation is entirely different. She is a country that has given birth to great masters, but failed to produce successors comparable to Turner and Constable—whose anticipation of significant elements in later painting is generally admitted. Yet she has continued to produce painters who enjoy international respect. Lacking both France's wonderful century and America's exhilarating decade, British art (with very few exceptions) has suffered relative neglect abroad, in spite of the efforts of the British Council, and even by British critics who in their treatment of the art of other countries have shown themselves perceptive and scholarly.

It was this situation, involving, as it seems to me, the unjust neglect and even denigration of modern English painters that prompted me to write about them. It is relevant to mention that certain of the subjects have been accorded far wider recognition and more comprehensive treatment since the publication of these volumes.

For such reasons, then, I undertook this series of studies of certain English painters for whose work I feel particular admiration. It does not, of course, pretend to be a history of the last century of

English painting; many painters of high talent have had to be omitted. But those artists treated do, collectively, illustrate at least one
quality that should command respect, namely an exceptional degree
of individuality: no mature work of any one of them could possibly
be mistaken for that of another. This is a characteristic less common
than might be supposed, even in the work of the most illustrious. It
is not always easy, for instance, to distinguish at a glance, between
the Cubist canvases of Braque and Picasso. In retrospect it is almost
always possible to discern 'period' characteristics in common. But
to a contemporary eye the painters discussed in the pages that follow
—even those closest to one another, such as Sickert and Steer,
mutual admirers, friends, exact contemporaries—have little in
common beyond the free brushwork that marked the recoil of
artists of the Impressionist generation from the linear techniques
that characterized neo-classical as well as most popular painting.
But most artists, however independent, show certain characteristics
common to their generation, and not only Sickert and Steer but
to a greater or less degree all the leading members of the New
English Art Club practised a 'painterly' technique until its rejection
by its successors, most militantly by Wyndham Lewis and his
Vorticist associates.

This generalization is true of the painters treated in my first two
volumes, but not, it seems to me, of those in the third, all of them
born in the present century when tradition has virtually collapsed
and painters accordingly emerge as more sharply differentiated
individuals than ever before. A figure such as Hillier, for instance,
whose work looks realistic, even traditional, has had to swim
against diverse and fast-flowing tides to realize his aims.

In view of the increasing prevalence of burglary, I have omitted
private owners' names from the first two volumes as I have from
the third.

JOHN ROTHENSTEIN,
Newington,
1976.

PREFACE

THE seventeen painters who are the subjects of chapters in this book are introduced strictly in the order of their appearance in the world. To insist upon an artist's identity with a group is to compromise his individuality. Groups have a way of dissolving under scrutiny, of proving to be more fortuitous in their composition and more ephemeral than they at first appeared. Unlike the individuals who compose them, they have no hard core. In earlier, less disintegrated periods, there was some meaning in the classification of artists according to the tradition to which they belonged, but in our time the general enfeeblement and even collapse of traditions has made the classification of original artists almost impossible: they exist by virtue of their individual selves alone. The chronological arrangement of the chapters that follow is intended to emphasize the individuality of their subjects by cutting them off from all fortuitous and ephemeral groupings.

My treatment of my various subjects has been deliberately varied. In the cases of painters such as Steer, Tonks, Pryde, Augustus John and my father, who are the subjects of adequate biographies either already available or in preparation, it has been mainly critical, or else directed towards the elucidation of some lesser-known or neglected aspects of their art and personalities. But when my subjects have been artists whose lives and personalities are in danger of being altogether forgotten, such, for example, as Ethel Walker, Gwen John or Gore, I have tried to reconstruct their personalities and to put down the principal landmarks of their lives. How necessary this is in the case of these neglected and vanishing figures may be inferred from the fact that the birth-date even of Augustus John, so far as I am aware, has never been precisely recorded.

I would emphasize, however, that not only, in some cases, do I omit biographical details or even landmarks, and do not always, in my criticism or appreciation of an artist's work, consider it from its beginning to its end. In the chapters on Sickert and on Steer, for example, I have been concerned to discuss their painting rather at those points at which, as it appears to me, it changed direction, and to concentrate my attention on the turnings that it took, and on other features of it that, as it seems to me, have been unduly neglected. The volume of critical and other writing on these two painters is already considerable. My own accounts of them – unlike the other chapters in this book – are in the nature of supplements, or, it may be, of correctives.

I have described them as English rather than British painters because (with the exception of Gwen John) England was their home and it was by the climate of England, intellectual, emotional, physical and social, that they were, all I believe, (with the exception of Pissarro) predominantly formed. Several of them were not English-born, and I have in fact dwelt at some length upon the effects of their place of birth and early environment – French in the case of Pissarro, Irish in that of Orpen and Scottish in that of Pryde. I have often been made aware that Scots at least are apt to draw a firm distinction between Scottish artists who have remained in the country of their birth and those who have settled in England. Only this week came a batch of Press cuttings from Scottish newspapers reporting that the chairman of an Edinburgh art society had stated publicly that the Tate had not on view a single example of work by a Scottish artist.

In writing of living artists, even when referring to their writings, I have taken the liberty of omitting any prefix. It seems to be arbitrary to reserve the honorific suppression of prefix to the illustrious dead.

For information, for permission to reproduce pictures and to quote from letters, for assistance in collecting the necessary photographs, and for help of many kinds, I am so deeply in debt that no full list of my obligations is possible. By gracious permission of Her Majesty Queen Elizabeth the Queen Mother, I have been able to reproduce Steer's *Chepstow Castle*. To the custodians of public collections and to private owners who have allowed me to include reproductions of their pictures I am indebted for their ready and invariable helpfulness. For exceptional help I am indebted to Mrs. Lucien Pissarro, Mme. Fourmaintraux-Winslow, Miss Olivia Walker, Mrs. Gilman, Mr. E. M. O'R. Dickey, Mr. H. L. Wellington, Mr. and Mrs. Augustus John, Mr. Edwin John, Mrs. Spencer Gore, Mr. Frederick Gore, Mrs. Alan Bazell, Mr. and Mrs. Matthew

Smith, Father Vincent Turner, Miss Grace English, Mrs. Silvia Hay, Mr. Norman Reid, Mr. Derek Hudson, Mr. Eric Westbrook, the Matthiesen and Mayor Galleries and Messrs. Arthur Tooth.

Finally, I must record my thanks to Mrs. Geoffrey Pooley, Miss Perdita Craig, Miss Jennifer Howard-Langton, Miss Jane Ryder and Miss Doreen Plunkett-Ernle-Erle-Drax for secretarial assistance of various kinds given in what would otherwise have been their leisure hours.

JOHN ROTHENSTEIN.

Newington.
June 1951.

MODERN ENGLISH PAINTERS

INTRODUCTION

IT is unlikely, it is hardly indeed imaginable, that the twentieth century will be accounted one of the great periods of painting. Yet painting in our time shows certain characteristics of surpassing interest. The waning of traditional authorities has encouraged an unequalled diversity in all the arts – a diversity which has been stimulated by the accessibility of a variety of examples of the arts of every time and place inconceivable in any previous age.

An artist working to-day has to accommodate himself to circumstances unlike any which have previously existed. A few prints after paintings by Michelangelo were sufficient to produce an intense and lasting impression upon the imagination of Blake; and I remember hearing someone describe the delighted agitation of Morris and Burne-Jones when, as undergraduates at Oxford, they happened to see a small coloured reproduction of a painting by Botticelli. How almost infinitely greater are the opportunities of the artist of to-day for acquiring knowledge! With what little effort can a provincial art student gather an impression of the sculpture of, say, the Etruscans or the Minoans, or of the present wall painting of the Mexicans! I am far from being persuaded that the advantage of easy access to the art of other ages and peoples – it can give to the student an unprecedented breadth of critical experience and to the lonely original artist precisely the examples he needs to justify and enrich his own vision – outweighs its disadvantages. Reproductions which in time past would have germinated new movements are now apt to be accepted as a matter of course and regarded with listless eyes. Even the most sensitive cannot respond to more than a relatively few reproductions any more than the most compassionate to more than a relatively few of the atrocious crimes against humanity of the prevalence of which we are aware. Indeed the vast multiplicity of the art forms by which the painter of to-day can hardly avoid being aware disinclines him from the intensive and therefore fruitful exploitation of the possibilities of a limited range of art forms, and tends to overwhelm his imagination and to prevent his opinions from becoming dynamic convictions.

The manner, nevertheless, in which gifted and resourceful painters have responded to a complex of circumstances that is in this and in certain other respects unique in the history of art, and, perhaps, uniquely unpropitious to the creation of great works, provides a subject which one would suppose to be of absorbing interest. In England, at all events, this has not proved to be the case. When we consider the serious character of more than a few of the English painters of our time, the numbers of perceptive writers interested in painting, and the avid and increasing interest of the public in the fine arts, the paucity of substantial writings devoted to the work of these painters is astonishing. Not long ago in one of the consistently intelligent London weekly journals there appeared a review by one of the best-known British art critics of a collection of reproductions of paintings and drawings by Augustus John prefaced by a longish essay by myself. The review ended with the observation that the various points I had made had been more extensively developed in previous books on the same artist. In preparation for writing my own essay I must have read most of what had been written about Augustus John, and was in a position to know that not only had no book upon this artist ever appeared, but how surprisingly little had been written about him. Two or three brief prefaces to slight volumes of reproductions, a handful of articles, none of them exhaustive, scattered references in books of memoirs, an informative entry in a foreign dictionary of artists, these represent approximately the extent – apart of course from innumerable reviews of exhibitions – of the critical writings on Augustus John.

The relative critical neglect of the most celebrated of living Engish artists – a painter whose work carries a strong popular appeal, who is also an eloquent writer and a dramatic personality – gives some measure of the neglect suffered by lesser-known painters, indeed by English painting in general. Of recent years there have been signs of awakening literary interest in this subject. Biographies as readable as they are authoritative have been published on Steer, Sickert and Tonks, and the Penguin Modern Painters are making widely known a number of our most gifted contemporaries.

Year by year, however, I have been expectantly awaiting some treatment of British painting of somewhat wider scope – some work in which the principal figures would be placed in relation to one another, their works compared and subjected to critical investigation. I have waited, so far, in vain, and in the meanwhile the notion of making some slight attempt at something of this kind gradually took hold of me, but it was a notion to which I yielded with reluctance, for I am very conscious of my manifold disqualifications. I lack, first of all, a clear-cut view of the subject. The view of Post-Impressionism adumbrated by Sickert and belligerently developed by Dr. Thomas Bodkin is not one which I find credible. 'The modern cult of Post-Impressionism', Sickert wrote, 'is localized mainly in the pockets of one or two dealers holding large remainders of incompetent work. They have conceived the genial idea that if the values of criticism could only be reversed – if efficiency could only be considered a fault, and incompetence alone sublime – a roaring and easy trade could be driven. Sweating would certainly become easier with a Post-Impressionist personnel than with competent hands, since efficient artists are limited in number, whereas Picassos and Matisses would be painted by all the coachmen that the rise of motor traffic has thrown out of employment.'[1]

However effective the machinations of dealers and other interested persons – if they have succeeded, that is to say, in suborning this or that influential critic, in securing the acceptance, or indeed the apotheosis, of this or that spurious artist – there still remains, in the Post-Impressionist movement and in its more recent derivatives, a consistency of vision and a logical coherence of doctrine which, even were I unimpressed by the painting and sculpture in which they are actually made manifest, would preclude my regarding them as other than spontaneous, even, perhaps, as historically inevitable developments.

Nor, on the other hand, can I fully accept the contrary view implicit in the critical works of Mr. Herbert Read. This writer, more interested, perhaps, in the philosophical ideas which may be supposed to underlie works of art than in the aesthetic or representational content of works of art themselves, has treated the principal revolutionary artistic movements of our time with a serious objectivity. But Mr. Read's pages, judicious though they are,

[1] 'The Old Ladies of Etchingneedle Street,' *The English Review*, January 1912.

unmistakably convey the impression that there is an inherent superiority in revolutionary art and that representational art is a curious
survival, condemned by its very nature to sterility and hardly worthy
therefore of the attention of the critic. For me, a canon of criticism
according to which, say, Hans Arp is accounted a figure of greater
significance than, say, Stanley Spencer, is one which takes inadequate
account of the evidence of one's eyes.

For Sickert the more 'advanced' schools of art were 'the biggest
racket of the century', for Mr. Read they are the whole of art now.
For me, as for Sickert, the ramp is a reality: I have seen it in action
at close quarters, but it does not seem to me nearly so influential
as it did to him. For me, as for Mr. Read, the advanced movements are the chief focus of interest, and they have in general
resulted from the activities of the most vigorous and original
personalities; but the wind bloweth where it listeth, and genius
shows itself in representational as well as abstract form.

I cannot therefore envisage the twentieth century either as a
period of retrogression or of progress, still less of stability. I am
mainly conscious of a complex interplay of innumerable personalities; of the action upon these personalities of numerous and
various forces – economic necessity, fashion, the momentum of
traditional aesthetic movements, social change, patronage, psychological and archaeological discovery and so forth – forces which
neutralize each other often and are, for the time being, incalculable
in their effects. With the passage of time much of what presents
itself to our eyes as confused will insensibly assume a settled
pattern; then there will be written a history of this period
accurate in perspective and secure in its critical judgements. But
I am not at all certain that the historian of that distant time who
looks back with justified condescension upon ours may not
perhaps envy a little the historian, however ludicrous his errors,
to whom the artists who are the common objects of their study
were familiar figures, known either directly or through their
friends. Therefore it seems to me that there is an obligation upon
those to whom has fallen the privilege of knowing artists, to place
on record something about their personalities and their opinions.
(Even if, at certain points, the portraits, like those in 'Modern
Painters', as Ruskin noted in the margin of his own copy, are

'drawn mild because . . . men are living'.) For the memory of these fades away with a pathetic swiftness. Some months ago an acquaintance told me she was engaged upon a study of Innes. This painter died only thirty-eight years ago, yet with what labour will the materials for her study be assembled!

But of what use is the study of an artist's personality? There are many critics who answer this question with an emphatic 'None whatever. The work of art transcends the artist; all that need be known of him can be learnt from the study of his work.'

It is a truism that we can be deeply moved by a work of art of whose creator we are entirely ignorant, as also indeed by works of art produced by societies that have vanished without other trace. But are we not moved yet more deeply by the works of art which we are able to see in relation to the personalities of the artists who made them, or against the background of the society from which they came? It is my conviction that we are, and that the more we know about both the artist and his subject the fuller is likely to be our comprehension of the work of art. It is difficult to think of any fact about an artist, any circumstance of his life, that may not have its effect upon his work. The idea that a painting or any other work of art can in fact transcend its creator is one which is tenable only on the assumption that the creative capacity of the artist is enhanced by a form of 'inspiration' derived from some source outside himself. Until we have some knowledge of the nature of such extraneous assistance it is reasonable to assume that the artist possesses within himself the power of giving visible form to his conceptions. If this assumption is well founded, in what sense can a work of art, which is the expression of a part of a human personality, be said to transcend the whole? For me, therefore, the artist is, in a sense, more not less important than any-thing he creates, which is not to say that the work of art may not be more comprehensible and more attractive than the man. (I remember, years ago, someone saying to my father, after meeting A. E. Housman, 'so far from writing "A Shropshire Lad" I shouldn't have thought him capable of reading it'.) Nor do I overlook the possibility of an artist's having an imaginative comprehension of certain qualities, magnanimity, for example, or singleness of purpose, which may enable him to realize them in his art but not in his conduct ; yet comprehension forms, nevertheless, an element in his own personality. In any case, the greater our knowledge of a personality, the better able we are to understand how apparently inconsistent and even irreconcilable elements form parts of a whole which can, roughly speaking, be considered one whole. And so it comes about that, with my doubts upon fundamental aesthetic problems unresolved (doubting, even, whether aesthetics, in the sense of a comprehensive system by which the value of a work of art may be judged, has any validity) and my ignorance of many important and relevant matters, I am decided to try to give some impression of certain of the painters who have been at work in England during my lifetime. It has come suddenly upon me, with a sense of shock, that Time's Winged Chariot is indeed hurrying near. That I am forty-seven years old; and that is to be full of years. Ten years ago I had occasion to reply to a girl who said that she believed I knew her parents, that this was the case, and that I knew her great-grand-mother. This great-grandmother was Lady Burne-Jones, but my artistic memories extend – tenuously it is true – still farther back than this, for I can remember, as a child, spending an afternoon with an original member of the Pre-Raphaelite Brotherhood, William Michael Rossetti. I still plainly see the darkened room, with blinds half-drawn, and, reclining upon a couch, an old man with a long grey beard and a sallow complexion, wearing a black alpaca cap, whose owl-like eyes, with dark pouches beneath, looked momentarily startled at our entrance. And I still see his relatives grouped solicitously about him and I hear my mother's voice saying: 'Dear Mr. Rossetti, pray don't get up.' The couch, which was large and of uncommon design, made an impression on me which I was unaware of having received. One morning during the flying-bomb attack on London, Mrs. William Michael Rossetti's daughter telephoned to me at the Tate to tell me that the Rossetti's house had been badly damaged and the family possessions, including Pre-Raphaelite pictures, were exposed to looters and the elements, and to ask whether I would take charge of them. 'And I'd be so grateful', she added, 'if you would take into your care also the couch on which Shelley's body was placed when it was taken from the sea.' Within a few hours the precious pictures arrived; also the couch. I instantly recognized it as that upon which, nearly forty years before, I had seen Dante Gabriel Rossetti's brother reclining. And I have had opportunities of coming in contact with a number of English painters who have been active during my lifetime, or of hearing first-hand accounts of their characters and ideas and aspects of their lives.

The exceptional complexity, if not the confusion, of the painting of our age, as it offers itself to my contemplation, will be, in one respect at least, radically simplified in the pages which follow. There are in Great Britain to-day practitioners of the fine arts to the number of about twenty thousand. Of these the merest handful will be noticed at length. It is relevant, perhaps, to say a few words about the principle upon which the choice will be made. There exist critics who claim to base their judgements upon consciously held critical canons. They may, for all I know, in fact so form their judgements, but I myself can hardly conceive of a mental process of such a nature. Indeed there is only one way in which I can conceive of judging a work of art, and that is the same as that which the greater part of mankind employs in judging their fellow-men: namely, instinct refined and sharpened and deepened not by personal experience alone but by those standards, created for us by experience through successive generations, which guide us even when we are hardly conscious of our inevitable appeal to their authority. We respond spontaneously to a fine work of art in the same way as we respond to a fine character, and it is only afterwards that we begin the process of analysis in order to try to account for our response. (Equally, of course, we are liable to be deceived by spurious work, as we are by a plausible but meretricious person.) And by the same means – although the process is inevitably more complex and protracted – do we judge the totality of an artist's work, that is to say, the artist himself.

The artists noticed in the chapters which follow have been chosen on account of a series of just such intuitive preferences – preferences founded, that is to say, chiefly upon personal response tempered by inherited canons of judgement. These painters, however, who appear to me to have distilled to its finest essence the response of our times to the world which the eye sees – by which I include both the outward and the inward eye – have few pronounced characteristics in common. A critic with a conservative bias might well object that they were almost all associated, at one time or another, with some innovating movement. That is true, for there does seem to exist some correspondence between inspired art and revolutionary art. Indeed the assumption that there is some such correspondence underlies so much current discussion about painting that it might well be suspect. But so far as Post-Renaissance art is concerned, it appears to be well founded. All the modern masters to a more or less marked degree were innovators, and all of them suffered a measure of contumely and neglect on that account. From Delacroix to Cézanne every great painter made his contribution to a revolutionary process, and the more closely we study the period the more completely is the assumption justified, and the more intimately are important painters, formerly regarded as conservative or even reactionary, understood to be implicated with change. The Surrealists, for example, have directed attention to the revolutionary elements in the early work of the Pre-Raphaelites, and Picasso to those in that of David and Ingres. In our own age, indeed, it is an unconscious assumption that the great artist is a man who innovates, who is original. Originality has become a part of the meaning that we assign to the word 'greatness'. It has not always been so. The outlook of Aristotle, for example, was rather that by 'experience' men discover the right proportion, say, or the 'right' way of doing something, or form and harmony that satisfy; and when it is discovered, it is there once and for all. An artist will be himself, no doubt, but only in abiding by 'the laws'. Is not this the assumption behind the practice, too, of classical Greek art – as it is also of, say, Sienese Quattrocento painting? In Post-Renaissance times, however, if not earlier, there has occurred a radical change in this respect. So that now it is a sign of an inferior gift if a man continues to do, however well, what has been done before. That there should seem to be some correspondence between greatness and innovation among the painters of modern Europe – in which change as radical as it is continuous has come to be accepted as an inexorable law of existence – is hardly surprising. The possessor of superior gifts is likely, in our change-loving age, to be indifferent towards continuing, with whatever distinction or success, procedures already current: his powers will predispose him to attempt what has not been attempted before. But this correspondence arises, I believe, from an impulse deeper than this. The great artist demands of his art that it should express the whole man. Therefore, more sensitive than his contemporaries, he is aware of the particular bias to which the art of his own time is subject, which incites him to a discontent – although sometimes a deeply respectful discontent – with the prevailing modes of seeing and which impels him to a conscious and radical reorientation.

Consider, for example, the origin of the discontent which brought about the new and unforeseen changes which may conveniently be taken as the beginnings of the chief contemporary movements, at the very moment when Impressionism appeared to have imposed itself as a great central tradition of Western painting, and to have established a kind of 'norm' of vision. The doctrines which crystallized around Impressionism were at least as lucid and compelling as those associated with Neo-classical art, which had dominated the academies of Europe since the Renaissance. The aims which it proposed were aims which represented the culmination of centuries of sustained effort on the part of a broad succession of European painters to represent the material world in the closest accord with the facts of vision; its exponents could hardly have been a more brilliant company, indeed they included the most considerable painters of their age.

These considerations were such as to attract any young painter into the Impressionist movement, which did in fact attract a mass following, and it ultimately became the acknowledged academic tradition. It was challenged only by a few of the most sensitive and independent painters of a younger generation, who, although they looked upon the great Impressionists with reverence and affection, were intuitively conscious of a certain incompleteness in their enchanted vision of the world.

The major aim of the Impressionists may be said to have been the representation, on the spot, and with the utmost truth, of a casually selected fragment of visible reality. Impressionist truth was different from that older conception of truth which expressed itself in the accumulation of meticulously rendered detail; it was on the contrary broad and comprehensive. Impressionist painters were not at all concerned with what Sickert used to call 'the august site'. Almost any fragment of the visible world, was, they held, a worthy subject for a picture, but such fragments, arbitrarily come upon, are inevitably without the elaborate balance of subjects either carefully selected or deliberately composed. The Impressionists, therefore, imposed upon their subjects a comprehensive unity of *tone* in the same way as Nature herself invariably binds together in a harmonious envelope of atmosphere any group of objects, however incongruous they may be or however awkwardly disposed. It was through truth of tone that they were able to achieve a new kind of accuracy. The power which they derived from their extraordinary command of tone, of giving unity to any stretch of landscape, to any group of persons, had the effect of inducing painters to visualize the world in terms of its surface and to be forgetful of the rock and bone beneath, to see, that is to say, in terms of colour rather than of form.

In order to set upon their pictures the final stamp of truth, it was logical that these should have the appearance of having been begun and completed at a sitting, under precisely the conditions of weather and light represented in the picture. In northern Europe these notoriously change from hour to hour, and as it is evident that large and elaborately 'finished' pictures could not be painted in such conditions, Impressionist paintings, in order to carry conviction, inevitably have something of the character of sketches.

Preoccupation with colour as distinct from form, and with verisimilitude of so exacting an order, inevitably excluded from Impressionist art many qualities, notably the reflective and monumental qualities which characterized most of the great art of the past. It was the absence of certain of these from the art even of the masters of Impressionism that provoked in the most sensitive and independent among those who were always proud to proclaim themselves their disciples an uneasy awareness of the qualities it lacked. Cézanne's often quoted remark that they must recreate Impressionism according to the art of the museums was an expression, not of a desire to return to a tradition but of a consciousness of how small a part of the whole man was expressed by Impressionist art, of how great a sacrifice had been made to its coruscating perfection. The masters of Cézanne's generation each tried to restore to painting one of the qualities sacrificed: Gauguin an exotic poetry; van Gogh a passionate humanity; Seurat monumental and elaborate

formal harmony, and Cézanne himself the rocky or bony framework
of things. The great Impressionists were themselves aware that, in
their intoxicatingly new approach to the actual appearance of
things, in their close pursuit of a beauty miraculous because it was
not an imagination or a dream but the tangible beauty of all created
things, their art lacked a certain massive reflectiveness. There came
a time when the bathers of Renoir became sculptural in themselves
and monumental in their composition, while Pissarro with a sublime
humbleness made experiments under the guidance of Seurat, one of
his own disciples, in directions clearly repugnant to his own innate
genius, and declared that Impressionism 'should be nothing more
than a theory of observation, without entailing the loss of fantasy,
freedom, grandeur, all that makes for great art'.[1]

Now that more than half a century separates us from the decade
when the principal painters of an oncoming generation were
manifesting their awareness of the failure of the art of their great
Impressionist teachers to express the whole man, it is not
difficult to understand the nature of the readjustment which was
taking place. But from that decade onwards how increasingly
difficult it becomes to perceive any 'norm' of vision or any central
traditions. From decade to decade confusion grows, and what
remains of the central traditions of Cézanne, of Gauguin and of van
Gogh becomes more and more dissolved into individual idiosyn-
crasy.

The heaviest emphasis has been laid by art historians on the
effect of monumental qualities in the painting of Cézanne upon his
followers, the Cubists in particular. We are given to understand
that upon the basis of the most austerely structural elements in his
painting and of his precepts a great 'Classical' art has come into
being. A return to Classicism is how the Post-Cézanne movement is frequently described.

'The idea behind the modern movement in the arts is a return
to the architectural or classical idea'[2] are the first words of Mr.
R. H. Wilenski's closely reasoned introduction to contemporary
art, and his whole book may be considered as an amplification of

[1] Camille Pissarro, 'Letters to his Son Lucien', edited by John Rewald, 1943,
p. 23.

[2] 'The Modern Movement in Art', R. H. Wilenski, 1927, p. ix.

them. This may well have been the Cubists' programme, but it is not easy to gather from the innumerable written accounts how far it was from being realized or how quickly it was abandoned. That certain of the early Cubist paintings had a severely structural character is obvious enough. They sacrificed in a passion of dour joy the shimmering surfaces of things in which Manet and Renoir had delighted, and which Cézanne, for all his preoccupation with structure, had striven so strenuously and sometimes, especially in his water-colours, with such breathtaking success to represent, and they created a new order of form, stark and subtle and, after the first brief 'analytic' phase, bearing scarcely more than a remotely allusive relation to the natural order. Among the best of these highly original and momentous works are a number by Picasso. In the light of this artist's subsequent development and the character of the intoxicating but disintegrating influence he has wielded, the fact is significant. But what have been, in fact, the effects of this group of Cubist paintings; the creations of the apostles of solid construction, of dignified, self-sufficient form? It can hardly be denied that they have been, in the main, disintegrating; that in their shadow has grown up an art as remote as any that could be conceived from the ideal of Cézanne 'to make out of Impressionism something as solid and enduring as the art of the museums'. The contrast between the spate of talk and writing about the rebirth of an architectural painting and of the classical ideal, and the overwhelmingly idiosyncratic character of the painting that was actually produced corresponds to the discrepancy, in the political sphere, between the proclamations, which grew thunderous upon the conclusion of both the World Wars, of international solidarity, and the persistent growth of aggressive nationalism. But whereas, in the larger sphere, the discrepancy between the ideal and the actuality is widely recognized and lamented, in the sphere of the fine arts a discrepancy not less startling is virtually denied, and the continuing chatter about 'architecture' and 'classicism' would lead a student who read about works of art instead of looking at them (a practice almost universal among students) to form radically different conclusions about the character of contemporary painting from those of anybody accustomed to use his eyes. Certain ideas about form implicit in the work of Cézanne and expressed in his rare sayings have gained the widest acceptance

1. WALTER RICHARD SICKERT. *Statue of Duquesne, Dieppe* (*c.* 1900).
Oil, 51½ × 39¾ in. The City Art Gallery, Manchester.

2. WALTER RICHARD SICKERT.
The New Bedford (1906–7).
Oil, 36 × 14 in.
Privately owned.

throughout the western world, but from the two other commanding figures of the Post-Impressionist movement, Gauguin and van
Gogh, also derive ideas, to a certain degree complementary, which
exercise a decisive influence. Upon the art of Germany and Scandinavia the influence of these two has been even more pervasive
than that of Cézanne. Between the ideas of van Gogh and of Gauguin
there are sharp distinctions, but their influence has been somewhat
similar in its effects. Both painters were acutely aware of the ex-
clusion from Impressionism of poetry and of the deeper human
emotions; both, too, made the discovery that the tonal technique
of the Impressionists, perfectly adapted though it was to the creation
of harmonies in colour and light, was too vaporous to lend itself
readily to the lucid expression of the poetic and dramatic emotions
of their own passionate natures. Gradually both therefore abandoned
the realism of the Impressionists and each evolved an art that was
predominantly symbolic.

From the Impressionists they had learnt to dispense with the older
type of formal, closely integrated composition; they early discarded
the tonal system upon which the Impressionists relied to give
cohesion to their pictures. The highly original poetry of Gauguin
and van Gogh was expressed in terms which proved as fascinating
to these artists' younger contemporaries as they were audacious and
novel.

In this expressionistic art the functions of form and colour were
to convey, symbolically yet forcefully, the emotion of the artist.
Expressionism and Cubism, and its later and highly logical development, Abstraction, have played, as already noted, complementary
parts in the history of contemporary painting, the one, essentially
subjective, with its emphasis upon the artist's emotion, the other,
rather more objective, with its emphasis upon the created form.
The one may be said to correspond to the Romantic as the other to
the Classical motive in the earlier art of Europe; certainly Expressionism took most vigorous roots in Scandinavia and the Germanic
countries, where the Romantic tradition had been persistent, and
Abstraction in France and the Latin countries, where the rational
values had always found a wider acceptance.

But just as the Abstract artists failed to fulfil the achievement of
certain of the early Cubists to build upon the foundation of Cézanne

an art of pure form, nobly defined and exact, so did the Expressionists prove unable to express anything beyond a narrow and, it would
seem, a continuously narrowing range of human emotions; with
the greater part of the human drama and of the poetry of life
Expressionist painters were unable or else unwilling to deal. The
Norwegian Edvard Munch showed himself, in a group of early
paintings, pre-eminent among the rare exceptions. There would
seem, in fact, to have occurred early in the period of which I am
writing a catastrophic change which has profoundly affected the
fine arts. The word 'catastrophic' has been applied to this change
both by those who regard it as the rejection of values which have
been long regarded as constituting the foundation of European
culture, and by those for whom such values represent, at the best,
a series of intrinsically undesirable but historically necessary ex-
pedients, at the worst, conventions which served no purpose but
that of confining the creative spirit in the interests of tyranny,
political, religious or academic.

The more closely we read history the more aware do we become
of the strength and intimacy of the relationships by which the fabric
of human society is bound together; the relationship between our
age and another of apparently opposite character, between two
factions, which at first seem irreconcilably opposed. We see, for
instance, how powerfully the forces which produced the Protestant
explosion in the sixteenth century were also active within the Catholic Church; we see how difficult it would be to define with exacti-
tude the issues which divided the North from the South in the War
between the American States. We may therefore take it that the
revolution in the arts which may be said to have begun with Post-
Impressionism in the last decade of the nineteenth century and has
gathered momentum progressively since, may present to the future
art historian an aspect perhaps less radical than it does to us. The
origins of phenomena which appear, even to learned and boldly
speculative art historians, entirely novel, will reveal themselves in
the course of time. '. . . Where, in the immediate ancestry of modern
art', asks Mr. Herbert Read, 'shall we find the forbears of Picasso,
Paul Klee, Max Ernst . . . ?' I suspect that the future art historian will
marvel at our want of perception and at the complacency which
allows us to attribute to our own art an unexampled uniqueness.

It is, however, difficult for someone writing to-day not to share, to a considerable extent, the impression that the characteristic art of our time is, in fact, the product of a catastrophic change. The European tradition of painting owes its cohesion largely to the persistence of two impulses; to represent, as exactly as possible, the visible world, and to evolve the perfect forms of persons and things. These impulses crystallized in what are frequently termed the Realistic and the Classical ideals. Both have asserted themselves throughout the whole history of European art; from the Renaissance to the decline of Impressionism, the development and the intimate interaction of these ideals have been continuous. But towards the end of the last century both began to lose their compelling power for numbers of the most reflective and highly gifted artists. They persisted with reduced vitality, but those who followed them travelled, more and more, along sequestered byways rather than along the high roads. The ultimate causes for the rejection of ideals which had been accepted for so many centuries lie deep in the history of religion, of philosophy, of politics and of several fields of scientific discovery, but certain of the immediate causes are obvious. Their achievement in representing brilliant light gave to the painting of the Impressionists the character of extremity and climax. It seemed that in this, the centuries-long ambition of European artists to represent in something of its fulness the world to which their senses bore witness had been fulfilled; the old excitement in the gradual approach to reality could hardly be experienced so intensely again. But the visible world exercised a diminished attraction over the artists of the Post-Impressionist era on account not solely of their predecessors' close approach to the limits of the possible, but of the doubts which they shared with their fellow-men about the ultimate reality of the world perceptible to the senses. Science has conjured up a world which the senses cannot apprehend, a world in which the stars themselves – to artists and poets for thousands of years the embodiments of an eternal and changeless beauty – have no longer any substantial existence, but are instead hypothetical entities, light rays curving back to the points where once shone suns for millions of years extinct. And the very substances of which the material world is made – even the simplest and most solid among them – are now assumed not to be the stable entities they seem, but on the contrary to be assemblies of whirling particles. But when a man of education rejects the time-honoured 'commonsense' view that things are more or less what they appear to be, it is hardly any longer possible for him to believe that the profoundest truths about the world can be expressed by the representation, however searching, of its deceptive surface. The dissolution of the artist's confidence in the reality of what his eye sees is destructive of both Realist and Classical ideals: for it is equally foolish to represent or to idealize a mirage.

In another age general revulsion against the close representation of the world which the eye sees might have had less 'catastrophic' consequences than it has to-day. (I speak tentatively because the whole history of art records no previous revulsion against realism either so widespread or so deeply felt.) The imaginative treatment of subjects from religion, mythology, or simply from the inward vision might have withdrawn painting beyond the understanding of all but a perceptive few, while preserving a degree of continuity; but the scepticism which has weakened the confidence of modern man in the reality of the world to which his senses bear witness has yet more radically transformed his outlook: it has made him doubtful of its validity. In contemplating the art of past ages we are conscious of how much of it testified to an irrepressible delight in the multitudinous aspects of the world and human society, in its Creator, in the beauty of nature and of man, in the exciting spectacle of the surrounding stream of life, so various and so dramatic as it flowed by. Even the most savage satire was inspired by the sense that mankind was sufficiently precious to be castigated for its own redemption. There would seem to prevail to-day, among artists, little of the sense of majesty of the world and the excitement of the human adventure. What has taken the place of the medieval artist's exalted conception of a God-centred universe in which every man and woman, and every created thing, had its value and its function? Or the Renaissance artist's intoxicating confidence that man, by the intense cultivation of his understanding, his inventiveness, his daring and all his faculties, might himself become godlike? Nothing, except an intense preoccupation with his separate and individual self. This individualism, historically, may be regarded as the culmination of the worship of the spirit of liberty. But now, in Western

Europe and America, there are no more Bastilles to storm. For the artist there is now but one criterion: his own satisfaction.

The history of modern art is constantly depicted in terms of a perpetual struggle against 'convention'. It is true that in the arts as in other spheres of man's activity there is a continuous tendency for the disciples of an audacious innovator to reduce his practice to a system of rules more or less tightly formulated, and in so doing to obscure the true significance of his achievement. Thus they distort something which was a heightening of human perception into a complex of rules which at best alienates those perceptive and independent natures by whom the audacious innovator would have most desired to be understood. The activities of the academic mind, by transforming that which was thrilling and elusive into that which is dull and docketed, is a continual source of misunderstanding. So much is plain; but of recent years it has been habitual to exaggerate the importance of the mischief which pedants have done to painting. Among the forces which form the natures of great artists and bring about the flowering or the decline of traditions these pedants have a minor place.

Time and again we see the man of genius in conflict with the academician, but the activities of the framer of conventions are not for this reason devoid of positive value. If his effect is frequently to provoke the man of genius by repressing him, he plays a necessary part in the education of less gifted men: he makes available to them, in a readily assimilable form, not only the accumulated technical experience of his predecessors but even something of their vision. In those rare ages when many masters are at work they themselves will diffuse directly their fertilizing influence, but in those far commoner ages when there are few or none, the function of the academician in preserving, systematizing and handing on the heritage of the past – even if in a desiccated form – is a useful one. Even though the academician's gaze is directed towards the past and his bias towards the form and away from the spirit, what, without him, would be the plight of the secondary artist, whose nature does not demand that he should have that immediate contact, intuitive or intellectual, with first causes which is one of the distinguishing necessities of genius? A distinctive, closely-knit tradition is the most favourable seed-bed of the secondary artist, just as a

C

profusion of these would seem to create the most favourable conditions for the emergence of genius. Thus the academician, invaluable to the secondary artist, makes his contribution, however pedestrian, however indirect, to the formation of the master also.

According to the contemporary history of art, 'convention' is the great positive evil against which all good artists have had to contend – a kind of artistic fascism – and new movements are explained by the necessity for 'breaking away from' or 'reacting against' such and such a 'convention'. As though the prime motive of those dedicated to one of the most exalted and most exacting of man's vocations was a bicker with obsolescent regulations! The fundamental causes for the new directions which the arts are forever taking under the hands of the masters are outside the scope of this book (although I have touched upon what I think is the most important of these, namely, the masters' preternatural sensibility to the respects in which the art of their times fails to express the whole man), but if there is one factor which plays no part in the formation of contemporary art it is the 'convention'. For 'convention', comparable to the older, clearly formulated, passionately upheld complexes of rules, can hardly be said to exist any longer. Some contemporary painters and a larger number of their advocates continue to behave as though there were still reactionary and, above all, realistic formulas against which they were under an obligation to struggle. But what restrictions are there upon the absolute liberty of the artist to please himself? The 'Old Bolsheviks' of the Cubist Revolution and their younger followers decline to recognize that they are tilting at a mirage, and aggressively asserting rights which for years nobody has dreamed of challenging. They do not tell us against what they are remaining in this state of perpetual belligerence. The truth is that the revolutionary impulse has largely expended itself, and for the very reason that there are no longer any objects for revolutions; all doors are open. What remains to be seen is whether art can, in fact, flourish without laws. 'Art', declared Ozenfant, 'is structure, and every construction has its laws.' The question is whether the abolition of every law but the satisfaction of the artist is not vitiating those deeper impulses necessary to the creation of great works of art. Modern painters have easy access to the knowledge of all traditions but the powerful support of none.

I say 'powerful support' because many, indeed perhaps all traditions, in attenuated forms, still persist. The present situation in this regard is thus concisely described by Mr. Read:

> . . . we have in some way telescoped our past development and the human spirit, which in the past has expressed itself, or some pre-dominant aspect of itself, diversely at different times, now expresses the same diversity, without any stress on any particular aspect, at one and the same time. I might refer, as a modest illustration of my mean-ing, to those metal cups made of a series of what mathematicians presumably call conic segments which when pressed together, collapse into concentric rings – what was once continuous and spread over several sections of space becomes discontinuous within one section of space.[1]

Mr. Read sensibly disclaims the implication that the human spirit is more diverse to-day than at any other time, but it is true that the very absence of authoritative traditions and of imposed discipline of any kind allows for a more untrammelled expression by the artist of his own personality than at any previous time. Prior to the nineteenth century most art served a religious or a social purpose which demanded some subordination of the artist's personality; whereas for the artist of to-day the expression of himself has become his sole, or at all events his overriding preoccupation. And this preoccupation was shared no less by the Cubists and other Abstract artists, whose work at first glance has an objective look, than by the Expressionists, whose work is frankly personal. 'Cubism differs from the old schools of painting', said Guillaume Apollinaire, 'in that it aims not at an art of imitation, but at an art of conception, which tends to rise to the height of creation.' But in what sense can the concepts and the creations of Cubists be said to be less exclusively the products of the artist's mind than the 'literary' concepts of Expressionists? Both are manifestations of the forthright and un-inhibited expression of personality which is the distinguishing characteristic of the art of our time. In the past artists have been inspired by exalted subjects, most of all by religious subjects, and their talents tempered and directed by tradition, but the artists of our own day rely upon neither of these external sources of strength: they are at once their own subjects and their own teachers. Their art

[1] 'Art Now', revised edn., 1936, p. 60.

therefore, in comparison with that of certain periods of the past, conspicuously lacks the sustained dynamic power which can result from the combination of an intrinsically inspiring subject and a comprehensive discipline; it resembles a river which has overflowed its banks. Paradoxically the perfect liberty of which so many artists have dreamed, now achieved, makes it the more difficult to realize the great work of art. But if in our own time the great work of art, rare in the most propitious circumstances, is exceptionally rare, that does not mean that our own highly personal and, in consequence, infinitely various art has not qualities which are precious and unique. We have become so accustomed to regard art as primarily the expression of personality and as being practised for the satisfaction of the artist himself, that we are apt to forget how recently in the history of the world such an art came into existence. Almost all medieval art exhibits an anonymous and collective character; only with the early Renaissance did the artist begin to emerge as a highly differentiated individual, and it was not until the middle of the nineteenth century that the conception of personal and self-sufficient art lately so widely accepted began to prevail. And we have no assurance that it is certain, or even likely, to continue to prevail even in Western Europe and the Americas. Within the last thirty years it ceased to be accepted by the rulers of three great States, Russia, Germany and Italy, and in their dependencies. In all these the arts were transformed overnight into instruments of political propaganda and education and could no longer be the unforced expression of the individual human spirit, and their criterion became, therefore, social utility instead of intrinsic worth. And the time may come sooner than we expect when the kind of art which, to one living in Western Europe or the Americas, is now taken for granted, may have come to an end. There have been in the past many tyrannies and many states where the rulers have employed artists for purposes which allowed only the narrowest scope for the expression of their personalities, yet art as an expression of human personality has always survived and generally flourished. Those who argue from the example of the past that this kind of art can still be pursued in the totalitarian state of the twentieth century fail to distinguish the radical difference between these and the older authoritarian states in which even subversive art was sometimes tolerated, and the consequences of this difference for the artist. This difference arises from the fact that modern totalitarian states have come into existence at a time when democracy has already established itself over large areas of the world and become – in spite of the effeteness of many democratically elected governments – an active and formidable principle. The governments of such states, which by their very nature cannot allow their authority to be challenged, even implicitly, are therefore compelled to control with unexampled vigilance and severity the popular opinion which they have displaced as the most powerful element in politics. There is no manifestation of opinion, however insignificant, which is hostile, or even indifferent, to these régimes which they can safely tolerate. Art, with its unique power over the mind, must be subject to the most rigorous control, or rather, to the most precise direction. To the modern absolutism personal art is at the best an irrelevant display of personal egotism, at the worst the germ of an alternative attitude towards life, and as such a subversive activity.

Let us therefore remember in considering the art of our own day that it is the most extreme expression of the Humanist tradition, which has always set a high value upon personality. Let us remember, too, that it may prove to be its last expression. Of recent years in particular there has been a tendency – an anticipation, perhaps, of what would seem to be the collectivist epochs ahead of us – to deplore Humanism's rejection of the anonymity that marked, during the Middle Ages, so many of man's activities. We may live to see the subordination of the individual to a totalitarian state and his merging in the anonymous mass.

At the beginning of this chapter I voiced my doubt whether the present would ever be counted among the great ages of painting, but its extreme expression of one aspect of Humanism, its astonishing variety and the unprecedented conditions with which its artists have had to come to terms give it, nevertheless, an extraordinary character. In this general interest in the art of our time many share, but very few indeed would seem to attach serious importance to the contribution of our own country. As I write I have before me a number of notices on the Tate Gallery exhibition of the last fifty years of British Painting which was shown at Millbank in 1946 after a tour of the principal capital cities of Europe. The Press, I think without exception, praised the representative character of the selection; but certain of the most responsible papers referred in cool or else frankly disparaging terms to the school of painting it represented. 'What are its characteristics?' asked 'The New Statesman and Nation'[1] and thus answered the question. 'Rarely original, even more rarely powerful, it is usually sensitive especially in colour.' The impression received by 'The Spectator'[2] was one of 'respectable talent, a general level of sensibility without authority. . . . For eyes other than British it is not an impressive period, for we spent most of it in the backwaters of streams already grown stagnant at their source.' Such quotations would seem to be typical not of ignorant but of informed and responsive elements of British public opinion. While nobody would be likely to maintain that during the period with which this book is concerned English painting could compare with French in richness, in perfection or in inventiveness, it must be remembered that the latter derives much of its vitality from forming a part of one of the most inspired movements in all the history of European art. At the beginning of the present century the great Impressionists were alive: with the death of Bonnard in 1946 the last of their disciples departed. And who remains active in France to-day? In my view two figures tower above the crowd, Rouault, the sombre suffering-haunted groping giant, and Picasso (who is not a Frenchman), the prodigiously accomplished and prolific master of all styles and all media; the one a blundering but God-guided sleep-walker, the other very much 'all there', the resourceful master of every situation. To Matisse, gifted though he is with a singing sense of colour, as a designer and as a pure yet engagingly informal draughtsman, and with the nature which so limpidly reflects the temperate gaiety of the French character, I doubt whether posterity will accord so pre-eminent a place as he occupies to-day. There is a flimsiness in the central principle which informs the art of Matisse, which will, I think, grow more apparent in the coming years. These three apart there seem to me to be no painters with serious claim to the title of master. Braque is a grave and beautiful artist whose work projects with a rare and serene distinction a pre-existing vision, but he lacks, quite simply, the magnitude of a master, the magnitude which is not, of course, dependent upon the scale on which an artist

[1] 10 May 1947.   [2] 16 May 1947.

works, and which is, for example, as manifest in a drawing by Rubens or an etching by Goya as in their largest paintings.

Is this commonplace of criticism – hardly less widely accepted here than abroad – that an immeasurable gulf still separates the painting of England from that of France in fact justified? Or is it an inevitable consequence of the dazzling ascendancy of France right up to the immediate past? And of the debt which every English artist of our age – with a single exception to be noticed later – owes to French inspiration in his formative years? I am conscious of the national prejudice, the parochialism, the personal affections that may have gone to the formation of my opinion, but I am conscious also of the obligation to place on record my conviction that no such gulf in fact exists, and that the English school shows no less excellence than the French and considerably more interest. It counts among its members a wide range of mature and highly individual personalities, and, although it cannot, of course, compare in inventiveness with the French School, it has shown a power, not conspicuous elsewhere, of applying the basic discoveries of the most original painters of Continental Europe to the representation of many of the traditional subjects of European art. Wyndham Lewis voiced the permanent disposition of many of his English contemporaries when he wrote, of his own attitude after the First World War:

> The geometrics which had interested me so exclusively before, I now felt were bleak and empty. *They wanted filling.* They were still as much present to my mind as ever, but submerged in the coloured vegetation, the flesh and blood, that is life. . . .

WALTER RICHARD SICKERT
1860–1942

SOME months before the beginning of the year 1900, which I have arbitrarily selected as my point of departure, Walter Richard Sickert left England, and did not return until five years later. Apart from being the senior among the subjects of these studies, Sickert was the most consistently and effectively articulate painter of his generation, who spoke with insight and authority and not on his own behalf alone. By taking him as my first subject (in spite of his initial absence from the main theatre of operations) I shall be enabled the more readily to refer without delay to ideas about painting current among artists. He himself has warned us 'to judge an artist by his works, not by his patter', but if patter is not to be accepted at its face value it is equally not to be ignored. Sickert's own placing of himself was very simple:

> I am [he said] a pupil of Whistler – that is to say, at one remove, of Courbet, and, at two removes, of Corot. About six or seven years ago, under the influence in France of Pissarro, himself a pupil of Corot, aided in England by Lucien Pissarro and by Gore (the latter a pupil of Steer, who in turn learned much from Monet), I have tried to recast my painting entirely and to observe colour in the shadows.[1]

This placing gives an indication of one of the causes of Sickert's authority among English artists: his familiarity with French painting. Since the early days of Impressionism the more independent artists in England had been increasingly aware of the momentous character of French painting and of the stature of Millet, Courbet, Manet, Pissarro, Degas, Renoir and Monet, but only to very few of them was the work or the personalities of these masters familiar. Of those few Sickert was one of the best informed. He went to France in 1883, in order to take Whistler's *Portrait of his Mother* for exhibition at the Salon. 'I have a clear recollection', he has told us, 'of the vision of the little deal case swinging from a crane against the star-lit night and the sleeping houses of the Pollet de Dieppe.'

[1] 'The New Age', 26 May 1910.

41

Although he was only twenty-three years old he was already well prepared to make the most of all he saw and heard in Paris. Oswald Adelbert Sickert, his father (1828–85), was a capable painter and draughtsman, who studied in Paris with Couture – and his father, Johann Jurgen Sickert (1803–64) was also a painter and head of a firm of decorators employed in the Royal Palace of Denmark. (The family was originally Danish, but Sickert's father acquired German nationality as a result of Germany's seizure of Schleswig-Holstein but was subsequently naturalized in England, where he settled in 1868 with his English wife.) Sickert himself was born in Munich on 31 May 1860. The family was harmonious and united, and Sickert therefore eagerly assimilated, instead of reacting against, as might otherwise have been the case, the sober, professional attitude towards the arts of his father and his grandfather. Of his father Sickert declared that he never forgot anything he told him.

At King's College, London, he must have laid the foundations of an excellent education, especially in the classics, for he read Latin and Greek with pleasure throughout his life. After going down he wished to become a painter, but his father warned him against the uncertainties of an artist's career; so he fell back upon his second choice, the stage. For three years he acted, on occasions in Irving's company, but although he took only minor parts his experience in the theatre was not an irrelevant interlude. It confirmed a love of the stage that lasted as long as his life, and, it is reasonable to assume, the histrionic elements in his own temperament. There was a sense in which, for Sickert, the world was always a stage, and he the player of many parts, but I think that Sir Osbert Sitwell is justified in his opinion that none of these was without a genuine foundation in his own character. In 1881 he became a student of the Slade School, under Alphonse Legros, but a chance meeting with Whistler caused him to leave the well-trodden path. 'You've wasted your money, Walter', he jibed; 'there's no use wasting your time too,' and Sickert went off to help Whistler print his etchings. By forsaking Gower Street for Tite Street, Sickert entered a new world, for in the studio of Whistler he found himself remote from the Slade and near to the mainstream of European painting. The at first almost daily association with Whistler was one of the two most important relationships of Sickert's life. For a time even his sceptical spirit was captivated by the Master, the capricious, scintillating dandy who held sway over courtiers whose subservience was as unexceptionable, if not, perhaps, as demonstrative, as that of the courtiers of Xerxes. Sickert once wished to introduce D. S. MacColl to him, and identified him as the author of an article in 'The Saturday Review' entitled 'Hail, Master!' 'That's all very well, "Hail, Master!" But he writes about Other People, *Other People*, Walter!' 'Of course', Sickert added, 'with Whistler there was always a twinkle.' In time the friendship waned. In 1897 Whistler, giving evidence against him in a lawsuit, described him as 'an insignificant and irresponsible person'. For a man of Sickert's independence, friendship on the terms which Whistler demanded could not have been of long duration, but there existed a still more active cause of disruption: Sickert's admiration for the Master became more and more tempered with criticism, until at last Whistler's art came pre-eminently to stand for some of the weaknesses which Sickert most abhorred. In 1882, he has told us, he began a campaign in the Press on the Master's behalf which he did not wind up until ten years later. Subsequent references to Whistler contain searching criticism; at last there appeared an article entitled 'Abjuro'[1] which was, in his own words, 'an explicit repudiation of Whistler and his teaching'. It is not, however, in 'Abjuro' that Sickert gives most explicitly his reasons for his repudiation. When the Pennells' 'The Life of J. McN. Whistler' appeared, Sickert reviewed it at length.[2] Here he gave his most considered estimate of his master. Insisting that Whistler's art is dominated by his taste he developed the theme that 'Taste is the death of a painter'. 'An artist', he contended, 'has all his work cut out for him, observing and recording. His poetry is in the interpretation of ready-made life. He has no business to have time for preferences.' In a later article[3] he indicted Whistler of a yet more radical defect. After a tribute to 'the exquisite oneness that gives his work such a rare and beautiful distinction' which he obtained by covering the whole picture at one 'wet', he proceeds to show how heavy a price Whistler had to pay for this quality. 'The thinness of the paint resulted in a fatal lowering of tone . . . and necessitated

---

[1] 'The Art News', 3 February 1910.
[2] 'The Fortnightly Review', December 1908.
[3] 'Where Paul and I Differ', *The Art News*, 10 February 1910.

an excessive simplification of both subject and background.' Sickert
then clinched his argument with an observation of the rarest insight.
'*Mastery*' (he had denied that in the proper sense Whistler was a
master), '*Mastery, on the contrary, is avid of complications*, and shows
itself in subordinating, in arranging, in digesting any and every
complication.' In a fourth article,[1] written twenty-five years after
Whistler's death, he put the whole of this indictment into one simple
sentence. 'Whistler accepted', he said, 'why, I have never understood,
the very limited and subaltern position of a *prima* painter.'

> [His] paintings were not what Degas used to call *amenées*', he continued,
> 'that is to say, brought about by conscious stages, each so planned as
> to form a steady progression to a foreseen end. They were not begun,
> continued and ended. They were a series of superimpositions of the
> same operation. . . .

I have quoted Sickert's criticisms of Whistler at some length for
two reasons. Whistler and all that he stood for may be taken as
Sickert's point of departure, and his progressive repudiation bears
a precise relation to his own development. This repudiation,
thoroughgoing though it was, was not absolute. There were qualities
in Whistler which he continued to revere and which moved him to
pay him this ardent yet discerning tribute:

> I imagine that, with time, it will be seen that Whistler expressed the
> essence of his art in his little panels – pochades, it is true, in measure-
> ment, but masterpieces of classic painting in importance. . . . The
> relation of and keeping of the tone is marvellous in its severe restriction.
> It is this that is strong painting. No sign of effort with immense result.
> He will give you in a space nine inches by four an angry sea, piled up
> and running in, as no painter ever did before. The extraordinary beauty
> and truth of the relative colours, and the exquisite precision of the
> spaces, have compelled infinity and movement into an architectural
> formula of eternal beauty. . . . It was the admirable preliminary order
> in his mind, the perfect peace at which his art was with itself, that
> enabled him to bring down quarry which, to anyone else, would have
> seemed intangible and altogether elusive.[2]

Nor was it only Sickert's admiration that outlasted his friendship
with Whistler; his personal devotion survived it also.

[1] 'The Daily Telegraph', 25 April 1925.
[2] 'Review of Life of J. McN. Whistler', by J. and E. R. Pennell, *The Fortnightly Review*, December 1908.

The diary of the painter's mother [he wrote] depicts the child the same as the man I knew; sunny, courageous, handsome, soigné; entertaining, serviable, gracious, good-natured, easy-going. A charmeur and a dandy, with a passion for work. A heart that was ever lighted up by its courage and genius. . . . If, as it seems to me, humanity is composed of but two categories, the invalids and the nurses, Whistler was certainly one of the nurses.[1]

If Whistler was Sickert's point of departure, Degas, for the greater part of his life was his ideal. 'The greatest painter of the age' is how, in a personal account, he described him.[2] This account is remarkable in several respects, in none more than for being a portrait entirely credible and entirely delightful, yet painted without a single shadow. I mean that for Sickert Degas was a being without defects. I am far from having the good fortune to have read everything that Sickert has written or even all his published writings, but I cannot recall a single instance of adverse criticism of Degas. He did not regard him, I take it, as of the stature of Turner or of Millet but, within narrower limits, as the perfect artist. Sickert reverenced Degas for his achievements, but there was one question of method over which he was passionately convinced, and it is impossible to read his writings without coming upon frequent references to it, just as it occurred frequently in his conversation. This was the question whether large pictures of more or less complex subjects should be painted on the spot, direct from life, or in the studio from preliminary studies or photographs. His opinion was, I think, first expounded at length (and with admirable pungency) in a book published in 1892 on Bastien-Lepage and Marie Bashkirstev. This has long seemed to me to be among the best of Sickert's writings, and I was surprised to find it omitted from Sir Osbert Sitwell's judicious selection.[3]

To begin with, [he said] it was thought to be meritorious . . . for the painter to take a large canvas out into the fields to execute his final picture in hourly tête-à-tête with nature. This practice at once limits your possible choice of subject. The sun moves too quickly, you find that grey weather is more possible, and end by never working in any other. Grouping with any approach to naturalness is found to be impossible. You find you had better confine your composition to a single figure . . . that the single figure had better be in repose. Even then

[1] 'The Burlington Magazine', December 1917.   [2] Op. cit.
[3] 'A Free House', 1947.

your picture necessarily becomes a portrait of a model posing by the hour . . . your subject is a real peasant in his own natural surroundings, and not a model from Hatton Garden, but what is he doing? He is posing for a picture as best he can and he looks it. That woman stooping to put potatoes into a sack will never rise again. The potatoes, portraits every one, will never drop into the sack. . . .

With these melancholy procedures Sickert contrasted those of Millet, based upon the conviction that, in the master's own words, 'Le nature ne pose pas'. 'Millet knew that if figures in movement were to be painted so as to be convincing, it must be by a process of cumulative observation . . . he observed and observed again . . . and when he held his picture he knew it, and the execution was the singing of a song learned by heart, and not the painful performance in public of a meritorious feat of sight-reading. . . .' 'To demand more than one sitting for a portrait is sheer sadism' is a saying that recurred in both his writings and his conversation. That the method of Millet and of the old masters should also be in this regard the method of Degas was a source of constant satisfaction to Sickert. There was no conviction that he held more fiercely than that there was no fundamental difference between the old art and the new, and that the history of art was therefore a history of additions, not of revolutions. 'There is no new art', he wrote. 'There are no new methods. . . . There can no more be a new art . . . than there can be a new arithmetic . . . or a new morality.'[1] Not even the painter who carried a large canvas into a field so much provoked him as critics who treated the new as though it superseded the old.

You are not to consider [he admonished them] that every new and personal beauty in art abrogates past achievements as an Act of Parliament does preceding ones. You are to consider these beauties, these innovations, as additions to an existing family. How barbarous you would seem if you were unable to bestow your admiration and affection on a fascinating child in the nursery without at once finding yourselves compelled to rush downstairs and cut its mother's throat, and stifle its grandmother. These ladies may still have their uses.

Sickert's sympathies towards artists who attempted new themes was readily kindled, but he remained steadfast in the conviction that the

[1] 'The International Society', *The English Review*, May 1912.

classic or academic method constituted the only durable framework.

Oddly enough, Degas, whom Sickert venerated, probably influenced him less than the master whom he abjured. In particular,
the low tones which Whistler taught him to use continued to distinguish his painting until after 1903, but his ready acceptance of the
accidental elements in life as subjects for painting, no less than his
preference for subjects drawn from popular life, it may reasonably
be assumed that he derived from Degas.

During the years 1899-1905 when Sickert, as already noted, was
living abroad, he sent a number of his best pictures to the New
English Art Club, which, as he observed, set the standard for painting in England. The Club was founded in 1886, in opposition to the
Royal Academy, by artists who had studied in Paris, for the purpose
of establishing a platform for realistic painting. Its earliest members
worked chiefly under Barbizon influence, but since about 1889 the
more enterprising among them had applied a colour vision derived
from the Impressionists to themes in general already accepted in
England. The preference of leading members, notably Sickert
himself, for 'low-life', no less than that of others, notably Conder
and Beardsley, for exotic and 'decadent' subjects outraged academic
opinion. Not since the earliest days of the Royal Academy had so
preponderant a part of the keenest and ablest talents of England been
gathered in a single institution, and the resulting interaction of one
temperament upon another issued in a widely diffused spirit of
audacity. Notwithstanding the diversity of temperaments which
found a welcome in the New English Art Club, the Club became
identified with a distinctive method of painting, which Sickert thus
described:

> Technically we have evolved, for these things are done by gangs, not
> by individuals, we have evolved a method of painting with a clean and
> solid mosaic of thick paint in a light key . . . and . . . a whole generation
> holds it in common. . . . [1]

Sickert here voices, incidentally, an opinion rare among artists –
namely, that art is largely a collective pursuit. Most artists have a
sense, often a blinding sense, of their individual uniqueness, and of
the solitary character of their struggle with refractory material and

---

[1] 'The New English and After', *The New Age*, 2 June 1910.

the buffets of Fortune, but to Sickert, who was always learning and always teaching, the collective aspect of their vocation was constantly present.

> It is well to remember [he declared] that the language of paint like any other language, is kneaded and shaped by *all* the competent workmen labouring at a given moment, that it is, with all its individual variations, a common language, and not one of us would have been exactly what he is but for the influence and the experience of all the other competent workmen of the period.

It is related that, when some pictures alleged to be by Sickert were coming up for auction, an interested person who doubted their authenticity telegraphed to him: *Did you paint the pictures signed with your name and at present on view at such and such auction rooms?* Other wits might have sent the reply; *No, but none the worse for that.* Sickert is the only artist known to me who might have meant it.

During the early years of the new century Sickert's painting underwent a gradual change. Previously many of his best works had had something of the character of coloured drawing. If we examine *Gatti's Hungerford Palace of Varieties, second turn of Katie Lawrence*,[1] of about 1888, *The Old Hotel Royal, Dieppe*,[2] of 1900, *The Horses of St. Mark's, Venice*,[3] of 1901, *The Statue of Duquesne, Dieppe* (Plate 1),[4] of 1902, *Rue Notre-Dame, Dieppe*,[5] of the same year, they are all of them, in spite of the elaboration both of their design and their colour, essentially drawings in paint. Their outlines are emphatic; the paint is lightly applied. The best works of the immediately following years reflect the movement, widespread among European painters, towards a certain massiveness, achieved by a more deliberate, more concentrated design, and by a thicker application of paint. Such paintings as *The Lady in a Gondola*,[6] of about 1905, *Mornington Crescent*[7] and *The New Bedford* (Plate 2),[8] both of 1907, *The Juvenile Lead*,[9] of about 1908, all show how closely Sickert shared its aims. With the exception of the first (which was, however,

[1] Privately owned. [2] Privately owned.
[3] Privately owned.
[4] The City Art Gallery, Manchester.
[5] The National Gallery of Canada, Ottawa (Massey Collection).
[6] The Ashmolean Museum, Oxford.
[7] The Art Gallery of South Australia. [8] Privately owned.
[9] Southampton Art Gallery.

painted in London), the subjects of all these later paintings were taken from Camden Town, where he settled on his return from abroad. This grim and often fog-bound but roughly genial neighbourhood of small, square, late Georgian or of tall, early Victorian long-windowed houses, soot-encrusted and built in crescents or straight rows, was one in which he delighted. In accordance with his habit, he rented odd rooms for working in. The nearby Caledonian Market was among his favourite haunts. One day he was seen there (according to an account which has reference to a later day) in an old trench-coat and a straw hat with a broken brim, with his trousers stuffed into brown leather Army boots that reached almost to his knees, and as the boots had no laces the uppers jumped backwards and forwards as he walked. He came upon an old piano. 'Mind if I try it?' he asked the owner of the stall. 'Go ahead, guv'-nor', was the reply. Thus encouraged, he rattled off an old music-hall tune and then spun himself round several times on the revolving stool. 'Very fine tone', he gravely assured the owner and wandered off into the crowd.[1] Of the four places where Sickert painted most, Camden Town, Dieppe, Venice and Bath, the first was the one which he most intimately understood. Yet Mr. Wilenski can bring himself to write:

> In painting these [the Camden Town] pictures Sickert was no more recording life in Camden Town than he was recording life in China-town. He let his North London cronies think that the locality had something to do with it. But in fact when he was painting, his mind was not in North London but in North Paris.[2]

The artist's mind, surely, is always upon his subject, and Sickert himself has repeatedly affirmed that 'serious painting is illustration, illustration all the time'. Sickert's sayings were sometimes paradoxical, but here he was voicing a tenaciously held conviction which had immediate reference to his own work. The quality which gives such peculiar fascination to the North London paintings is the application to subjects conspicuously shabby and anecdotal of procedures which resume, with consummate erudition and taste,

[1] 'Sickert', ed. and with an essay on his life and notes on his paintings, by Lillian Browse, and with an essay on his art by R. H. Wilenski, 1943, p. 17.

[2] Op. cit.

the distilled wisdom of the foremost masters of the age; not only of Whistler and Degas, but of Pissarro, Vuillard and Bonnard. And not of his own age only: his colour, especially his muted but resonant pinky-carmines, shows to what good purpose he had lately spent his time in Venice. When I applied, just now, the attribute of *taste* to Sickert, I was aware that it was an attribute which he himself would have disclaimed with aversion, as also, at his behest, would certain among his admirers. Sickert's own view of taste – that it is the death of an artist – I have already noted. He spoke constantly of painting as 'a rough and racy wench'.

> The more our art is serious [he declared with studied deliberation] the more will it tend to avoid the drawing-room and stick to the kitchen. The plastic arts are gross arts, dealing joyfully with gross material facts. They call, in their servants, for a robust stomach and great powers of endurance, and while they flourish in the scullery, kitchen, or on the dunghill, they fade at a breath from the drawing-room.[1]

Except where this question of taste is concerned I believe all the opinions of Sickert's which I have cited hitherto to have been objective opinions, which may be accepted at their face value. But about this question he protests too much. It is true that an artist cannot relish a tasteful 'arrangement' he has thought up for himself as keenly he can something suddenly perceived (either by the outward or the inward eye), any more than a man can fully enjoy, as Sickert used to say, a meal that he has cooked himself. It is true that many of the greatest artists have ennobled some of the grossest subjects; but that there is any necessary connexion between serious art and – even in the broadest meaning of the word – the kitchen, is a notion which the history of art shows to be false. The great Italians, from Giotto to Tiepolo, to whom we owe so disproportionate a number of the masterpieces of the world, had scarcely a glance to spare for scullery or kitchen; nor had Van Eyck, El Greco, Poussin, Watteau, Delacroix or Turner. The cooks of Velazquez are not finer than his infantas or his *Virgin of the Immaculate Conception*. To persuade us of the truth of the view he had propounded, Sickert wrote as though the drawing-room were the only conceivable alternative to the kitchen, but this is no more than a dialectical device, and a transparent device at that. Why should

[1] 'Idealism', *The Art News*, 12 May 1910.

Sickert, a critic of the rarest insight, have persisted in so questionable a generalization? He gave us, I believe, a clue when he wrote:

> To the really creative painter, it must be remembered, the work of other men is mainly nourishment, to assist him in his own creation. That is our reason why the laity are wise to approach the criticism of art by an artist with the profoundest mistrust.[1]

The answer to this question is, I believe, that Sickert was himself essentially a man of taste, and, in consequence, acutely aware of the vitiating effects of taste once it becomes predominant in a man's work. The acerbity and the frequency of his warnings against the dangers of taste suggest that Sickert had had personal experience of them. An artist of robust stomach, wholly at ease in dealing with gross material fact, a Rubens or a Rowlandson, would be disposed to regard taste not with animosity, but rather as a minor, but on the whole an enviable sensibility. The circumstance which, as I understand the matter, so peculiarly exacerbated Sickert's animosity towards taste, was his own discipleship of Whistler. He came gradually to realize that he had come near to worshipping, in his first master, the very quality against which he should have been most vigilant. And was it not this circumstance, too, that gave eventually a personal twist to his especial dislike of the predominance of taste in Whistler himself? May not his feeling have resembled the gradual and galling recognition by a child of a defect in a parent from which he also suffers? It was not that Sickert was lacking in robust qualities, but detested Taste was always at his elbow with his plausible ways. . . . You have only to look at his painting and drawing to see how strongly sheer taste was always working in him; the delicate slates and violets, and the lemons, and the muted carmines of Tintoretto. And there were occasions when he capitulated altogether to his taste: he forgot his sarcasms about the 'august site' motive, and took a ticket to Venice, and painted St. Mark's under a star-hung midnight heaven. Could any paintings be remoter from the scullery than Sickert's Venetian subjects, whether they be St. Mark, Santa Maria della Salute, or for that matter La Giuseppina herself. It would be difficult, I believe, to show that Sickert's paintings of Venice – and, one might add, of 'august sites' in Dieppe, aspects

[1] 'The English Review', March 1912.

of the venerable Church of St. Jacques, or of the stylish hotels
along the seafront or of the spacious arcading by the harbour –
were inferior to the shabby interiors of Camden Town. An intensely observant, or, as he himself said, 'a breathlessly listening'
artist, he divined the history, the social ambience and everything
which goes to make up the distinctive 'atmosphere' of a place, which
enabled him to paint and draw it – 'beautiful' or 'ugly' – with
extraordinary comprehension.

It was, I suppose, in the best of his Camden Town pictures that
Sickert came nearest to realizing his aims as a painter. His criticism
of Whistler for accepting the subordinate position of a prima
painter, for persisting in the 'trial and error' method, has already been
noted; also his corresponding praise of Degas for his deliberateness,
resulting in the growth of the power to begin, continue and end
pictures according to a minutely pondered plan. Sickert's abhorrence of the sketcher's attitude towards painting, and in particular
of this attitude in Whistler, like his abhorrence of taste, derived, it
is reasonable to suppose, from the knowledge that he himself shared
with his first master something of the sketcher's temperament. The
summary character of a considerable part of his early work would
suggest that this was the case. I have already drawn attention
to the fact that several of his largest as well as his finest Venice and
Dieppe pictures have the character of drawings rather than of
paintings. They may be said to be impressions rather than constructions. Constructions are precisely what the best of the North London
pictures are. The *Mornington Crescent* already mentioned and *The
New Home*,[1] of about 1912, are pictures of this different kind: there
is nothing summary about them; they are deliberate, compactly
designed and thickly painted. Painting of this kind probably did
not come easily to Sickert; it was the result of a prodigious effort
of will, inspired by tenacious conviction. In general, it was the more
summary method that he employed, but even with this he experienced difficulties the existence of which it is at present unfashionable
to admit. Sickert is freely spoken of as a master of his craft, and,
more especially, as a master draughtsman. He was an artist of the
highest intelligence and, in consequence, of the most exacting
standards, but not, it seems to me, a natural master. Drawing

1 Temple Newsam, Leeds. (Correct date 1908).

did not come to him as it came, for instance, to Augustus John, as a gift of the fairies. How poorly, even at the height of his powers, he could on occasion draw is apparent not only in acknowledged failures, but in such a widely admired picture as *The Camden Town Murder*, of about 1907.[1] The torso of the recumbent woman, a confusion of clumsy planes which fail to describe the form, would do no credit to a student; the hands of both woman and man are shapeless. This picture shows in its extreme degree the innate weakness as a draughtsman and summariness as a designer against which he fought a lifelong, but in the main a glorious battle. That by the exercise of constant self-discipline and of his superb intellect he made many splendid drawings, and painted pictures which are marvels of reflective construction, is an indication of how powerfully the creative will worked in Sickert – a will which ever draws strength from the difficulties which it overcomes.

In the course of Sickert's Camden Town period, which lasted about nine years, and ended with the outbreak of the First World War in 1914, his work underwent a radical change. This may be considered as a manifestation of the increasing influence in England of Cézanne, van Gogh, Gauguin, Seurat and those other artists who repudiated important parts of the teaching of their revered Impressionist masters. The manner, or, more precisely, the timing of this change was singular, for the Continental Post-Impressionists were familiar to Sickert long before their influence was felt in England. Why should he have continued year after year uninfluenced by it until it began to attract the excited attention of his juniors? Sickert's was a highly complex, and, in many respects, a secretive character, and this question is one to which I would hesitate to give a confident reply, but upon which I would offer an opinion. One of the mainsprings of Sickert's actions was love of change – of change simply for its own sake. From his childhood to his old age he would abruptly sever relations with old friends and companions, and welcome new ones; the variations in the character in which he presented himself to the world are legendary. In the conduct of his life he responded with a freedom that verged upon irresponsibility to his love of change. In his work this love is sober and discreet, unobtrusive, but manifest. Sickert had the habit of making friends

[1] Graves Art Gallery, Sheffield.

younger than himself. This was in part due also to the desire for change, in part to his passion to teach and to lead the young, and in so doing, perhaps, to renew the illusion of youth. When he settled in North London he began to gather about him a new group of young friends which included Spencer Gore, Harold Gilman, Henry Lamb and a contemporary, Lucien Pissarro, and later on Charles Ginner and Walter Bayes.[1] The interest of all these in one or another aspect of Post-Impressionism was electrified by the Post-Impressionist exhibitions held in London in 1910 and 1912. Sickert, I surmise, was excited by his two-fold love of change and of leadership into a belated (as well as a reserved and transitory) participation in the Post-Impressionist movement. When I say 'excited' I am far from meaning 'stampeded': the article he wrote on the Post-Impressionists[2] – which contains a noble tribute to Gauguin – shows all his accustomed independence and wisdom.

Sickert's relations with the English Post-Impressionists eventually became embittered, and he left them. The association had, however, lasting effects upon his own work: it led him to heighten his tones, to observe colour in shadows, and to lay on his paint in small mosaic-like patches instead of long strokes and large patches, hitherto characteristic features of his style. To the end of the Camden Town period belongs one especially notable work: *Ennui*,[3] of about

---

[1] Painter, principally within the tradition established by Sickert; also a teacher and critic. Born 31 May 1869 in London. Attended evening classes at the City and Guilds of London Institute, Finsbury, 1886–1900, and at the Westminster Art School under Frederick Brown, for a few months about 1902. Taught at the City & Guilds Institute, at Camberwell School of Arts & Crafts; Headmaster of the Westminster Art School from 1919 until 1934. As a critic he rendered to his fellow artists what Sickert called 'the incalculable service of speaking the truth as he conceives it'. In 1906 he succeeded Fry as art critic to 'The Athenæum', a position he held until 1916. He was a contributor to 'The Outlook', 'The Saturday Review' and 'The Week End Review'. His writings are pugnacious but sometimes obscure. 'I have read your Athenæum article', Sickert would tell him, 'read it three times and I believe, I am proud to believe, that I understand it.' He has also written three books, 'The Art of Decorative Painting' (1927), 'Turner, a speculative Portrait' (1931), and 'Painter's Baggage' (1932). He has also occasionally designed for the theatre. He has held one-man exhibitions at the Leicester Galleries (1918 and 1951) as well as the Goupil Gallery and Carfax.

[2] 'The Fortnightly Review', January 1911.

[3] The Tate Gallery, London. Smaller versions in the coll. of H.M. Queen Elizabeth the Queen Mother and at the Ashmolean Museum, Oxford.

1913. This, although it is lightly painted and has a certain superficial appearance of slightness, is a scrupulously composed and a highly finished work: a work which could in no way be altered or added to without loss. An air of deceptive simplicity veils the artist's mastery, rather as the unaffected manners of the man of the world may veil his accomplishments. In this picture, too, with even more than his customary skill, the artist has disguised his own weaknesses; first of all his difficulty in coming to close grips with form – in describing it with fulness and precision. Its large scale and noble proportions, however, and the economy of means with which so much is forcefully conveyed, make *Ennui* the culmination of the entire Camden Town series. Only once again did he achieve so splendid a major work. This is the *Portrait of Victor Lecour* (Plate 3),[1] of about 1922, in which Sickert's finest qualities, his rich, sardonic sense of human dignity; his power of conveying, not only the atmosphere of a room, but the life which has been lived in it; his adroitness as a designer; and his vivid understanding of the essence of the European tradition – all are radiantly present. I know of no late Sickert to compare with it; I detect, in fact, a steady decline in his powers after the beginning of the First World War, and *The Soldiers of Albert the Ready*,[2] of 1914, I take to be the first symptom of it. There is much to suggest that his vital powers were waning. There was a change in his method of painting which was profoundly symptomatic of decline. About 1914 he began to rely upon photographs and old prints rather than upon his own drawings and cumulative observation. In the early nineteen-twenties he began gradually to abandon drawing, although now and then he produced a drawing or an etching, such, for instance, as *The Hanging Gardens of Islington*, which show all the old mastery. In a letter to 'The Times'[3] he asserted that 'a photograph is the most precious document obtainable by a sculptor, a painter or a draughtsman', but he had many years earlier expressed the qualifying opinion that

> the camera, like alcohol . . . may be an occasional servant to a draughtsman, which only he may use who can do without it. And further, the healthier the man is as a draughtsman, the more inclined will he be to do without it altogether.[4]

[1] The City Art Gallery, Manchester. [2] The Graves Art Gallery, Sheffield.
[3] 15 August 1929.   [4] 'The English Review', January 1912.

The decline in Sickert's power did not show itself in a steady diminuendo, but in wild fluctuation. At no time did he paint or draw more finely than in the *Portrait of Victor Lecour* or in *The Hanging Gardens of Islington*, but there are also among his later works paintings in which no trace of his rare spirit is apparent. I do not refer to the failures which every artist abandons or destroys, but to works exhibited, frequently reproduced and authoritatively praised. What, for instance, has *Sir Nigel Playfair*, of 1928[1] – a work without a single merit – in common with the other works hitherto discussed in these pages? What are the *Echoes* – with one specified exception – of the late nineteen-thirties, but trivial pastiches barely held together by Sickert's knowledge and taste? Yet so responsible a critic as Sir Osbert Sitwell has said that there are among them 'paintings more magnificent than any that the artist had hitherto achieved'.[2]

The cause of the acceptance by many people, ordinarily of independent judgement, of any work by Sickert, however ill-conceived and ill-executed, as a masterpiece can only be the extraordinary power and fascination of his personality.

It was indeed an elusive personality, remote and detached, yet also entirely of the world, needing alternately to hold himself aloof and to enjoy the bustle of the world and the influence and affection that his manifold gifts ensured. Solitude was necessary for his work; he must also have been conscious that his withdrawals made the enchantment of his presence the more enjoyed – an enchantment which he heightened by his legendary changes of 'character' – from dandy to fisherman, from gamekeeper to chef, each one perfectly sustained. Latterly he preferred a free and fantastic version of his 'workaday' self. I recollect, for instance, his coming to meet me at Margate Station in the summer of 1938 wearing a huge, long-peaked grey cap, a suit of bright red, rough material (the coat with long tails and the trousers egregiously ample) and an outsize pair of khaki bedroom slippers. The taxi in which he drove me to his house at St. Peter's-in-Thanet resembled, in construction and even in smell, an ancient brougham.

Sickert's presence, which seemed to hold out the promise of the sunniest intimacy, conveyed simultaneously the threat of ruthless sarcasm and cold displeasure. What a fabulous subject for a Boswell!

[1] Privately owned.   [2] 'A Free House', p. liv.

But Sickert had no Boswell, and he moved elusively from one to another of the painting rooms he collected, and showed constantly differing aspects of his own subtle complex self. In spite of an ultimate heartlessness, he was capable of intimacy – I have rarely read letters so self-revealing as two or three among those he wrote to my father in the late 'nineties – but intimate relations between him and his friends were apt to be transitory or intermittent. With this power of disconcerting by mingled charm and threat, he possessed an extraordinarily retentive memory. In consequence he was able to quote at length and minutely describe in a manner which held his listeners spellbound, the artists, actors and writers, as well as low-life 'characters' he had known, and to discourse upon the most fascinating aspects of their private lives or their most abstruse ideas and their loftiest achievements. It enabled him to draw easily upon a wide range of reading, for he devoted, I suppose, as many hours each day to reading as to painting and drawing. (He was as familiar with the classical writings of Italy and Germany as of Greece, Rome and England.) His personal ascendency is now being prolonged by the republication of his writings. The incisiveness, independency and dry, racy wisdom of these have equipped him to advocate the traditional values in the arts, as Chesterton advocated the traditional values in theology and morals, so as to delight, even if not to convince, a generation which has grown up in the belief of the inevitability of continuous revolution and is apt to confuse novelty with progress. But the effect of his writings upon his reputation as an artist may prove deleterious. For his prestige is now such that to criticize his work with candour is considered scandalous. But his reputation as an artist must ultimately depend upon the best of his Dieppe, Venice and Camden Town paintings, of his Degas-inspired music-halls, upon *Victor Lecour* and his best etchings and drawings. The inclusion of reproductions of such pictures as the wretched *Camden Town Murder* and *Sir Nigel Playfair* already referred to and the (by any standards) derisory *Signor Battistini*[1] in serious publications does his memory a grave injustice. For Sickert was at his best a master: a master of sober and exquisite colour, who could suggest the atmosphere of places with a certainty and fulness which none of his contemporaries has been able to approach, as none has been able to perceive beauty so

[1] Privately owned.

abundantly in places and objects generally considered ugly. Without a trace of idealization, Sickert has the power of showing us, in a row of sooty Islington houses, a piercing beauty. That is true glory. To claim that he portrayed with exceptional insight the life of the ordinary man is the starkest nonsense. He produced (I am now considering his work as he, like Hogarth or Keene, wished it to be considered, as illustration) merely intriguing vignettes: incidents which provoke our curiosity. But he could do no more than this, for, as Roger Fry observed, 'things for Sickert have only their visual values, they are not symbols, they contain no key to unlock the secrets of the heart and spirit'. Sickert lacked the emotional power that would have given reality to his figures. As it is, they are inert puppets, though marvellously, sometimes touchingly, resembling human beings, but they feel neither hunger nor thirst, neither love nor hate, only, perhaps, indifference, which at bottom was his own attitude towards his fellow men.

PHILIP WILSON STEER
1860—1942

THE generalization made in the Introduction of this book
upon the neglect of English artists does not apply to Steer.
MacColl's authoritative and spirited biography, tightly packed
with information and pertinent comment, is but the epitome of a
vast Steer legend. The innumerable authors of it range from George
Moore to fellow artists and students who break for the first and last
time in their lives into print to add yet another to the formidable
sum of recorded anecdotes about the idiosyncrasies of Steer: his
solicitude for his health, his modesty, his love of cats and his inarticulate wisdom. I do not refer to the existence of this legend to call in
question its essential truth, but because the dense aura of 'respect'
which it engenders has made more difficult the just appreciation of
the artist's work. What is of far greater consequence is the possibility,
even the probability, that it had adverse effects upon the artist himself. George Moore's portrait, for example, gives several indications
of how heavy with solicitude and adulation the atmosphere around
Steer became. Upon the completion of Steer's portrait of his old
housekeeper, *Mrs. Raynes* (Plate 6),[1] Moore describes[2] how, as he
and Tonks stood before it, he asked if the blue vase on the shelf did
not seem a trifle out of tone, and Tonks 'said in an awed voice:
"It will go down" and begged me not to mention my suspicion to
Steer. . . .' Moore speaks, too, of friends who 'bring an abundance
of love and admiration somewhat disquieting to the master', and
he surmises that, in the recesses of Steer's mind,

> If not a thought at least a feeling is in process of incubation that perhaps
> Ronald Gray's appreciations lack contrast, the humblest sketch being
> hailed in almost the same words as the masterpiece that has taken
> months to achieve.[2]

It is no part of my purpose to provoke scepticism as to the
general verisimilitude of the huge, composite portrait of Steer (to

[1] The Tate Gallery, London.
[2] 'Conversations in Ebury Street', 1924 and 1930.

which I have myself contributed a detail here and there) which so many of us cherish with affectionate admiration. Personal acquaintance with Steer, extending over a number of years, and the circumstance that a warm friendship subsisted between him and my parents for the greater part of their lives have given me opportunities of comparing fact and legend, and observation and direct report have for me confirmed and rounded out the portait which can be discovered in the pages of Moore, MacColl and its other delineators.

From these there emerges a big, small-headed, slow-moving, comfortable man, a lover of the quiet and the familiar, an impassioned valetudinarian ('Steer dreads getting wet even as his cat', wrote Moore, 'and he dreads draughts; draughts prevail even in sheltered nooks, and draughts are like wild beasts, always on the watch for whom they may devour'). A man with his feet planted firmly upon the material world: an assiduous and successful follower of the fluctuations of the stock market, and an economical man. Yet one who did not allow his preoccupations with property to impinge upon his paramount preoccupation. An instinctive and disinterested collector

> instigated [to quote Moore once again] by a love of beautiful things, so pure, that he would collect Chelsea figures and Greek coins though he knew of a certainty that no eyes but his own would see them.

A man of chaste life but of a Rabelaisian humour, usually cosy, but illumined on occasion by a flash of wit. At an evening party an artist who had lately been charged with an attempt upon the virtue of a servant entered leaning upon a stick. A lady asked Steer what was wrong with the new arrival; 'Housemaid's knee' was his reply. But above all Steer emerges as an instinctive man, according a superficial wondering respect to the intellectual processes of his friends, but fundamentally sceptical of the value of ideas: indeed, for Steer ideas were hardly realities at all. Notoriously, when the talk of his intellectual friends departed from familiar ground – the technique of painting, connoisseurship, gossip – and took a philosophic turn, Steer slept. By instinct he was a Tory, insular, independent, incurious, unimpressionable. As a student in Paris he seems to have had little liking for the French, almost no interest in their language, literature, or in their history. He did go to see

3. WALTER RICHARD SICKERT. *Portrait of Victor Lecour* (1922).
Oil, 23½×31½ in. The City Art Gallery, Manchester.

4. Philip Wilson Steer. *Girls Running: Walberswick Pier* (1894).
Oil, 24¼×36½ in. The Tate Gallery, London.

5. PHILIP WILSON STEER.
Chepstow Castle (1906).
Oil, 35½ × 47½ in.
Coll. Her Majesty
Queen Elizabeth
the Queen Mother

6. PHILIP WILSON STEER. *Portrait of Mrs. Raynes* (1922).
Oil, 27×22 in. The Tate Gallery, London.

Gambetta lying in state, 'which', he characteristically reported, 'was not anything much'. The ignorance of French, by which he was insulated from Parisian life, and which even prevented him from becoming aware of the very existence of the Impressionist school of painting, eventually brought his studies to a sudden end. In order to bring about a reduction in their numbers, the Ecole des Beaux-Arts imposed upon its foreign students the obligation to pass an examination in French, for which Steer felt himself unqualified to sit, with the result that, in 1884, he returned to England. Such, in brief, is the legendary Steer. It is an authentic but a superficial likeness, which does no more than hint at an infirmity in him which is manifest in his art, a radical infirmity of which his aversion from the processes of conscious thought, from what Rossetti called 'fundamental brainwork', and his sheer incuriosity were symptoms. This infirmity was a strain of laziness, and it was perhaps his instinctive consciousness of it which disinclined him from any activity, intellectual or physical, liable to divert his limited energies from his painting. His other activities were conducted in an easygoing fashion. He read desultorily. Social intercourse, being invariably the one 'qui se laisse aimer', he was able satisfactorily to sustain with the minimum of sacrifice and effort.

His duties as a teacher from 1893 until 1930 at the Slade School made even slighter calls upon him. There are stories of students awaiting the criticism of their teacher seated behind them, and turning round at last to find him asleep. If a student said, 'I'm in a muddle', he would reply, 'Well, muddle along then'. Because he was apt to go to sleep and to make comments of such a kind, he was not without value as a teacher – in fact, the contrary was the case. He showed at moments a power of imparting, by a benevolent, homely phrase, something of his own instinctive wisdom; and his fame as a painter and the massive integrity of his presence made what he said memorable for his students. Like his agreeable social life, his teaching was conducted with the least possible exertion.

Steer's habitual lethargy of mind, and, to a lesser degree, of body also, exercised a far-reaching effect upon his human relations. He possessed most of the qualities which make a man lovable: a benign largeness, an instinctive modesty, a slow, unaggressive geniality, an impressive calm; he also possessed, from early days, the prestige accorded to extraordinary powers. In most times and places such a combination of qualities would by themselves have assured him a sufficiency of affectionate regard; his lethargy immeasurably enhanced their appeal, for it put to sleep that most deadly source of contention between artists, the spirit of rivalry. In spite of his manifest superiority over the majority of the artists with whom, in the course of his long life, he was associated, he probably excited less jealousy than any artist of his generation. It often happens that the evident satisfaction which a successful rival derives from the exercise of his superior powers is even more provoking to his friends than his possession of them. Steer not only disclaimed possession of superior powers; he persisted, sometimes beyond the verge of absurdity, in denying that anybody had ever supposed him to possess them. The lengths to which he was prepared to carry his pretensions were exemplified in connection with his appointment, in 1931, to the Order of Merit. He was at first unwilling to accept it, but after much persuasion on the part of friends he agreed. On the morning when he received the royal offer he took it to show to Tonks, whom he greeted with the enquiry, 'Have *you* received one of these?'

With equal resolution, Steer disclaimed higher ideals than his fellow artists. He referred habitually to his own activity as 'muddling about with paints' and let it be understood that he regarded painting as an ordinary 'job', like any others, in connection with which the expression of any high ideal was out of place. He once complained of my father, whose exalted sense of the artist's vocation sometimes irritated him: 'Will Rothenstein paints pretty much like the rest of us – but from higher motives, of course.'

Steer's egalitarianism sprang partly from a genuine sense of his own shortcomings confronted with the infinite and never-diminishing difficulties of painting, partly from his instinctive wisdom in withdrawing as far as possible from the field of contention the huge bulk of his talent, and thereby preserving it against distracting animosities. This difficult manœuvre could hardly have been executed more adroitly: Steer, who was scarcely more inclined to put himself out for his brother artists than he was to criticize them, became the personification of benign modesty. So much is apparent from the various authoritative writings about Steer. What has been, so far as I am aware, totally ignored is the question whether his intellectual lethargy, which involved a reluctance to recognize the value – it might almost be said, the very existence – of ideas, was detrimental to his life as an artist. I am persuaded that it was.

Not until Steer's life had neared its end did it occur to me that neither the familiar legend nor the accepted estimate of his art, according to which he was the Constable of our day – a Constable who had studied Gainsborough and Turner to some purpose – accounted fully either for his character or his art.

One day in 1942 Mr. G. E. Healing, the possessor of a collection of Steers, called at the Tate Gallery with a picture which he was prepared to sell. The picture was *The Beach, Walberswick*, of 1890. I can see it clearly still, propped up against the pink hessian of the sandbagged temporary quarters into which the staff had been driven by the bomb-wrecking of our permanent offices; I can see it clearly and well remember the electric effect it had upon me. Could anything, I asked myself, be more different than this from the green, opulent, complacent pictures generally accepted as characteristic Steers? There was no hint of greenness, opulence or complacency about the three intent, lanky but rather stylish young girls with their backs towards the spectator and gazing out across a boldly curving spit of sand to a sparkling sea. The elegance and the poetry of the scene had something of Whistler about it, yet more of Elstir, but nothing of the later Steer. And there was a suggestion of Lautrec in the incisively drawn boots of the girl on the left, and the indication that the long legs of this at first glance ethereal creature are planted on the sand with an almost startling energy. The picture revived the vague admiration I had felt on seeing reproductions of some early Steers in the collection of the late Sir Augustus Daniel, and, upon my earnest recommendation, *Walberswick Beach* was purchased for the Tate. A further visit to the Daniel Collection, and above all the opportunity which this afforded of seeing his *Girls Running: Walberswick Pier* (Plate 4), of 1894, convinced me that here surely was the masterpiece of what I had come to regard as the most important period of Steer's production. It is not one of those pictures that imparts a considerable volume of information. It does not touch any of the deeper chords of human experience; still less does it contain any intimation of the life of the spirit. It represents, on the contrary, a spectacle in itself in no way extraordinary: two young girls running swiftly along a pier away from the sea. Yet the whole scene has been apprehended with an almost apocalyptic intensity. It has been seen as though by a blind man vouchsafed the gift of sight the moment the two girls started to run towards him; it has been set down with visionary splendour. The composition is unremarkable, nor are the figures finely drawn, yet there they are, animated by an odd, incredible energy, racing towards us across the wide planks, the white, broad-sashed, rather formal dresses touched with the glory of the day. They are strange girls; so much is at once apparent; and why are they running so fast? There is something memorable about this picture. Had Renoir painted it, the effect might have been of greater breadth and resonance; if Lautrec, the strangeness of the girls might have been defined for us, yet as it is there is a freshness, an immediacy, an angular, unsophisticated grace which, added to the intensity of feeling manifest in every inch of this picture, make it memorable. Compared with works by either of these or by any of the other great Impressionists, it is marked by something of the lanky candour of adolescence, but it springs direct from the same vital source. The owner of this picture rejected the overtures I made with a view to its purchase for the Tate,[1] but this made me the more determined to strengthen the Gallery's representation of Steer's early work. It was not long before other and only slightly less dazzling opportunities presented themselves. *The Bridge at Etaples*, of 1887, a small oil, of two figures against a luminous background of lemon and grey river and sky, the Tate had purchased the year before, but this work, for all its pensive beauty, had not at the time struck me as expressing anything of the audacious vision of the painter of *Girls Running: Walberswick Pier* and *The Beach, Walberswick*; later it seemed to me their reticent, less positive counterpart. From the Steer sale at Christie's the Gallery acquired *The Swiss Alps at the Earl's Court Exhibition*, a sketch in which echoes of Whistler and of Japanese colour prints are dashingly blended, and a much more personal work, *Southwold*. Both pictures were painted in 1887. Although it is not in quite the front rank of the artist's early pictures, this *Southwold* does more conspicuously than any other early Steer manifest the exulting spirits, the extremism, by which most of them are marked, and which most

[1] It was however presented to the Tate Gallery in 1951 by Lady Daniel.

sharply distinguishes them from all his later work – so conspicuously, in fact, that there was a moment when I wondered whether it could indeed be by Steer's hand. The theme of this picture too is figures against the sea. The way in which the brilliant colours are laid on in ribbons, rapidly and thick, in immediate response to strong, uncensored emotion enables us to compare *Southwold* without absurdity with a van Gogh. Steer's emotion was slighter in volume, less deep and purposeful in its nature, and the ribbons of paint were appropriately thinner, but at the moment when he painted this picture the two artists were not remote from each other. There is something of a trumpet-call of defiance in the excessive size and redness of the head of the schoolgirl on the left: a sign of how little he cared for the aggressively complacent opinion of the British public. In MacColl's biography the principal critical chapter is headed by a remark made by Steer to an interviewer: 'They said I was wild.' The biographer's intention in prefacing with such an opinion his final summing up of his friend's achievement and place in history was evidently ironical. Yet what sign of wildness could be plainer than this oversize, empurpled, intrusive head?

During the same year protracted negotiations were in progress for the acquisition of yet another early Steer. *The Swiss Alps at the Earl's Court Exhibition* and *Southwold* I purchased quite simply on my own initiative at the Steer sale at Christie's, relying upon the enlightened mercy of the Trustees of the Tate to confirm my action at their next meeting, but *Boulogne Sands*, of 1892, was elusive from the first.

When Frederick Brown, Steer's frequent summer painting companion, Tonk's chief at the Slade, a gruff old survivor of the early days of the New English, died in 1942, I paid a visit to Ormonde House, Richmond, where he had spent the latter part of his life. My expectation of finding some remarkable pictures in the house of this old incorruptible of somewhat circumscribed but intense loyalties was not disappointed. The walls of the dark but finely proportioned room were covered with paintings and drawings by his friends and associates of the New English and the Slade. Two of these at once attracted my attention: a small self-portrait by Gwen John, to which I shall refer later on, and a large beach scene by Steer. This was in a lamentable condition, but between innumerable cracks and beneath a heavy coat of yellowed varnish could still be discovered what MacColl had thus beautifully described just fifty years before when the picture was first shown in its pristine brilliance:

> The children playing, the holiday encampment of the bathers' tents, the glints of people flaunting themselves like flags, the dazzle of sand and sea, and over and through it all the chattering lights of noon – it is like the sharp notes of pipes and strings sounding to an invitation by Ariel.

I told Miss Ellen Brown that I was convinced that this picture ought to hang in the Tate, and she allowed me to show it to the Trustees, who were of the opinion that it represented an opportunity on no account to be missed. After many setbacks the Tate Trustees successfully appealed to the National Art-Collections Fund, by whom, in November 1943, the picture was at last presented to the Gallery. The audacious and sparkling character, the overtone of tense, mysterious exaltation manifest in the early paintings of Steer of which I have been speaking, *Girls Running: Walberswick Pier,* and in those acquired by the Tate Gallery between 1941 and 1943, is shared by a number of other pictures by Steer painted between 1887 and 1894. Among the most notable of these are *On the Pierhead, Walberswick,*[1] of 1888, *The Ermine Sea, Swanage,* of 1890, *Beach Scene, with Three Children Shrimping, Boulogne,* of 1890 and *Children Paddling, Swanage,* of 1894, all three of which belonged to Sir Augustus Daniel, and *Cowes Regatta,*[2] of 1892.

Now whether these works, according to the accepted opinion, are considered to constitute the awkward exploration, under the fugitive spell of Manet and the Impressionists, of a blind alley, or, as I suggest, a splendid beginning precipitately and mysteriously abandoned, the differences between them and the most characteristic works of the artist's later life are so radical as to be apparent to the least practised eye. Indeed, so radical that it would be difficult to distinguish any qualities common for example to *Girls Running: Walberswick Pier* and the characteristic masterpieces of his maturity,

---

[1] Privately owned.   [2] Privately owned.

Richmond Castle,[1] of 1903, and *Chepstow Castle* (Plate 5),[2] painted two years later, apart from a certain looseness of handling which had become widely prevalent with the diffusion of Impressionist influence. Yet this almost total transformation of Steer's outlook, which appears to me to be the most important event in his life, has remained – so far as I am aware – unnoticed or ignored by all those who have written on his work. This is the case even in the authoritative biography by his lifelong intimate, D. S. MacColl. Perhaps the very closeness and continuity of the relations between the two rendered the changes in his subject almost imperceptible to the biographer. MacColl seems almost unaware of the revolution in Steer's vision; a hint here and there, however, suggests that, in spite of his deeply convinced and comprehending defence of Steer's early work when it was first publicly shown, he regarded most of it as slight compared with that of his maturity. He alludes to the collection of the artist's work built up by Charles Aitken at the Tate as having been enlarged and – evidently with reference to the acquisitions already described – 'even diluted'. Elsewhere he notes with surprise the interest evoked by the early work in the memorial exhibition of 1943. Even granted the fullest allowance for the inevitable difficulty in distinguishing the changes which succeed one another in the life of an intimate contemporary, there is something singular in the failure of the possessor of so sharp a critical faculty as MacColl, as he looked intently backwards over his friend's life, to note the change in the whole character of his art which took place about 1900; MacColl, who justifiably reminds us of his critical severity towards his friends. How can he have failed to note the contrast between the profoundly purposeful spirit which informs these early works, the intensity of the running girls, the vivacity of the paddling children, the intentness of the seaward-gazing girls, the subdued tension of the couple on the bridge, and the inanity of his later figure subjects? A predilection for inane gestures and vaguely allusive subjects showed itself early. In *The Pillow Fight*,[3] of 1896, the girl with the solemnly lethargic face aiming the pillow wide of its archly posturing target has been 'posed'

[1] The Tate Gallery, London.

[2] Coll. H.M. Queen Elizabeth the Queen Mother. There is another version in The Tate Gallery, London.

[3] Privately owned.

so as to be incapable of throwing it at all. For this 'promising romp' MacColl complacently notes that he was in part responsible, having sent the artist a reproduction of a Fragonard as an incentive. In *The Mirror*,[1] of 1901, described by MacColl as one of Steer's two most memorable double-figure compositions, the attention of the woman reflected in the mirror is elsewhere, nor is that of the woman holding it engaged in what she is doing. In *Golden Rain*,[2] of about 1905, and *Reclining Nude*,[3] of 1905 (to mention two at random), naked women – who are never anything but studio models – loll inconsequently in incongruous or indeterminate surroundings. In writing of these pieces, Steer's biographer extenuatingly alludes to his 'disinterest in event'. Artists have at all times exercised the right of modifying history and nature in the interest of their creations. Veronese could hardly have pushed to a greater extreme of improbability his huge representation of *The Supper at the House of Simon the Pharisee* at the Accademia in Venice; Turner declared that no one should paint London without St. Paul's, or Oxford without the dome (*sic*) of the Bodleian. It is nevertheless true to say that the most serious artists have in general modified objective fact for the purpose of making their representation of it more not less convincing. Steer's later figure compositions, however, were the merest pretexts for representing one of those aspects of nature in which he most delighted – soft, rounded female bodies. So did Renoir, but Renoir's nudes, while they are hardly more purposefully employed than Steer's, are adolescent girls, with lips parted for an eager intake of breath, or who you would know are smiling notwithstanding their averted faces, or great elemental women, who might be the mothers of the human race; while Steer's are usually Chelsea models; old man's pets, not made for generation and love.

It would be difficult, on account of the sporadic character of Steer's development and the scarcity of evidence as to his innermost convictions about painting, to trace with anything like precision the radical change and, as I believe, the deterioration, of his creative faculties which unmistakably showed itself around the year 1900; yet its causes, principal and accessory, are tolerably clear. It may reasonably be supposed that in Steer's early years the effects of his

[1] Privately owned.
[2] Privately owned.   [3] Privately owned.

lethargy of mind (and to less conspicuous degree of body also) were minimized by the exuberance of youth, and by the quickening sense of adventure which belongs to the beginning of the career of an artist of exceptional powers, and by the invigorating wind blowing from Paris. Even in those years he seems, as one critic has observed, to have responded to the achievements of other masters in much the same manner as he responded to nature. Many of his early paintings clearly indicate the source of their inspiration: the paddling pictures, Monet, *A Procession of Yachts*,[1] of 1893, Seurat, probably by way of Pissarro, *Mrs. Cyprian-Williams and Children*,[2] of 1891, and the *Self-Portrait with Model*,[3] of 1894, Degas. In all these pictures, and still more conspicuously in the *Girls Running: Walberswick Pier* and others noticed earlier, Steer took the work of other painters as points of departure, but in every instance, in spite even of a naïve imitation of idiosyncrasies (witness the truncation of the artist's head, Degas-fashion, in the *Self-Portrait with Model*), it may fairly be said that he has made what he borrowed unquestionably his own. But by 1900, when Steer passed his fortieth year, his youth lay behind him; painting, if still a continual joy and a continual agony, was a breath-taking adventure no longer. The fruitfully disturbing proximities of Degas, Manet, Monet, Pissarro and Seurat were only memories to be faintly stirred by the endless, reminiscent monologues of his friend, George Moore. The fact was that Steer had entered another world, a closed world in which the air was stuffy with adulation. Here there was nobody to temper the intellectual sloth which so firmly asserted itself, or the lazy, good-natured contempt for all investigation into the causes of things. There were, on the contrary, friends ready for ever to see something impressive in his defects, and their continual bluff, bachelor jokes depicted him as the great man of action properly indifferent to the chatterings of theorists. Steer's propensity for being sent to sleep by the serious conversation of his friends was a favourite theme: it was indeed an endearing trait. The harm done to Steer was not the work of sycophants – he was quick to discount anything they said – but of intimates of high intelligence and high integrity, ardently devoted to his interests, whose

[1] The Tate Gallery, London.
[2] The Tate Gallery, London.   [3] Privately owned.

pervasive attitude could hardly have been without effect. At a
critical moment in his life, Steer was surrounded and jealously
guarded by friends who made of his deadliest weakness an engaging
virtue. His very supineness excited a species of possessiveness in
them, fierce and enduring. I remember conversations with several
of them in the course of the organization of the Memorial Exhibition at the National Gallery in 1943 (for which I was the official
responsible) not long after his death, and how anger kindled in them
at the idea of anyone outside the little closed circle of 'cronies'
concerning themselves in any way with Steer: they had staked out
their own claims over the big, immensely gifted but supine personality. In conversation with some of these, a sudden, envenomed hiss
would warn the unwary that he had unwittingly touched a vested
interest in some episode of the artist's life, some personal characteristic or opinion. The impassioned possessiveness of 'Steer's
friends' clashed in the extensive but closely contested 'no man's land'
of the artist's personality.

From the time when I first became convinced of the extraordinary
merits of Steer's early paintings until the first of a short series of
visits which I paid him shortly before his death on 21 March 1942,
the problem of the change in his outlook remained only vaguely
present to my mind. Two of these visits I partially recalled in a note in
'The Burlington Magazine'.[1] Some years had elapsed since I had been
to his house, and I was at once aware of changes in him. His eyesight
had grown worse; but although he was almost blind it was wonderful to see the ease with which his large figure moved on the narrow
stairs and in and out of the rooms, very dark that winter's morning,
crowded with pictures and with the miscellaneous pretty objects he
had accumulated in a lifetime of collecting. This ease was evidently
due to his intimacy with the house where he had lived and worked
for more than forty years. I had heard, of course, of his increasing
blindness, and the courage with which he accepted it did not
surprise me. I was, however, unprepared for the comprehensiveness
of his interests and still more for his detachment from the opinions and
attitudes attributed to him in the legend that has grown up about
his name. He showed the liveliest interest in public affairs, especially
in the conduct of the war, in history, in literature and music. Unable

[1] 'Two Visits to Steer', August 1944.

to paint, he listened to the news on the wireless, to discussions, to concerts, and daily to the evening service. 'Flo', his devoted house-keeper, and his friends read to him constantly. And, unlike other illustrious men in their old age, he seemed interested in the present rather than the past. To a lady who had said to him that she would like to see the strange world which would take shape after the war, Steer responded with an emphatic 'So should I'. And the satisfaction he took in exercising his mind and reaching his own conclusions without the intervention of his clever friends was gradually borne in upon me, by what stages I cannot now recall. One incident remains clearly fixed. I had come to see him, to discuss the question as to who should write the introduction to the volume to be devoted to his work in the series on British artists that I was editing for the Phaidon Press, and I told him that I believed that this work should be undertaken by one of the younger critics, who would attempt to make a fresh assessment of his work in a spirit more detached than would be possible for one of the intimates who had so early discovered and so consistently proclaimed his merits. The energy with which he expressed his concurrence came as a surprise. 'My old friends', he declared, 'have written well about me, and I'm grateful for their encouragement, but they've written enough.' I then explained that the person I had in mind had hitherto made no special study of his work, and would even approach it in a positively critical spirit, but he was excellently equipped to consider it against a broad background of European painting. 'He sounds to me just the man', Steer said, his face lighting up. 'Who is he?' I explained that he was Robin Ironside, a colleague at the Tate. 'Very well then: bring him to lunch, any day you like.' Then, as though welcoming an occasion for speaking about matters which had troubled him, he referred to the project, which I knew had been under consideration for some time, for an authorized biography. 'The idea of my life being written doesn't appeal to me', he said. 'Lives have a way of leaving out what's really important. Perhaps they have to.' Referring to various writings on Tonks, he said:

'Tonks was a big man, and big men have conspicuous faults as well as conspicuous virtues; but there seems to have been a sort of conspiracy to discount Tonk's faults. In any case, my own life has been very pleasant, but not very interesting. But my friends tell me that something of the sort will eventually be done, and that it had better be done by someone I don't disapprove of too much, and I expect they're right. There's one thing, though, I'm clear about: I don't want it done by someone who's already said his say about me. I'm tired of the old opinions, the old stories. In the last years, when I've been more alone, I've come to see many things differently; there are things I've only just begun to think out.'

The impression his attitude made upon me at the time was that, in spite of his affection and admiration for Tonks, Steer derived a conscious satisfaction from his present independence of the influence of a friend whose energy, strength of purpose and intellectual grasp so far exceeded his own. This I placed on record in my 'Burlington' note, but on account of Steer's recent death, the occasion seemed to me inappropriate for dwelling upon imperfection in a complex of friendships of a singularly wholehearted and enduring character. Nor would I do so now were I not convinced that Steer had come to recognize the source of these imperfections, to realize that certain of his intimates, by flattering his own supine attitude towards the 'fundamental brainwork' necessary to the perfection of the work even of the most instinctive artists, and by persistent argument, had impaired the activity and narrowed the range of his mind, and had imposed their own ideas upon him, to the detriment of his art. Certainly he seemed to lose no opportunity of qualifying his affectionate loyalty to his old friends by an attitude of marked detachment from them, and most emphatically from their opinions. To me, familiar ever since I was of an age to speculate about human relationships with the solidarity and the exclusiveness of the circle in which Steer was enclosed, these utterances were a surprise. It was they which caused me to call in question those parts of the legend which represent him as an artist so unerring in his intuition as to have no need for a reasoned apprehension of things. It became clear to me that Steer, no longer able to paint and brooding upon the past, had become aware of the baleful part which certain of his friends had played in fostering his intellectual inertia.

Even if the jealously possessive circle in which he lived after the 'cronies' had closed in upon him, and the numbing blend of adulation and bluff fun disposed him to ignore the causes of things, even the causes of the effects in which he most delighted, and robbed his figure painting, especially, of the vivid purposeful character which had distinguished it, he remained nevertheless a memorable figure, and one of the great landscape painters of our time. This, indeed, is the opinion of his painter friends, of the critics, accepted by a substantial part of the public which concerns itself with painting. Steer's reputation is so high, and the fervour of his advocates so fierce, that to dwell upon the shortcomings of his art is still to invite the imputation of questionable taste. For those prepared to brave this imputation it is necessary to insist that he lacked the artistic will of the greatest masters, and that he was tempted too readily to see nature in terms of other painters. I remember how easily visitors at the Memorial Exhibition of 1943 recognized which master he had had unconsciously in mind in representing given subjects. The absence of a consistent personal vision left him without a firm basis for logical and sustained development, while his lack of intellectual convictions and his delicate receptivity were apt to leave him at the mercy of chance memories. Few phases of his art, therefore, bear a logical, necessary relation to those which precede or follow them. But though a highly personal vision and logical growth may be said to be characteristic of the great masters, the relative want of both in Steer does not invalidate the high claims put forth on his behalf. The art of Delacroix was affected not less than that of Steer by the art of other masters; the unfolding of Turner's vision, owing among other causes to his love of emulation, would seem to have been as arbitrary at many points. There were moments when Steer, inspired not by particular works but rather by the spirit of Constable and Turner, painted landscape in which piercing observation goes hand in hand with a splendid poetry. I have in mind, besides such masterpieces as *Chepstow Castle* and *Richmond Castle*, already mentioned, *In a Park, Ludlow*,[1] of 1909, and the two versions of *The Horseshoe Bend of the Severn*,[2] both of 1909. Turner taught him to see the majestic, the rhythmical and the glowing qualities in landscape; Constable the beauty of noonday light, of the glistening surfaces of wet foliage

[1] Privately owned.

[2] The City Art Galleries, Manchester and Aberdeen.

and grass, and of the contrast between white cloud and angry sky, between rainbow and thunder-shower – in fact, of the living texture of nature. In these majestic, darkly tempestuous or glowing landscapes can be caught traces of a devoted discipleship of Rubens and Gainsborough also. Around his middle fifties, a change of style, corresponding to an inevitable ebb of physical energy, became apparent in his work. The epic mood and the massive mottled surface were slowly dissolving into something approaching the opposite of them: a long series of landscapes frankly inspired by the lyrical, thinly and limpidly painted sketches made by Turner as a result of his last visit to Rome twelve years before his death. Of the scenes Steer made at Harwich, at Bosham in 1912–13, of Shoreham, 1926–7, misty, subtly coloured visions, it would be no exaggeration to say that they are a worthy tribute to the miraculous originals of the master to whom he was faithful to the end. These subjects are nearly related to his productions in water-colour. This medium he used from about 1900, at first occasionally; then, as he abandoned the practice of completing large canvasses outdoors, he made use of it as a means of accumulating material for works to be completed in the studio. He became entranced, however, by the medium itself, and gratified by the success it brought him. Eventually he evolved a remarkable style, compounded of Turner, Alexander Cozens, Claude, with a faint but intriguing touch, as Tonks noted, of the Oriental, and dependent upon an astonishing dexterity.

Towards the close of his life, his water-colours had come to be widely regarded as his principal achievement. In spite of the almost miraculous quality of the finest of them I believe this to be a mistaken view, and that his fame will ultimately rest securely upon three phases of his paintings in oils: namely, his early figure subjects, the epic landscapes of his early middle years, and the liquid, lyrical visions of his old age, and a single portrait, the tenderly wrought face and figure of his grim housekeeper, *Mrs. Raynes.*

ETHEL WALKER
1861—1951

CAMILLE PISSARRO was quoted earlier in these pages as describing Impressionism as a way of seeing compatible with the free play of the imagination. But he expressed this opinion at a time when, under the promptings of Seurat, he had lately become convinced that the *original* Impressionism, by its acceptance of the scene accidently come upon, and of the necessity for completing the picture on the spot, before the light changed, in a word, by its acceptance of the *sketch* as the highest artistic ideal, did of its very nature circumscribe the imagination. He made the assertion, in fact, with the new, consciously constructive Impressionism in mind, of which he was just then a transient advocate, rather than the earlier movement. It was clear enough that this latter was not readily compatible with a deeply ranging imagination. After its first wonderful flowering and within the lifetimes of its founders, it was rejected by the most imaginative of the younger painters, and it dwindled eventually into the most tepid and unexacting of academic traditions.

Ethel Walker was the first in point of seniority of those English painters who were impelled, by an imaginative temperament, to reject Impressionism; or, rather, to modify it radically to suit her own highly personal ends. In her sense of the primacy of light she was innately Impressionist, but the Golden Age of her highest imaginings could not be represented with sufficient clarity by a system of tones; it demanded contours.

In the chapters on Sickert and Steer I was able to proceed quickly to the consideration of their work. Both were well known personalities; both are the subjects of illuminating biographies, as well as of extensive mythologies. Ethel Walker was certainly 'the best-known woman artist', but there has been no serious attempt to appraise either her art or her personality; or even, so far as I have been able to ascertain, any attempt at all. In order to find out what had been written on this artist, I visited the two principal art libraries in London. The subject index of one recorded the existence of four catalogues of one-man exhibitions, the other of a single sketchy article in a recent issue of a monthly periodical. Not much after nearly ninety years' original, aggressively independent living, after more than sixty years of increasing and effective dedication to painting. And now, it is too late to obtain from her certain important facts about her life and opinions. The last time I saw her, during the early days of 1950, it was plain that her memory had failed. She was able to recollect little and confusedly, except for a few incidents which she cherished rather as landmarks in the gathering darkness than for their intrinsic worth. One such was connected with the first occasion when she exhibited a picture. I had picked out from among the many curled and yellow photographs that were propped against the mirror above the mantelpiece one of an interior with a girl wearing a long white dress turned away from the spectator. It was from a painting, I explained, which I had long regarded as one of her best, but of which I had never seen the original.

'Oh, I'm glad you like that,' she said, 'it's very beautiful. It belongs to a relative of mine, to——I can't remember his name. It was the first oil painting I ever made. There was an exhibition in Piccadilly. At the private view George Moore came in and looked attentively at something of mine. "You've got somebody new who's good," he observed to Steer. "There she is," Steer answered. "Come over and meet her." At that time I had no studio, so Moore invited me to his flat at Victoria Street, and told me I might work there whenever I wished. So one day soon afterwards I brought a model from Pulborough in Sussex, where I was living, and took her to Moore's flat. No sooner had we arrived than a dense fog closed down. We tried a pose or two, but it was almost dark. "It's no good," I said to the model in despair. As she turned away she took so beautiful a pose beside the fireplace, with her full white dress flowing away behind her, that I was inspired, and set feverishly to work in spite of the darkness.'

Where the exhibition was she was unable to recall. It was probably at the Dudley Gallery, where this picture, entitled *Angela*, was shown in 1899. This is not only a beautiful but a mature painting, and cannot possibly (quite apart from her admission that Moore had been attracted by a previous work) have been her first. I would have liked to ask her about this and other matters, but I was reluctant to tax her failing memory.

I shall not forget that last sight I had of Ethel Walker. The previous November she had held, at the Lefevre Gallery, the last exhibition of her work in her lifetime. She was very old; she was illustrious; she had not long since ceased to paint, but the exhibition was virtually ignored both by the public and the Press. I had learnt that she was ill and indigent. But I should have been surprised to find her discouraged, for no artist I have known has ever felt so assured of the immortality of her work – or of the salvation of her soul.

When I came into her studio, unannounced and for a moment unheard, the scene before me epitomized the confident delight of Ethel Walker in the work of her hand. Beside an iron stove in which a large fire glowed, she crouched, in order to keep warm, but sideways, so that she could look out into the room. All round, upon easels, propped against chairs, upon chairs, in fact upon every level space with some kind of support behind it, every one of them turned towards their creator as a flower towards the sun, stood a dense and various assembly of her own paintings and drawings. At them she was gazing enrapt, with pride and wonder. For her, in that dark afternoon they shone like stars in the firmament. The scene lasted for but a moment. Seeing me, she got up and welcomed me, as though she had received an eagerly awaited visit from an intimate friend, instead of an unexpected visit by an old acquaintance. Presently, forgetful of her age and infirmity, she was lifting and moving her pictures to enable me to see them in the best light, just as she had when I first called upon her in that same house nearly twenty years before. Perceiving the admiration which her activity aroused, she abruptly told me her age. 'I'm eighty-six. I was born on 9 June'. 'Were you eighty-six last birthday', I enquired. 'Last birthday', she said. That made 1863 the year of her birth; hitherto she had given it as 1867. She was born in fact in 1861.

Except for the orientation of the pictures, the large L-shaped studio overlooking the river, on the first floor of 127 Cheyne Walk, which she had occupied for the past forty years, was little changed. It had silted up with her miscellaneous possessions, odds and ends of china, medicine bottles, photographs, letters, and the like, and the dust had settled still more thickly upon them. It was typical of the room that the reflections yielded by the few mirrors it contained, although these were not particularly old, were foggy and reluctant. The room had changed little because its occupant had changed little. She had grown smaller and forgetful and infirm, but these were superficial changes: the deep voice, the courage, the benevolent indifference towards other people, the restless energy and above all the unquestioning conviction of her own greatness were as conspicuous as always. That conviction was always expressed so frankly that each new manifestation of it had long been received with a partly admiring and partly malicious enjoyment. As a member, for instance, of a hanging committee of an exhibition, she would remove pictures already hung in favourable positions, replace them with her own, and walk out with an air of satisfaction at having contributed rather more than her share to the collective wisdom of the assembly. She would write to me from time to time to suggest that this or that other picture in some current exhibition would be a particularly appropriate addition to the national collection. 'I would remind you', she wrote on one occasion, 'that every purchase of my work strengthens and enriches the sum of good pictures at the Tate Gallery.'

The declaration, several times repeated during this last visit of mine, of her belief in reincarnation gave me a less unsympathetic insight into her limitless vanity. In support of it she quoted Walt Whitman: 'As to you, Life, I reckon I am the leavings of many deaths'; she urged it as the only valid explanation of genius, of all superior qualities. Therefore she regarded herself not so much as a unique phenomenon, but as the last of a long succession of previous 'incarnations', to whose remarkable merits she owed her own. Her pride, as I now understand it, resembled the family pride of the aristocrat rather than the wholly self-regarding pride of the upstart. But how constantly and how candidly she displayed it! I have never seen anyone so transported with delight by pictures as Ethel Walker by her own. Such exclamations as 'That's beautiful, isn't it?' or 'Even though that is a little sketch, it has the scale of a great picture' formed a continuous pæan of praise. She was sublimely confident that the admiration of others equalled her own. When one of her aunts died, the widower reproached her for neglecting to send a letter of condolence. When at last she wrote, it was to say that she was 'very sorry that Aunt Maud did not live to see my *Resurrection*, as she would have loved it so'. And when Steer died she said, 'Now he and Sickert are gone I'm the only artist left'.

Late on the afternoon of my last visit the fire of life died down in her, and I prepared to leave.

'I owe a good deal to Sickert,' she observed: 'he confirmed me in the habit of working fast. I've always worked fast, especially when I'm painting the sea. Sometimes, at Robin Hood's Bay, I've waited for weeks for a certain effect, a harmonious fusion of water and cloud. When it comes I rush to my canvas and paint furiously with the tide, for the sea and the sky won't wait for me, and, when the effect has gone, I never touch the canvas again. And Sickert taught me to paint across my forms, and not into them. I once said he was generous with his knowledge. Sickert, hearing of it said, "But she never takes any notice of what I say."'

The deep voice died away and we said goodbye. As I stood by the door and turned for a last look at the small figure in the red jacket and gilt buttons, white blouse and black bow tie crouched once again over the fire, at the amphitheatre of pictures and all the disorderly accumulations of forty years, scarcely visible now in the failing light, she spoke again, quietly, without looking round: 'A painter must be brave, must never hesitate. Timidity shows at once. I've always been brave – but now I've given away my palette and brushes.' She had nothing more to say and I went quietly out. I never saw her again. She died in that house on 2 March 1951.

◦   ◦   ◦

When we consider her character, her freedom from the ordinary conventions, her fanatical independence, her habit of uttering her uncensored thoughts and her domineering ways, it is perhaps odd that she led so relatively tranquil a life. It is now the fashion to assume that artists live entirely for their work, which constitutes their only relevant biography. I remember hearing H. G. Wells assert that the life of the average commercial traveller was more eventful than that of the most adventurous artist. But that is not invariably the case. The life of Sickert, for example, would make a fantastic saga comprising half a dozen secret lives, fascinating relationships with the illustrious and the forgotten; nor has the life of Augustus John been barren of event. Even Delacroix, who led, if ever a man did, a life dedicated to art, confessed that in his earlier days 'What used to preoccupy me the least was my painting'.[1]

That Ethel Walker's impact upon her generation has been slight (the only influence she has exercised has been upon the gifted spinsters, the 'matriarchs' of the New English Art Club) and her life little more eventful than Steer's is due to the completeness of her self-absorption. People affect others principally because, consciously or not, they wish to. Such was her self-absorption that, given models and the sea to paint and a generous ration of admiration (and some dogs), she could have lived happily, so to speak, in a vacuum. She has looked attentively at reproductions of the cave paintings at Ajanta, at the Blessed Angelico, Botticelli, Whistler and, longest of all, at Puvis de Chavannes, the Impressionists and Gauguin. And she has looked with tender respect; yet these works have been important in her eyes not so much on their own account as incitements to her own imaginative life. She speaks of her friends, however interesting their personalities, solely in relation to herself. Of George Moore, for instance, I once heard her say: 'He was in love with me; he tried to get into my bedroom and I threw him down the stairs. "You have the affection of a porcupine", he protested, "unconscious of its quills as it rubs against the leg of a child."' But her profound self-absorption was not inconsistent with constant and practical kindness to the afflicted and to animals. Of all religious bodies she most approved, I think, of the Salvation Army, on account of its special solicitude for the poor.

◦   ◦   ◦

Ethel Walker was the younger child of Arthur Abney Walker, a Yorkshireman, and his Scottish second wife Isabella, born Robertson, widow of a Presbyterian minister. At the time of Ethel's birth her parents resided in Melville Street, Edinburgh. One of her ancestors, Hephzibah Abney, had assiduously practised the art of water-colour; his daughter, Elizabeth, married her first cousin, Henry Walker, of Blythe Hall, Nottinghamshire, and Clifton House, Rotherham,

[1] 'Journal', 11 October 1852.

and their son, born in 1820, was Ethel Walker's father. The Walkers were ironfounders, and built old Southwark Bridge. About 1870 Arthur Walker left Clifton House, the large, bleak building where he was born and which now serves as Rotherham's municipal museum, and settled with his family at Beech Lodge, Wimbledon. Ethel attended a strict but excellent school kept by the Misses Clark in the then rural neighbourhood of Brondesbury. At this academy she attracted the particular attention of Hector Caffieri, the drawing-master, who was the first person to encourage her tentative but growing interest in painting. His connection with the school came, however, to a sudden end. A train in which the Misses Clark, accompanied by a number of favoured pupils, were travelling with edifying purpose happened to draw up beside another train, in which Mr. Caffieri was observed seated in a third-class compartment and smoking a pipe. There could be, of course, no question, the Misses Clark thereupon decided, of a person capable of such conduct being permitted to continue as a member of their staff. But about this time Ethel formed an intimate friendship with a girl named Claire Christian, whose family were neighbours of the Walkers in Wimbledon. Claire Christian shared Ethel's principal interests, and one consequence of their friendship was a heightening of their preoccupation with the arts. About 1878, in the company of an aunt, Ethel paid her first visit to France. In the early 'eighties, with Claire Christian, she attended the Putney School of Art. By this time art was her vocation: after a day's work at the school the two girls assiduously studied anatomy and drew from casts of Greek sculpture. Later they visited Spain together and made copies after Velazquez in the Prado. On their homeward journey they stopped in Paris, and, prompted by George Moore,[1] saw for the first time the work of Manet and the Impressionists.

There comes early in the life of most artists the miraculous moment when they look with understanding upon the work of a great master. I have more than once heard Ethel Walker declare that Velazquez taught her to paint. It does not appear to me that Velazquez affected her painting in any perceptible sense, and I am inclined

---

[1] Both Ethel Walker and Claire Christian, and their relations with George Moore, are described at some length and often in the latter's 'Hail and Farewell' under the pseudonyms of Florence and Stella.

F

to think that her often repeated avowal of her indebtedness was a recognition, not of any specific debt, but of her awakening to a realization, under the first impact of his genius, of all that painting could signify.

The atmosphere of Beech Lodge, although she was adored by her mother and her old nurse, was not conducive to her studies: with Claire Christian she went into lodgings in Wimbledon and later rented a cottage at Pulborough in Sussex. She worked under Frederick Brown at the Westminster School, and she followed him in 1892 to the Slade School when he was appointed to the Professorship, where she remained for two years.

The early life of Ethel Walker presents one curious feature. She seems to have been talented. From an early age she seems to have been possessed by the idea of becoming a painter. Her family's circumstances made her free of the necessity to support herself. She was endowed with a singular power of will. How was it, then, that, in these highly propitious circumstances, her beginnings were desultory and she came to maturity late? She had reached her late twenties before she went to the Putney School of Art; she was over thirty when she followed Brown to the Slade. The painting which she described to me and to others as her first, *Angela*, was probably done, as it was certainly shown, in 1899, when she was nearly forty. To this question I can offer no answer. But once she had reached the degree of maturity represented by *Angela* she developed rapidly in a highly personal direction, and won an increasing measure of recognition among her fellow painters.

Angela is an example, although an admirable one, of a kind of painting that was being done at the New English rather than an individual creation. The subject, a girl in a white dress, comes straight from Whistler, the Club's irascible patron saint, only it is represented, quite consciously, in a rougher, more homely style than the Butterfly's: the interior is less deliberately arranged, the thick paint is more loosely applied. It would not be difficult, in fact, had it borne their signatures, to accept it as the work of Steer, of Tonks or of several other leading members of the Club.

It was not long before Ethel Walker abandoned her pre-occupation with the representation of figures solidly modelled in sombrely lit Victorian interiors. The best of these paintings exhibited a truth of tone, a grasp of form, a grace, and a bold, easy handling of paint which gives them a place only just below the best of their kind, Brown's *Hard Times*[1] or Steer's *Music Room*,[2] for instance. But they are no more than admirable essays in a kind of painting already fully evolved, and even displaying symptoms of exhaustion.

The paintings of Ethel Walker's maturity differed in every important respect from those of her apprenticeship. Instead of representing facets, shadowy or shady, of the real world in terms of what might be termed the common vision evolved by the New English Art Club, she became absorbed in the contemplation of a Golden Age of full if gentle light, which she represented after a highly personal fashion. Instead of the building up of solid form, she aimed now at the creation of forms which were delicately shimmering and evocative, rather than descriptive, and, more generally, at an art not based directly upon observation but upon observation frankly transformed by a poetic imagination. Here I am thinking chiefly of what I consider to be her principal works: namely, her figure compositions, for in a considerable part of her painting – in a quantitative sense, indeed, the larger part – she continued to represent the visible world. But like her compositions, her later portraits of girls and her paintings of the sea, her two favourite subjects, reflected the radical changes which transformed her outlook during the first decade of the new century. Like the compositions, they are no longer modelled in terms of light and shade, but in delicate and brilliant colour; her preoccupation with surface design is more, and with design in depth less marked.

The transformation in her art was due to two factors: the impact of Impressionism[3] from without and the steady growth within of her vision of a Golden Age. From Impressionism she learnt how to illuminate the groups of virginal figures in their vernal settings which became more and more the focus of her most intense imaginings. Although the influence of the Impressionists upon her was mainly technical, the contemplation of their sunlit landscapes must also have illumined her inward vision. In her pictures painted directly

[1] The Walker Art Gallery, Liverpool.   [2] The Tate Gallery, London.
[3] The love of brilliant colour which she first learnt from the Impressionists was strengthened by her contacts with the Belgian painters Leon de Smet, Marcel Jeffreys, Emil Claus and Marcel Hess when they were refugees in England during the First World War.

from life – the long, enchanting series of portraits of girls and of agitated seas off the Yorkshire coast – she showed herself a disciple of the Impressionists, but in her imaginary compositions too she used certain of their technical methods, direct painting in small disjointed brush strokes of pure colour without subsequent retouching, besides modelling in colour instead of tone, but for purposes remote from theirs. Her frankly ideal visions of a Golden Age, elaborately constructed and painted in her studio from studies, had little in common except their colour with the objective studies of the Impressionists in which the thing seen was accepted with slight modifications and completed on the spot. What I have called the Golden Age of Ethel Walker's imagining was not in itself an original conception; it had haunted the imaginations of numerous European painters ever since the Renaissance. Of Ethel Walker's older contemporaries, Puvis de Chavannes had portrayed it with most conviction, and he must therefore be counted among the chief among her masters.

The two paintings in which this vision is most completely expressed are *Nausicaa* (Plate 7),[1] of 1920, and *The Zone of Love*,[2] of 1931–33, both imaginative compositions. Like all her compositions, these were based upon numerous drawings made from carefully posed models, freely transposed into an imagined world of beauty: a rainbow-hued springtime world peopled by slender young girls, naked, dreamy and innocent. These two big tenderly wrought paintings are original creations.

In this ideal world, the spirit of Ethel Walker was ecstatically at home, but how delightful a contrast it made with the studio in which her earthly body had its being – with the accumulated disorder, the long-gathered dust. How much nearer to reality that other world was in her eyes, how oblivious she herself of her earthly surroundings was suddenly revealed to me when she exclaimed: 'I can't work to-day. I'm like the old Chinese artist who couldn't work if the smallest particle of dust in the air annoyed him.'

[1] & [2] The Tate Gallery, London.

HENRY TONKS

1862—1937

A CONVERSATION which took place in 1892 between Frederick Brown, the recently appointed Slade Professor of Fine Art at University College, London, and a thirty-years-old doctor named Henry Tonks, to whom he presently offered the post of Assistant at the Slade School, had important results. The doctor abandoned his profession and became instead a painter and draughtsman, also a teacher of drawing – the most inspiring and influential, in fact, of his generation. This alone would entitle him to a place in the history of English art. But I make no apology for noticing Tonks in these pages as an artist in his own right as well.

Tonks was a phenomenon that has become rare almost to the verge of extinction – namely, an academic artist. And by an academic artist I do not mean one who supinely accepts whichever of the well established conventions happens currently to prevail but one whose art is based upon traditional canons, clearly apprehended. Academies during the past century or so have become more and more conspicuous for the disregard they have shown for the fundamental traditional values; it is therefore no accident that when the real academic artist, the Alfred Stevens, the Henry Tonks, does appear, he is rarely counted among their members. Always traditional and scholarly in his orientation, Tonks deliberately chose his side when values upon which the art of Europe had hitherto been based seemed to him to be challenged. Throughout his life as an artist he was an assiduous and a reverent student of the methods of the great masters.

Tonks was a late-comer to art, and the road he followed, as he himself has told us, was a strangely devious one. He was born of a solid, cultivated family, the proprietors of a brass-foundry in Birmingham, at nearby Solihull, the fifth of eleven children, on 9 April 1862. There must have been many illustrated books in his father's library, as the son claimed to have been familiar 'from infancy' with the draughtsmen of the 'sixties, with Charles Keene and Wilhelm Busch and, thanks to the catalogue of the 1857 Exhibition at Manchester, with the Pre-Raphaelites. Sadistic ill-treatment at the High Church preparatory school to which he was sent left him with a lasting aversion to dogmatic religion; at his public school his career was undistinguished and he was scarcely less unhappy. 'I only began to live', he declared in old age, 'when I left that damnable Clifton.' His interests shortly turned towards medicine, and in January 1880 he entered as a pupil the Sussex County Hospital at Brighton. At school he was sensible of a vague attraction to the artist's life, but there is no record of his having shown a special predilection for drawing. One faculty invaluable to an artist he early possessed: a retentive visual memory. How precisely and how vividly this enabled him to evoke, years later, incidents from boyhood and youth! The particular use, for instance, of the cane by the headmaster of his preparatory school:

He was a tall, powerful man, and he had an ingenious way of lifting the boy up the better to adapt his clothing to the punishment, and swinging him round at the same time, so that all could see the result of his prowess.[1]

Or the early stirrings of romantic sensuality:

If I had met you, as I did not, as a little girl going for a walk in Kensington Gardens, that spot would have remained sacred for me, just as the sea end in Montpellier Road, Brighton, has a meaning for me, because once I saw up the street a girl who excited my passions (my word, she was a dull girl really but just like a ripe peach).[2]

At Brighton he made drawings, which he attempted without success to sell at half a crown apiece from the window of a small shop; he also made his first attempt at painting, which he quickly abandoned in discouragement. Eighteen months later he transferred to the London Hospital, where he remained for three years, devoting himself to anatomy and physiology. During all this time he became more and more absorbed by drawing, taking as his subjects both the living and the dead, until it gradually became his ruling passion.

[1] 'Notes from Wander-Years', by Henry Tonks, *Art Work*, Winter, 1929.

[2] From a letter to a friend, quoted in 'The Life of Henry Tonks', by Joseph Hone, 1939, p. 22.

One winter he visited Germany. At Christmas in Dresden occurred one of the critical moments of his life.

One of my family sent me as a present 'The Life of Randolph Caldecott' [he wrote, recalling it]; the flat in Moscincksy Strasse, my room, the position in it of the bed, and the moment of the night when I read how he had, almost by chance, from being a bank clerk, found the way to become the charming artist he was, come back to me with extraordinary vividness. I will not say that I registered a vow at that moment, but the determination of making myself into an artist then became fixed.[1]

On his return, although he won his Fellowship of the Royal College of Surgeons and was appointed Senior Resident Medical Officer at the Royal Free Hospital, he quickly found his way to the 'truly comic and dirty little studio', as he described it, 'which under Frederick Brown became the centre of a revolution which has done much to destroy the powerful vested interests of those days', the London County Council's Technical Institute, Westminster. The association between Tonks and Brown led shortly to the appointment, earlier referred to, which had a decisive effect upon the career of Tonks and upon the draughtsmanship of several generations of students in England.

For the rest of his life Tonks was obsessed by his having reached the age of thirty before he was able to devote his whole energies to drawing and painting. The disadvantage under which he fancied himself to labour on account of a late start in his chosen vocation seems to have aggravated his innate diffidence, and the strain of irascibility he inherited from his father, for he became, especially where his drawing and painting were concerned, a secretive and touchy man. Criticism of any kind was liable to provoke his resentment and to bring him to the verge of despair. No doubt, unknown to them, his angry suspiciousness must have been provoked continually by three of his most intimate friends: by Steer, on account of his wonderful natural gifts, by George Moore, notorious for a strain of obtuseness in his human relations, and by D. S. MacColl, most inveterately critical of men. Moore's criticisms corroded the friendship of Tonks, to whom his death, as he confessed to his intimates, came as a relief. MacColl's more deeply informed judgements

[1] 'Notes from Wander-Years.'

sometimes caused coolness between the two, but they also bore positive fruit in a series of water-colours, *Mr. MacColl visits Heaven and Criticizes*,[1] made during the First World War, which exhibit Tonks's satirical humour and flexible draughtsmanship.

Irascible suspicion, an ingenuity in finding pretexts for offence, with its issue in coolnesses, quarrels and separations, pronounced though they were, did not dominate Tonks's human relations. He possessed, on the contrary, a particular talent for friendship. In social contacts of a casual or routine order, he was inclined to be sarcastic and aloof; he was mostly content to reserve his sociability for the friends of his choice. These he met constantly; with them he maintained a regular correspondence, sometimes, late at night, pursuing by letter the subject of a conversation only just ended. During the latter part of his life he set aside a part of each day, often as much as two hours, for correspondence with his friends. Of them, the closest was Steer, for whom he showed a devotion which never wavered. Among others with whom, at one time or another, he was particularly intimate were, besides Moore and MacColl, Sir Augustus Daniel, already mentioned as the possessor of the finest of Steer's early paintings, for whose judgement he had an exceptional regard, the brothers Laurence and Leonard Harrison, Sargent's sister, Mrs. Ormond, and my father – for whom his friendship turned suddenly to enmity, apparently upon the unwarranted suspicion that he had written a flattering letter to Sargent with a view to securing his election to the Royal Academy[2] – C. H. Collins Baker, and, towards the end of his life, St. John and Mary Hutchinson.

The duality in his nature, which revealed itself in a capacity for friendship of the most constant and intimate kind, together with a proneness to suspicion, secretiveness, jealousy, touchiness and even malignity, was evident in other apparent contradictions. A dour, puritanical strain, revealed by the thin-lipped, sour mouth, the chilly stare, and a fussiness in the ordering of his daily life (he smoked, for instance, at fixed times of day, usually with reference to his watch), seemed incongruous with his sometimes Rabelaisian humour, the faint strain of impropriety apt to reveal itself in his conversation, and the sheer prettiness of much of his art.

[1] Privately owned.

[2] 'Men and Memories', by Sir William Rothenstein, Vol. II, 1932, pp. 192–3.

With his students his relations were mostly as happy as they were fruitful. The famous sarcasms, which provoked so continuous a profusion of tears among the women students, and for which he has sometimes been blamed, caused little lasting pain, and were, in fact, a characteristic expression of an exhilarating personality whose impact upon the Slade was that of a bracing wind. To students whom he considered to be of promise, in particular, his kindness was proverbial, although his ability to distinguish great talent from promise was far from unerring. He recognized with reluctance the genius of Augustus John (whose influence as a student at the Slade exceeded his own), while the modest geese whom he acclaimed as swans were many.

Tonks was so quintessentially, so almost, on one side of him, parochially English that the discovery that he read with diligence the French intellectual periodicals, and was conversant with the ideas of Valéry and Proust, seemed to me, in spite of the voracity of his intellectual appetite, as hardly less odd than the knowledge that one of the most intense and solemnly high-minded of my painter friends not only never missed the now discontinued Radio Rhythm programme, but was familiar with the careers of even minor composers of swing music.

During the years 1910 and 1912 there occurred events, which will be described at a more appropriate place in these pages, which had a decisive effect upon the outlook of Tonks, and upon perhaps the majority of his generation. These were the two exhibitions of Post-Impressionist painting held at the Grafton Galleries, at which the work of van Gogh, Matisse and Cézanne was first introduced to the British public. Until that time, Tonks's eager intelligence had ranged freely among the arts, in general taking a logical and rather detached view of things. The New English Art Club, where he first showed in 1893 and with which he was closely identified, although conservative by Parisian standards, had been a rallying point, since shortly after its formation, for the most brilliant and adventurous talents. Tonks therefore inevitably counted himself a man of 'progressive' affiliations and sympathies. The presence of serried ranks of Post-Impressionist pictures, fiercely coloured, vehement, harsh, and, to an even greater degree, I imagine, the general aesthetic theories deduced from them by Roger Fry and their other sponsors and

supporters, provoked in Tonks a violent revulsion of feeling which
resulted in a settled antipathy towards contemporary art, and the
conviction that it was the negation of the traditional values to which
he had pledged his loyalty. 'I don't believe', he confessed to Daniel,
'I really like any modern development.'[1]

By 1910 Tonks was nearly fifty years old, and the character of
both his art and his teaching had assumed a rigid pattern. Had he
been content to allow that the new modes of expression were outside
his province and even his sympathies, as one who had made up his
mind long since upon fundamental principles, and that they posed
problems to which younger generations must apply themselves, he
would have ridden, with dignity and without adverse effects for
himself, the storms which Post-Impressionism raised. But he was
not content with an attitude, however critical, of detachment:
instead, with sour monotony he elected to condemn. I am not at
this point concerned with the degree of justification he had; only
with its effects upon himself. These I believe to have been harmful,
in that his attitude of condemnation raised a barrier between himself and the most gifted of his younger contemporaries. The last
twenty-two years of his life – he died on 8 January 1937 – were
spent in an exasperated insulation from the issues which agitated
the most creative minds. Was he not, he once disarmingly enquired,
'a crabbed old hopeless piece of wood that had been taken by the
flood into a backwater'? Tonks constantly talked and occasionally
wrote in denigration of the new directions in the arts; he never, I
think, defined his own attitude so lucidly as he did in the course of
some reflections upon Proust:

Artists are perhaps as likely as any to come nearer to the meaning of
life: why I hate Post-Impressionism or any form of subjectivity is
because they, its followers, do not see that it is only possible to explain
the spirit as long as we are in the world, by the things of the world,
so that the painting of an old mackintosh (I don't pretend to explain
how) very carefully and *realistically* wrought may be much more
spiritual than an abstract landscape. There is no short-cut to poetry, it
has to be dug by the sweat of his brow out of the earth, and it comes
to a man without his knowing it; in fact one must never look for it.
Of course it sounds absurd seeing the dreadful things we do, but a
painter who is not a poet ought to be put in the stocks.[2]

[1] Hone, p. 191.   [2] Op. cit., p. 272.

One great quality Tonks possessed in common with his friend Moore: an inflexible will to succeed. Both were almost without natural talent; both, by sheer effort of will, made themselves serious artists. The early works of Tonks, drawings and paintings alike, were dry, slight and affected, self-conscious Pre-Raphaelite echoes, *A Lady in her Garden*, for example, of 1894, which belonged to Frederick Brown, is characteristic of his work during his early years at the Slade. The late start, which he so frequently lamented, was, I suspect, the spur that pricked him remorselessly onwards. He drew, he painted, he studied the methods of the masters; he was never satisfied, no artist was less complacent than he. Slowly his drawing began to express his hardly won grasp of construction and gesture, and his painting the solidity and the variety of light-suffused colour and the vernal, romantic atmosphere for which he struggled. Among his own paintings I fancy that *The Crystal Gazers*,[1] of 1906, was the one in which he considered that his aspirations were most nearly fulfilled. Most, perhaps, of Tonks's admirers would incline rather to agree with Mr. Collins Baker that none of his works stands so surely for his highest endeavour as *Spring Days*,[2] of about 1928–9. In any case, the two pictures have much in common. The themes of both are pairs of young girls in sunlit rooms, of whom one is absently engaged upon a domestic task, the other withdrawn in dreamy meditation. Both pictures the artist has succeeded in endowing with a certain enchantment. The enchantment fades a little, it seems to me, under close scrutiny. In the earlier picture, for instance, the figure of the girl holding the crystal is perceived to constitute a vast and shapeless mass, in itself ungainly to the point of absurdity and bearing no proportion to the shapely head and shoulders. In drawing this figure, the artist, evidently working close up to the model, has been mesmerized by his ruler and has neglected to use his eyes. The effect of the foreshortening of the corresponding figure in the later picture, although less flagrant, is to make it awkward and bunchy; and the two figures, moreover, have only the most perfunctory formal relation to each other. It is not, however, errors in drawing and other technical defects, serious as they are, which arrest the spectator's delight in pictures which abound in obvious beauties; it is something more radical than these. In the passage just quoted

[1] Privately owned.   [2] The Tate Gallery, London.

from Tonks's writings, he observes with wisdom that 'there is no short-cut to poetry . . . it comes to a man without his knowing it; in fact one must never look for it'. How interesting an anthology could be made of wise precepts, and of instances of their authors' neglect to observe them! For surely in no two pictures has poetry been looked for with so obvious and, it may be said, with so laborious a pertinacity; never has every short-cut been more assiduously explored, lovely girls young and dream-rapt, enveloped in an atmosphere of sunlight and elegance. Nor is there any earth for the poetry to be dug from. Even Mr. Collins Baker would hesitate to claim that the hardly-won poetry in these two pictures came to the artist 'without his knowing it'. Superior to both these pictures is, I think, a cracked ghost of a picture, *The Hat Shop* (Plate 9),[1] of 1897. In this work, so ardently admired by George Moore, from the earth, so to speak, of an ordinary hat-shop the artist has dug up authentic poetry, compounded of elegance and a mysterious, almost haunted spaciousness. Another and much later picture in which he has wonderfully succeeded in a similar feat is *An Advanced Clearing Station in France*,[2] of 1918, a monumental work in the authentic academic tradition.

Tonks cherished a passionate belief in poetic painting. ('A painter who is not a poet ought to be put in the stocks.') There would seem to be something in common between the strenuous aspirations of Tonks after poetic painting and the sense of obligation felt by many English artists of the late eighteenth and early nineteenth centuries to paint historical pictures. If only they had been content to represent closely observed contemporary subjects instead of personified virtues and vices, how much anguished perversion of talent to unsuitable ends and how many pretentious failures – even from the brushes of Hogarth and Reynolds – would have been avoided. *Spring Days* is a far better picture than *Sigismunda Mourning over the Heart of Guiscardo*, or the various versions of *The Snake in the Grass*, yet when I see one of the too rare examples of the kind of painting for which Tonks's qualities best adapted him, it seems to me that these poetic pictures are the fruit, if not of their perversion, at any

[1] Privately owned, acquired and restored by the City Art Gallery and Museum, Birmingham, 1951.

[2] The Imperial War Museum, London.

7. ETHEL WALKER. *Nausicaa* (1920).
Oil, 72×144 in. The Tate Gallery, London.

8. ETHEL WALKER. *Portrait of Jean Werner Laurie* (1928–30).
Oil, 23¼ × 19½ in. The Tate Gallery, London.

9. HENRY TONKS. *The Hat Shop* (1897).
Oil, 26×36 in. The City Art Gallery & Museum, Birmingham.

10. LUCIEN PISSARRO. *Ivy Cottage, Coldharbour* (1916).
Oil, 20¾ × 24½ in. The Tate Gallery, London.

rate of their diversion from their proper ends. I refer to the small series of interiors with figures of friends or familiars, such as *Steer at Home on Christmas Day with Nurse*,[1] of about 1928, *An Evening at the Vale*,[2] of 1929, and *Sodales: Mr. Steer and Mr. Sickert*,[3] of 1930. These paintings, which are closely related to his own caricatures, derive from the satirical group-portraits of Hogarth, Reynolds and Patch. The satire is gentle, almost tender, in *The Evening at the Vale*, although Moore wrote angrily that he had been represented as 'a flabby old cook' and the artist himself as 'an elegant young man striking an attitude like a demi-god against the mantelpiece, and he is nearly as old as I am'. In *Steer at Home on Christmas Day with Nurse*, where his friend is shown pouring tea for his formidable house-keeper, Mrs. Raynes, and for her friends, the satire is broader but not less affectionate; in *Sodales* it is uproarious.

All these paintings abound in 'earth', from which the artist has dug to good purpose, and, in unaffected innocence, has discovered abundance of genial and acutely perceptive poetry. Because he has worked in a vein so entirely natural to him, and because he has followed so closely his own wise precepts, the spectator is conscious of nothing of the painful strain under which he laboured in order to create, or rather, perhaps, to piece together, the various beauties in the ostensibly 'poetic' pictures. The figures, on the contrary, fall so easily into place that they seem to be real people, inevitably, indubitably present. The three more elaborate pieces, on account of the expressive and harmonious formal relations between the sharply contrasting and incisively characterized personalities, and of the intimate atmosphere which unites them, take their places among the best conversation-pieces of our time. *Sodales* presents the critic with a more difficult task, in that there is a puzzling disproportion between the means and the effects which they produce. The means in the 'poetic' pictures are of a formidable elaboration. In *Sodales*, they are elementary and at points frankly imperfect. The drawing of Steer is woolly; Sickert is incompletely related to his background, and the whole composition is too shallow for comfort. Yet how little these imperfections appear to compromise the effect of richness,

[1] The Slade School, London.
[2] The Tate Gallery, London. Another version exists.
[3] The Tate Gallery, London.

energy and character that the picture unquestionably has! Perhaps it is, after all, the very detachment of Mr. Sickert from his surroundings which so eloquently depicts him as a bizarre wanderer who, just for an hour or two, has blown into the snug world of Mr. Steer. It is my own belief, at all events, that it is upon these too few conversation-pieces that the reputation of Tonks as a painter will principally rest.

LUCIEN PISSARRO
1863—1944

THE path of Lucien Pissarro was as straight and untrammelled as Tonks's was circuitous and beset by chance. Of all contemporary painters at work in England, Lucien Pissarro was the most completely prepared for his profession. From his infancy it was assumed, in the face of the stubborn opposition of his mother, that there existed only one vocation for him, and as soon as he was able to hold pencil and brush he was taught by Camille Pissarro, his father. Whenever the two were separated, the father addressed to the son a stream of letters, which, when they were first published in 1943, were immediately recognized as documents of the first importance to students of nineteenth-century painting.[1] In these almost daily letters written for the instruction and encouragement of his son, Camille spoke with perfect candour and illuminating insight of his contemporaries, especially his great fellow Impressionists, and with unrivalled authority of the problems of vision and technique which preoccupied them all. So that when most of his own contemporaries were groping in provincial obfuscity, Lucien was the recipient of a continuous inner history of the art world of Paris during the most brilliant epoch of modern painting from the pen of one of its masters.

Lucien Pissarro was born in Paris on 20 February 1863, the eldest of seven children, of whom all five brothers became artists, but he spent his boyhood at Osny near Pontoise, where his parents lived. All the boys showed at an early age powers of observation and draughtsmanship in which their father frankly delighted, but their mother, too familiar with the privations and griefs which harass the lives of materially unsuccessful artists, was bitterly averse to their following her husband's vocation. In order in a small measure to alleviate his family's poverty, Lucien left his school at Pontoise at the age of fifteen and went to work in Paris for a firm which sold English fabrics, but his employer eventually told his father that he

[1] 'Camille Pissarro: Letters to His Son.' Edited with the assistance of Lucien Pissarro by John Rewald.

was an excellent boy, but lacking any trace of talent for business. In 1883 he was sent to London to learn English, where he lodged at the house in Holloway of his uncle by marriage, Phineas Isaacson, whose wife was half-sister to Camille Pissarro, and supported himself by working with Messrs. Weber & Company, music publishers, at 84 New Bond Street. This employment stimulated his musical taste: he regularly attended concerts and gained a fair knowledge of the works of the classical composers. He did not continue long in this occupation, for in the following year his parents moved from Osny to Eragny, a village not far from Gisors, and they required his help, both in this undertaking and on account of their unusually straightened circumstances. Not long after the family was established in their new home, he went to work in Paris with the lithographers Manzi Joyant. This experience proved invaluable, for in the studios of the firm he became familiar with the various processes of colour reproduction. In the evenings, with his friend, the artist Louis Hayet, he either drew from the model at an obscure school in the Rue Brequel, or frequented cafés and music-halls to make studies; in addition, he continued to paint. Slowly he began to make a modest reputation. In 1886, for instance, he was commissioned by the editor of 'La Revue Illustrée', F. G. Dumas, to make four woodcuts as illustrations for 'Mait' Liziard', a story by Octave Mirbeau. These woodcuts clearly show the influence of Charles Keene, who was admired in the Impressionist circle and whose engravings for 'Punch' Lucien collected.

It was in that same year that Lucien, together with his father, came to be intimately linked with Seurat and Signac, and an enthusiastic participant in the Neo-Impressionist movement of which these two were the originators. Already in the following year, Camille Pissarro – deeply implicated in the Impressionism of which the new movement was in some measure a repudiation, and the possessor of a temperament too spontaneous and a hand too vigorously expressive not to feel cramped by its rigid procedures – began to recede from it. But it was not until some years later that he abandoned the practice of divisionism. Upon Lucien the impact of Neo-Impressionism was lasting in its effects. He belonged by birth to the generation which was acutely conscious of the disorderly, fugitive elements in the earlier, in what his father termed 'romantic', Impressionism; his personal relations with Seurat, Signac and Félix Fénéon, the principal literary advocate of Neo-Impressionism, were close. What is more important, Lucien was without the particular qualities which the discipline of the movement repressed. He was thus able to continue in harmony with the most vigorous and fruitful impulse of the time – that of restoring the imagination and conscious architectural design to their rightful places in painting – and in harmony with his friends. And in harmony, above all, with his own particular vision. But he was not infected by the air of pedantry which hung about the movement. It is to be expected that the son of a master, especially when he has much in common with him, should be dismissed as a shadow of his father. Lucien Pissarro, on account of his innate affinities with a father who inspired in him an unreserved and unclouded devotion and his own modest, unassertive character, was particularly exposed to denigration of this sort. In comparison with those of Camille, his gifts were of a secondary order: he was an altogether tamer, less creative figure, but to call him a mere shadow is to do him much less than justice. His father, for all his devotion to his favourite son, praised him sparingly. He told him, however, that delicacy and distinction were his outstanding qualities, and that he possessed naïve good faith and a discreet reserve. These certainly are not the supreme attributes of a painter, but, cultivated with the single-heartedness and sober judgement of Lucien Pissarro, they produced an art which was sensitive, dignified and consistent. In the best of his paintings the forms, thoughtfully disposed, scrupulously realized, scintillate with a sober, even luminosity. This artist's vision had reached its maturity by the time he was in his early twenties, and he spent the remainder of his life in the unremitting effort to strengthen and purify it.

Lucien Pissarro was represented with his father, Degas, Mary Cassatt, Berthe Morisot, Gauguin, Redon and Seurat at what was, in fact, the eighth and last Impressionist Exhibition (although, on the insistence of Degas, the word 'Impressionist' was omitted from the announcement of it), held above the Restaurant Doré at the corner of the Rue Lafitte and the Boulevard des Italiens from 15 May to 15 June 1886.

In November 1890 he took the decisive step of settling permanently

in England; in 1916 he became a British subject. The most compelling of the several reasons which prompted this migration was
fear of his father's influence. Letters show how the effects of Camille's
mighty talent upon theirs, tentative and unformed, preoccupied
both father and sons: 'I know you fear my influence, but there is
such a thing as going too far'; 'It has to be England, for here I am a
hindrance to you all'; 'I feel you are still too close to my work'.
But Lucien was also moved by other considerations, of which the
chief was his want of success in Paris as an illustrator of books. Only
the commonplace in conception and the mechanical in execution, it
seemed to him, were acceptable in France. England, on the contrary,
he regarded as the country where the inspiring revival in the making
of books, which originated with William Morris, was still in
progress. From this movement he expected to learn and to it he
aspired to make his contribution. He took a small painting-room and
tried, without success, to support himself by giving lessons in drawing and engraving to private pupils. Thanks to introductions from
Fénéon and Mirbeau, he met English writers and artists. One of
these was the poet John Gray,[1] author of 'Silverpoints', who was soon
to enter the priesthood of the Catholic Church. Gray performed
a valuable service to Lucien by introducing him to Charles Ricketts,
for many years his closest English friend and most influential
mentor. Through Ricketts the world of book illustration, typo-
graphy and binding was immediately open to him. Ricketts and his
intimate friend, Charles Shannon, invited him to contribute to their
elegant and esoteric journal, 'The Dial', illustrated with woodcuts,
the first number of which was published in the previous year. Woodcuts by Lucien appear in the second number, published in February
1891. In 1892 he married Esther Bensusan, a distant relative, and
Camille Pissarro came over for the wedding. After a visit to France,
the young couple settled in April 1893 in Epping, at a house in
Hemnall Street which he called Eragny, in honour of his father.
Here, in 1894, he established the Eragny Press. He had already
printed two folios of woodcuts, of which the second, *Les Travaux
des Champs*, contained six subjects designed and drawn upon the
wood by his father. The first book to issue from the Eragny Press,

---

[1] Erroneously described by John Rewald as an artist. 'Camille Pissaro: Letters
to His Son Lucien', p. 137.

'The Queen of the Fishes', was handwritten and the text reproduced by process. Of the thirty-five books produced by the Press, a series of sixteen was printed in the Vale type, designed by Ricketts, who lent it to the Pissarros (for Esther quickly showed herself a conscientious and skilful assistant), and a later series, similar in number, appeared between 1903 and 1914, in the Brook type that Lucien designed.

It was not long before he took an honourable place in the small group of artist-craftsmen-printers, of which Morris was the first and Ricketts, at the time of Lucien's arrival in England, the most active. 'Unity, harmony, such are the essentials of fine book building', Ricketts declared. 'A work of art is a whole in which each portion is exquisite in itself yet co-ordinated.' Of them all, Lucien strove the most uncompromisingly after the unity of which Ricketts spoke. In his later books, he not only designed and cut the type, but he designed and, with the help of his wife, engraved the illustrations and embellishments, thus dispensing with the services of the professional wood-engraver (upon whom even Morris had depended), and he made their bindings.

This is not the place to dwell upon the achievements of Lucien Pissarro as a designer and maker of books, but the feature of it most nearly related to his painting calls for mention – namely, his use of colour. It would have been surprising if an artist so deeply imbued with Impressionism had not expressed it in his books as well as his painting, and in fact the distinguishing feature of the products of the Eragny Press was their delicate colour and tone. His double preoccupation with unity and with colour led him on occasion to knit his coloured woodcuts closely to his text by printing it, instead of in black, in muted greens and greys. His successful use of colour as a primary element within a completely harmonious whole was his most enduring achievement in this field.

The Pissarros remained at Eragny House, occupied chiefly with the making of books, until 1897, when they moved to London, living at 63 Bath Road, Bedford Park, until 1900, when they settled at a house known as The Brook at Stamford Brook, where they made their home until the death of Lucien on 10 July 1944 at Hewood, Somerset. The stables at The Brook, a pleasant Georgian house, were adapted for a studio.

During its earlier years the Eragny Press absorbed the greater part of his energies, but he was continuously active as a painter. At Epping his contacts with his fellow painters were comparatively few, but his establishment in London marked a change – gradual, but eventually notable – in the position he occupied among them. As a young man he was inclined at times to be irresolute in his aims and fitful in his habits of work. In the 'Letters' there is evidence of his father's awareness of these defects. After Lucien's illness in the spring of 1897, for instance (when Camille had come to England to bring him, Esther and their daughter Orovida back to Eragny), it seemed to him that his eldest son was prolonging his convalescence unduly. 'I hope that now you are back in your own circle', he wrote,[1] 'you will be able to work. You must give proof of will-power; it is also a question of habit. With a little courage you will succeed.' But as Lucien passed from youth to middle age his self-confidence and his industry increased. As the fame of the Impressionists grew steadily in England, the son of one of the most illustrious among them came to be regarded with a kind of reverential respect. Before, however, he was able to speak with authority as his father's son and out of his own experience as a painter, a valued friendship had to be broken. Increased knowledge of Impressionism, while it inspired the ablest among the younger painters, confirmed in their seniors a bitter prejudice against it. Among the militant sharers of this prejudice was Ricketts. Camille Pissarro was concerned at the 'Italian influence of Ricketts' over his eldest son: '. . . you give me the impression that you listen only to him', he complained.[2] The influence of Ricketts over Lucien as an engraver and a maker of books, as a typographer above all, was constant and valuable; as a painter it was negligible. The eager susceptibility Lucien showed on the one side and the indifferent imperviousness on the other has puzzled certain of his admirers, but I think with little cause. He was consistent in each instance in that he adhered to the more vigorous tradition, but his course was determined by consistency upon a deeper level than that where conscious judgements are formed. As a boy he had given himself heart and mind to the Impressionism taught him by his father. As a young emigrant in England, he had also identified himself, and with scarcely less reserve, with the

[1] 23 October 1897.   [2] 12 July 1900.

tradition of William Morris as an engraver and a maker of books. To have abandoned either would have been at variance with the unyielding constancy of his nature. Lucien's quiet adherence to the principles of an eminent father was understandable, a trait even to be respected in a young man, especially as they long continued to be little understood. But as gradually these principles made more of a stir in the world, and gained numerous adherents, and Lucien, no longer a reserved youth, became their respected advocate, the days of his friendship with Ricketts were numbered. How easy to understand the growing coolness towards his young friend of the dictatorial Ricketts, hostile to realism as the enemy of the imagination, and impatient of rival preachers, especially young disciples of his own who set themselves up in middle life as preachers of heresy! It is not therefore surprising that the day came when Ricketts passed Lucien by without recognition.

Lucien continued, as I have said, to produce books until the closure, in 1914, of the Eragny Press, but for the better part of a decade painting may be said to have been his most constant preoccupation. His vision was steady and sensitive rather than original, and his technique was solidly adequate rather than brilliant, but everything he did was marked by a delicate perceptiveness and a gentle candour. A certain unworldliness, a detachment from intrigue, are somehow mirrored in his art. The paintings of Lucien did not excite either passionate admiration or passionate censure, but they were held in a constantly growing regard. And the artist himself, his earlier hesitancies and want of urgency gradually outgrown, exerted a positive and fruitful influence, not only upon Sickert, but upon the chief personalities of a younger generation. But as learning is more important than teaching, I will defer treating of his influence until I come to write of the school of painters which he helped to establish.

After his first penurious years in England, he never consented to give formal instruction in drawing or painting, but he used to invite serious students who approached him to bring their work to his studio. His quick and accurate discernment of the needs of students, and his quiet, modest fashion of responding to them, spread his influence among a widening circle of younger painters.

From the time of the return of Sickert to England from Venice in 1905 and for several years afterwards Pissarro and he were on close and friendly terms. The focus of their association, the focus, too, of the activities of the most gifted among the younger generation, was the memorable meetings at 19 Fitzroy Street. Each member of the group which formed here around Pissarro and Sickert had the right to a rack to store his pictures and to an easel upon which to show them to the numerous persons who became interested in this novel point of contact with honoured exponents of the Impressionist tradition and a group of young painters of conspicuous talent, in this novel means of circumventing the dealers with their burdensome commissions and the exhibiting societies with their rigid and undemocratic constitutions. Saturdays were the days when the 'members' entertained their friends, showed and sometimes sold their work. At lunchtime they would adjourn to the Etoile in neighbouring Charlotte Street. These 'Saturdays', Ricketts's and Shannon's 'Friday evenings', and the second and fourth Sundays in every month when Lucien entertained his friends at The Brook (in fair numbers for tea; a smaller company of the more intimate were privily invited to remain to supper), became the principal events of his social life. At his own somewhat studious but hospitable evenings, spent in serious talk and study of his excellent collection of prints and illustrated books, among the most regular guests were his associates of 19 Fitzroy Street, Thomas Sturge Moore, the poet, Campbell Dodgson, Keeper of the Print Room of the British Museum, Ethel Walker, William Rothenstein and, until the final breach, Ricketts and Shannon. Pissarro exhibited with the Camden Town Group (which grew out of 19 Fitzroy Street) in 1911, with the New English Art Club from 1906, at the Allied Artists, and his first one-man exhibition was held at the Carfax Gallery in May 1913. The last considerable exhibition of his work to be held during his lifetime at Millers in Sussex, 'Three Generations of Pissarros', in which his father and his daughter Orovida were also well represented, I had the privilege of opening. I remember how proud I was to have been invited to perform the ceremony, and how he behaved as though it were they who were indebted to me. I can see him very clearly against the Pissarro paintings and drawings, among the crowd which had gathered in Lewes from all parts of Sussex, his short, stout figure, his full white beard shot with black, his cloak, his black wide-brimmed hat, and, behind the thick lenses of his spectacles, his slightly protuberant dark eyes; I remember the grave and gentle expression they radiated. Just as he had nothing of 'the melancholy, harsh and savage' elements which his father noted in his own temperament, or of his pungency as painter or writer (it would never, for instance, have occurred to Lucien to say, with reference to his politics, 'Gauguin . . . is always on the side of the bastards'), so his art differed from that of Camille. The father's was fluent and direct; the son's was conscientious and constructive. Lucien derived his palette from his father as a boy at Eragny, and his conception of design – the forthright, somewhat rigid system of design partly imposed upon, partly discerned in nature – from his Neo-Impressionist contemporaries, Seurat and Signac, but he gradually modified the uncompromising divisionism which they taught him. No new impulse would seem to have affected his tranquil, sensitive and deeply honest development of an outlook and of methods acquired early in his life. His painting therefore changed little – his brush strokes became rather shorter, less vigorous, but more sensitive as he grew older, and the quality of his paint a trifle drier – but the centre of gravity remained precisely where it was: no painter at work in England during the present century showed a greater consistency of aim than Lucien Pissarro.

JAMES PRYDE

1866–1941

THERE are certain painters about whom I find it difficult to determine whether they succeeded in expressing some important element in human life, or whether they produced, with whatever integrity and accomplishment, what are, in the last analysis, mere variants of existing works. I catch myself peering, as it were, into the faces of artists living or remembered, whose works I have pondered, and trying to read there the answers to my doubts – doubts which a future historian will find it easy to resolve – into the venerable face of George Clausen,[1] nobly marked by sixty years of humble and devoted dedication to painting, or at the fresh handsome face of Charles Shannon,[2] which carried even into old age the same unsullied spiritual look it had worn when he was a youth, I am conscious of a painful sense of arrogance in ignoring in these pages their solid, honourable achievements. But I am compelled to the conclusion that the art of the one is an unreflective projection of the art of Bastien-Lepage and that of the other of the art of Watts,

[1] *Sir George Clausen*, 1852–1944, figure and landscape painter of scenes of rural life, influenced by the French plein-air school and Impressionism; also author of occasional decorations. Born in London, 18 April 1852, son of a decorative painter of Danish descent. Studied at South Kensington under Edwin Long, and in Paris at the Académie Julian. Also visited Belgium and Holland. An original member of the New English Art Club, 1886; A.R.A., 1895; R.A., 1908; R.W.S., 1898. Professor of Painting in R.A. schools, and author of 'Six Lectures on Painting', 1904, and 'Aims and Ideals in Art', 1906. Knighted, 1927. Died 23 November 1944 at Cold Ash, near Newbury, Berks.

[2] *Charles Haslewood Shannon*, 1863–1937, painter of figure subjects and portraits, illustrator and connoisseur. His paintings often reveal a scholarly indebtedness to the Old Masters, especially to the tradition of Titian and Giorgione. Born at Quarrington, Lincolnshire, 26 April 1863, son of the Rector. Studied at the Lambeth School of Art, where he met Charles Ricketts, his lifelong companion, with whom he collaborated in the Vale Press and the *Dial*. A.R.A., 1911; R.A., 1920. Incapacitated after a fall from a ladder in 1929. Died at Kew, near London, 18 March 1937. The greater part of the works of art he and Ricketts had collected was left to the Fitzwilliam Museum, Cambridge.

both of which lack the principle of organic growth; that they belonged to that category of artists whom Northcote described as cisterns rather than living streams. I am the more conscious that my judgement may be at fault in that I propose to consider an artist who, in comparison with Clausen and Shannon, was deficient in creative power and in skill and, what was worse, in belief in his own vision – in fact, a failure, James Pryde. My justification is the originality and the consistency of the vision that was his, which, however, he lacked both the intellectual power to organize and the energy to develop.

James Ferrier Pryde was born in Edinburgh on 30 March 1866. The circumstances of his early life conspired to foster, if not to stimulate unduly, a highly romantic imagination. Every important element in his vision derived from his earliest days, and it is no exaggeration to say that no subsequent experience changed or added to it. The house in which Pryde was born, and where he spent his first two years, was as tall and sombre as a building in one of his own paintings. After an eight-year suburban interlude, his parents established themselves in Fettes Row, where they lived for twenty years, first at No. 22, moving two years later to No. 10. This house, also high, narrow, dark, was lit by a chilly north light; its narrow staircase mounted steeply up and up through a sombre half-light. This narrowness, gloom and perpendicularity made an impression which deepened with the passage of the years. At either end of Fettes Row stand two churches which would further have encouraged his predeliction for the tall and the impressive, and made him aware of the dramatic possibilities of columns and steps. Although it offers the sharpest contrast in architectural style to the New Town in which Pryde passed his boyhood, the Old Town, with its narrow streets of gaunt and gloomy tenement buildings and washing fluttering from the windows, ministered to his same abiding sense of the beauty of grandiose dereliction. There was one particular object, the great four-poster bed of Mary Queen of Scots at Holyrood, that haunted his imagination for at least as long as he was able to paint. The importance of Edinburgh in the shaping and furnishing of his mind, apparent to any student of his art, is acknowledged in a brief autobiographical fragment. 'To me,' he wrote, 'it is the most romantic city in the world. . . . I was very much impressed with the spirit of Holyrood, the Castle, and the old houses and Close, in the High Street.'[1]

But there must have been thousands of young men and women in Edinburgh whose imaginations were stirred by the sombre architecture of that wonderful city; environment moves readily enough to poetic imaginings, but rarely, of itself, to their transmutation into art. There was one improbable circumstance of Pryde's home life which made him familiar with the idea of transmutations of such a kind: his whole family, from his father, Dr. David Pryde (from 1870 Headmaster of the Edinburgh Ladies' College) downwards, was stage-struck. Irving had played in Edinburgh in the 'fifties, and the admiration which Dr. Pryde then formed for him, communicated to his wife and children, became a hysterical family cult. There is reason to suppose that James Pryde, besides participating in the solemn rites of Irving worship, was addicted to more popular devotions in the shape of attendance of the 'penny gaffs', the boisterous shows held in street booths behind the Royal Scottish Academy. Besides giving him an insight into a living art which made the prospect of his becoming an artist appear an immediate possibility instead of a perilous voyage into the unknown, his associations with the theatre made a deep and manifold impression upon both his life and his art. They inspired in him the ambition, intermittently and lamely realized, of becoming an actor himself; they began a connection with the theatrical world which lasted until the end of his life, and they stamped his personality with something of the actor, and his painting with the character of stage scenery.

By his early twenties he would seem to have been possessed of almost all his assets as an artist. At what periods of his life he became familiar with Hogarth, Velazquez, Guardi and Piranesi is unknown. The study of the work of all these artists was of manifest value to him. From them he must have gained an enhanced confidence in his own highly personal way of looking at the world; from them he evidently learned much about the making of pictures, and, it must be said, a repertory of pictorial mannerisms. Pryde's biographer discovered, for instance, that he possessed a photograph of Velazquez' *View from the Villa Medici: La Tarde*, and he considers it

[1] 'James Pryde', by Derek Hudson, 1949, p. 20.

probable that it was from this picture that Pryde appropriated several of his favourite themes, notably the high archway, boarded up in a manner to give it a look of dereliction, the tall cypresses, the eroded statue, the balustrade with the drapery hung over it. But although by his twenties he had reached the fulness of his growth, the time was not yet come for him to blossom in his fulness as a painter. How gifted and serious an artist he was is apparent from the charcoal drawing he made about 1886 of *Miss Jessie Burnet*,[1] a study of a young girl which puts one in mind of a Gwen John, only it is fuller, and finished with the conscientiousness of a beginner.

After the end of Pryde's desultory studies at the Royal Scottish Academy School and a brief visit to Paris without apparent consequence to his art, he settled in 1890 in England. Chance, however, at first directed his energies not towards painting but to the designing of posters. Mabel, one of his five sisters, an original character, met William Nicholson, a fellow student under Herkomer at his imitation Beyreuth school at Bushey, and after a singular courtship the two were married, and they established themselves in the spring of 1893 at The Eight Bells, a small former public-house at Denham, Buckinghamshire. A day or two after their arrival James Pryde came for a week-end and remained for two years. The visit led to the fruitful collaboration of Pryde and Nicholson as 'J. & W. Beggarstaff', who designed the best posters that had been seen in England. There is a sharp division of opinion as to whether Pryde or Nicholson was the dominant partner. That question is outside the scope of this book. The chorus of well-merited praise of the Beggarstaffs' posters has obscured the probability that the collaboration was prejudicial to Pryde's prospects as a painter. Pryde was lazy, and the habit of imagining in such broad, simplified terms as poster-designing demanded and his dependence upon his energetic brother-in-law to do the greater part of the executive work must have fostered a laziness which showed itself in the emptiness of much of Pryde's later painting, and in a disposition never to do for himself what he could persuade others to do for him.

In the autobiographical fragment earlier referred to, Pryde observed that the early impressions gained in Edinburgh did not affect his work until considerably later. It was about 1905 that the

[1] Privately owned.

emotions with which his early years in Edinburgh had charged his mind began to show themselves – emotions which, during the fifteen years or so since his departure, had been growing, as it were underground, in strength and clarity. With a curious suddenness, they fused into a vision romantic, dignified, sombre and highly personal, which, for the next twenty years, was expressed in a series of paintings of imaginary architectural compositions with small figures. Owing to Pryde's habit of giving the same title to several pictures, which may have been due to carelessness, perhaps even to a deliberate intention to mystify, the dates of his pictures are difficult to ascertain. The earliest of his architectural compositions was probably *Guildhall with Figures*, first exhibited in 1905, purchased by Sargent and subsequently lost. The architectural compositions are beyond question Pryde's original contribution to painting. Thirteen of them had as their principal feature a great bed, based upon his early memories of the bed of Mary Queen of Scots at Holyrood.

At first sight there is something deeply impressive about the best of these compositions; there is something about them which, even after the critical faculty has been provoked, lingers in the memory. It would hardly be possible to forget the way of seeing which Pryde for a few moments compels even the most recalcitrant to share. For to Pryde belonged one of the qualities of a great imaginative artist of imposing his vision by the force of sheer conviction. Augustus John, in the course of a brief description of his visits to Pryde's studio, indicates the particular character of these architectural pictures.

This studio [he wrote] had the lofty, dignified and slightly sinister distinction of his own compositions. Upon the easel stood the carefully unfinished and perennial masterpiece, displaying under an ominous green sky the dilapidated architectural grandeur of a building, haunted rather than tenanted by the unclassified tatterdemalions of Jimmy's dreams.[1]

The tall, derelict buildings, the high rooms, darkly painted and harshly coloured, convey a powerful suggestion of a malignant and inescapable fate overhanging man. Pryde has been likened to Poe, but he is closer to Hardy. But even the best of Pryde's paintings will not

[1] 'James Pryde', by Derek Hudson, p. 82.

withstand scrutiny. The general impression they leave is lasting, because there was something memorable and unique about his way of seeing, but it may be fairly said that never, in one single instance, did he succeed in giving it form which will long satisfy an exacting eye. I remember years ago saying of a picture in the presence of Gordon Craig that it was too theatrical for my taste, and how sharply he rebuked me with the words, 'And why shouldn't it be theatrical?' The answer which I was too slow to give is, I suppose, that the quality of theatricality, with its appeal to ephemeral emotions, is proper to a play, because when the curtain is rung down nothing remains, but improper in a work of art intended for prolonged scrutiny. And the defect of Pryde's painting is its theatricality: it is designed to make only a momentary impression. The spectator, suspicious of the degree to which his emotions have been played upon, becomes coolly critical, and his attitude hardens as he notes, one after another, the crude devices the artist has employed. The unvarying and excessive disparity in scale, for instance, between his buildings and his human beings is perceived to be grotesque. The doors are so vast that nobody could push them open. He notes, too, the slipshod manner in which these crude devices are constructed, the poverty and flimsiness of forms which at first seemed so imposing, and the way in which most of the pictures are designed, according to a formula, in three planes parallel to the picture surface, each separated from the other by a pace or two, like drop-scenes in a theatre. The art of Pryde, in fact, is lacking in all the qualities of good, let alone of great painting, except for the vigorous and consistent vision which he was never able fully to realize. Or, rather, which he was not equipped fully to realize in paint. Pryde's gifts fitted him ideally for the theatre, where his particular defects would not have mattered. The theatre was alive to his talents: both Gordon Craig and Lovat Fraser were deeply in his debt, and after he had all but ceased to paint, his theatrical sense was recognized by an American producer, Miss Ellen Van Volkenburg, who induced him to design the scenery for Paul Robeson's 'Othello' at the Savoy Theatre in 1930. Pryde himself was always drawn to the theatre; from time to time he played a small part himself. In the summer of 1895 he toured with Gordon Craig, taking the part of the priest in the last act of 'Hamlet', and another priest in 'Villon', a one-act play.

> As an actor [wrote Craig] he never really existed: but the idea of
> acting, the idea of the theatre – or rather the smell of the place – meant
> lots to him. Yes, I think he got much 'inspiration' from the boards –
> and the thought and feel of it all, as of a magical place. . . . There were
> little moments when in a bar or in the street he would put on the actor,
> as it were. He thought well of his own 'stage personality' off the stage:
> on it, it all vanished. But I'll swear he saw into the marvellous pos-
> sibilities.[1]

Pryde not only thought well of his stage personality; he came to
regard the world as a stage. Four sentences from Augustus John's
account of him, already quoted from, bring back to abounding life
the Pryde of the later years:

> Jimmy had been an actor and he still seemed to be playing a leading
> part in some robust old melodrama. Whatever his role might have
> been, it was a congenial one and he hadn't seen fit to remove his make-
> up. The performance in fact was non-stop and must have put a strain
> on even his constitution. When I last saw him in 'Rules', Maiden Lane,
> it looked as if it were almost time to ring the curtain down.[2]

My father has noted his passion for dressing up as Pierrot, and another friend described him so dressed and playing the harmonium
on Southwold beach. His everyday appearance continually engaged
his attention: his attitudes were studied and practised, and his dress
was the product of serious thought. He took pleasure in the contrast
between the bohemian appearance of his brother artists, sporting
ear-rings and hobnailed boots, beards and cloaks, and his own
dandified and dignified but not less distinctive appearance in a long
maroon overcoat with enormous buttons, and a velvet collar and
a plush top-hat such as cabbies wore.

The contrast which Gordon Craig observed between Pryde's
inability to act and his enchantment with the idea of acting and
his sense of the theatre as a magical place, is in some degree paralleled
by his inability to find forms to express, nobly and exactly, his sense
of the grandeur of a towering dilapidated building or of a high,
curtained bed and the littleness of the human figures which they
overshadow. In a moment of exultation, his biographer acclaimed
Pryde as the greatest painter since Turner. For making this and other
high claims for his subject, Mr. Hudson was taken to task by various

[1] Op. cit., pp. 37–8.   [2] Op. cit., p. 82.

reviewers. The suggestion that Pryde could hold his own with Turner as a painter will not, of course, bear an instant's calm reflection, but a comparison between Pryde the painter and Turner the poet, would not be irrelevant; between the series of high, derelict buildings and rooms and beds, sombrely shadowed and gloweringly lit, and the inept and never completed 'Fallacies of Hope'. To press the comparison would be unfair to Pryde, but the painting of Pryde, like the poetry of Turner, conveys, for all its imperfection, intimations of a vision more powerful and more deeply felt than its maker was able to express. It is for the occasional glimpses they afford of a harsh, gloomy but authentic poetry that the best of Pryde's paintings deserve to be remembered.

The comparative study of the careers of artists shows how little, by themselves, even high gifts of mind and hand are able to achieve unless they are directed by an unfailing purpose. In every generation many artists gifted – and gifted sometimes abundantly – with the first two, but who lack the last, vanish without trace. Pryde lacked it totally, so that neither the power and consistency of his vision nor his skill as a draughtsman availed to arrest his premature decay as an artist. Very early in his life he showed a broad vein of irresponsibility not only towards his obligations as a citizen, but also as an artist. It mattered little that he upset coffee-stalls upon their owners and patrons, that he engaged in street fights or that he was frequently in hiding from his creditors or that he drank heavily. Artists who have been guilty of all these and more, from Benvenuto Cellini to our own time, have succeeded, notwithstanding the diversion of creative power involved. But Pryde neglected to cultivate with assiduity that sombre, grandiose vision of his. To name a single instance of this neglect, though possibly the gravest: he was a painter of architecture, yet, his biographer informs us, he only admitted having painted a single building 'from the life'. This may not have been literally true, but the repetitiveness, the absence of development, an airlessness and a want of definition at key points are clear indications of his neglect to refresh his vision by the study of nature. At the heart of his failure lay, I think, the simple and awful fact that he slowly lost interest in painting.

Between 1915 and 1918, in the middle of that period of his life which his biographer calls his 'years of achievement', which extended from about 1905 until about 1925, a friend of mine saw Pryde frequently. She was one of a small circle of intimates of which Pryde was the focus. The members met several times a week at the houses of one or another of them, and often at his studio at 3 Lansdowne House, Holland Park – lent to him by Sir Edmund Davis, a wealthy patron of the arts – where he settled in 1914 after his separation from his wife. The studio, dark and lofty as one of his own compositions, was furnished like them with deep-red hangings and ornamental columns, and elaborately arranged to give an impression of careless, opulent profusion. On an easel stood the 'carefully unfinished and perennial masterpiece' noted by Augustus John, which, my friend assured me, during those three years underwent no perceptible change. His friends, she said, exerted as much pressure as they dared in the face of his aversion from talk about painting to revive his manifestly languishing interest in his vocation, but he gave at times the impression of positive boredom with painting, and of awaiting, with eager anticipation, the hour when he would foregather with his friends. He accomplished nothing of consequence, and during the last ten years or more of his life he appears to have done nothing at all. His languishing energies were directed towards dignified and gentlemanly forms of begging, whether it was writing to friends to purchase a picture or choosing, at public gatherings, the company of those most likely to stand him drinks or to drive him home. On rare occasions, when pressed for debt, and unable, for some reason, to extract the requisite sum from a friend, he would take up his brushes as a last resort.

By a curious stroke of fortune, it happened that early in the nineteen-twenties, at the very time when his creative energies began to fail, his reputation blossomed. Perhaps this combination of circumstances was not so curious after all. His most productive and fruitful years lay immediately behind, and the fact that he spent his time at the Savage Club, bars in the Strand and other places much frequented by journalists instead of at his easel, resulted in the wide-spread fanning by gossip-writers of a merited reputation. He became a sort of legendary king of bohemia. When sober he was inclined to be taciturn, at other times his conversation delighted those privileged to hear it. He showed occasionally flashes of wit. One night some years earlier, at the National Sporting Club, a friend, indicating

Augustus John, who looked a Christlike figure in those days, asked Pryde, 'How old is Gus?' Pryde looked across the ring. 'I don't know', he answered, 'but it must be getting dam' near time for his crucifixion.'

His friends, devoted and exasperated by turns, expected, his biographer tells us, to find him one day lying dead in his own four-poster with the curtains in tatters around him and the cobwebs spread over his special possessions: a last great dramatic tableau. But when he described himself as having 'one foot in the grave and the other on a banana skin', he showed greater prescience than his friends. Early in 1939, infirm in mind and body, he was taken to St. Mary Abbots Hospital, Kensington. Here he spent his last two years in a ward for old men, sucking sweets and reading detective stories. Here he died on 24 February 1941, aged not, as his friends supposed, seventy-one, but seventy-four. The old actor had consistently lied about his age. The Providence which ordained that he should not die in his four-poster had prepared a stupendous tribute to the vestiges of greatness in the lazy old inebriate who had lost his memory. As he lay dying, the earth trembled under the impact of falling bombs, black smoke covered the city and flames leapt up the shattered buildings. For an apocalyptic moment, nature, whom Pryde had neglected to his infinite cost, was transformed according to his vision.

H

FRANCES HODGKINS
1870—1947

IN the late nineteen-twenties the public was made aware of a new talent by an exhibition held at the now defunct Claridge Gallery. The works shown were oils and water-colours in a handwriting assured, sometimes to the verge of carelessness, and marked by arresting combinations of colour. It was not easy to decide whether they were the emanations of a simple or of an artfully sophisticated mind. Original some of them evidently were. It was presumed that an artist hitherto unknown and so easily familiar with contemporary modes of seeing must be young. This impression was strengthened by the appearance of work by the same hand in exhibitions representative of the avant-garde, and it was deliberately fostered by the artist herself. It was, however, erroneous: the dashing arrival was almost sixty years old. In her determination to preserve unimpaired her identification with the younger painters whose ideas, after a lifetime of painting, she had come to share and whose admiration she deeply valued, Frances Hodgkins was inclined to suppress and distort the facts about her life before she was, so to speak, reborn. These attempts to mislead the inquisitive were deliberate, but not systematic. After the acquisition of her first picture by the Tate Gallery in 1940, I asked her for certain biographical facts, which she readily gave, and, I believe, accurately. These included the precise date of her birth, which has not, I think, been recorded, not even in Miss Myfanwy Evans's excellent essay.[1]

Frances Hodgkins was born in Dunedin, New Zealand, on 28 April 1870, the second daughter of William Matthew Hodgkins, a solicitor born in Liverpool, who had gone out as a young man, spending some years in London and Paris on the way. In the artistic and intellectual life of the colony he played a zestful part: he helped to establish the Art Gallery, was founder and first President of the Otago Art Society, and well known as a topographical water-colour painter in a politely modified Impressionist style. He also gave

[1] 'Frances Hodgkins', The Penguin Modern Painters, 1948.

lectures, and he and Mark Twain, Miss Evans has told us, once changed platforms without warning; 'a joke', she cryptically adds, 'that was not as successful as they had hoped'. Her father taught both his daughters to paint in water-colours, but it was not Frances who was considered to have the talent, and not until the 'nineties, when her sister married, did she inherit the status of 'the artist of the family'. The presence in New Zealand of Girolamo Nerli, a dashing Italian portrait-painter, had the effect of setting up a professional standard and of sharpening the discontent of artists with the pleasant but still amateurish culture of New Zealand. Nerli had twice painted Robert Louis Stevenson in Samoa and been a quickening influence upon Charles Conder and other painters in Australia. At Dunedin he taught at the art school, but his instruction was dilatory and intermittent. 'In the morning I open the student', he said, 'and then I go over to the public-house and rest. In the afternoon I shut the student up. Good to get the salary, but I do not like the Accademia – too much work.' Her occasional contacts with this bizarre person seem to have been without profit, but a certain conventional competence, by one means and another, she evidently acquired, for a picture of hers, *Maori Woman*, painted in 1900, was bought by the National Gallery of New Zealand. I have never seen this painting, but I understand that it is capable but commonplace and affords no hint of the direction in which her art eventually developed.

Before the end of the century, her father had died, and she had made up her mind to go to Europe. Although he had lived well, he died poor, and she had to exert herself in order to earn sufficient for the expensive journey. She gave lessons in water-colour painting and piano lessons, and she drew illustrations for the 'Otago Witness', her first published works. According to Miss Evans, these 'manage to show both her distaste and her capacity'. In 1900 she went to Europe, and spent two years in travel, visiting Brittany, Holland and Morocco. It was in Morocco, she used afterwards to say, that she had her first glimpse of her way ahead. Here she found the subjects that she had drawn with her father, in the mountains and the bush at home, moving figures in bright light, but in Morocco the moving figures were strange and more vivid than any she had seen before and they made a sharper impression. (The circumstances of the life she led were of a kind to exercise a bracing effect upon a temperament as adventurous as hers. With a woman friend, she joined a native caravan and went to Tetuan, where she had to remain for three months because the place was besieged by bandits.)

The work of her first dozen years or so in Europe is scattered, lost and difficult to see, but the impression I have of it (based, let me insist, upon very little evidence) is that it reflects a personality bold, energetic, eminently capable, but lacking entirely the delicate poetry of her later years. And lacking more than this, for I also detect a distinct strain of vulgarity. It was a symptom of this insensibility, I fancy, that Miss Evans had in mind when she wrote (of her work of a slightly later period) that Frances Hodgkins 'had felt the influence of the gipsy-caravan storm – that purely English-bohemian thunderstorm . . . that was still shaking such diverse trees as . . . Brangwyn and Lovat Fraser'.

In 1902 she settled in Paris, where her particular qualities won her considerable success. She was asked to join the staff at Colarossi's (where no other woman has taught, I believe, either before or afterwards, and where there have been few teachers who have never themselves attended any school) as a teacher of water-colour. Eventually she opened a school of her own. Her work seems to have been welcomed wherever she chose to send it, the 'Internationale' (which was traditionally reluctant to accept work by women) and the 'Société des Aquarellistes' among others. Sudden, unexpected success (I am not speaking of the success that crowns a life or a great achievement) is an experience that enslaves certain temperaments by a process of intoxication, but others it repels. Those others seize the chance of seeing it at close quarters, and decide that they do not want it on the terms on which it is to be had. It is significant that Frances Hodgkins's progressive isolation from the world and her living more intensely within herself began with her first taste of success. But it often happens that success, when treated with reserve, redoubles its attentions. In 1912 she returned to New Zealand, and held exhibitions there and in Australia. The work of 'the girl from "down under" who conquered Paris' (as she was called by Australian newspapers) was purchased for public collections and was presently sold out altogether. After her visit home, she returned to Paris to her painting and her teaching, but it was not long before the First World War was declared, and she left for England, where she made her home. She lived in St. Ives from 1914 until 1919; after the war she travelled, living at various times in London, the Cotswolds, Bridgnorth, and also abroad, chiefly in France and Spain. From 1922 until 1926 she lived in Manchester, where she worked without any notable success as a designer for the Calico Printers' Association, and conducted a painting class. The fact that she had joined so whole-heartedly in everything that was going on made her regard the rejection of her works, when the City Art Gallery organized a large inclusive exhibition, with a bitterness, Miss Evans has told us, out of proportion to its consequence. But there were compensations at hand. After many vicissitudes, she began at last to discover the peculiar angle and range of vision, the strangely singing colour, the fluid composition from which sprang the seemingly artless poetry (which was in fact the result of calculation and industry) that became so memorably her own. All this was plainly apparent to discerning visitors to her first one-man exhibition in London, especially (to her delight) to the younger painters. It consisted of twenty-five water-colours, four drawings and nineteen oil paintings, and was held at the Claridge Gallery in the spring of 1928.[1] The enhanced status that the exhibition conferred upon Frances Hodgkins was confirmed the following year by her election to the membership of the Seven and Five Society, a small group, notably free of dead wood, to which the ablest of the younger artists belonged. From this time onwards she was so completely identified with her much younger contemporaries that new acquaintances perceived with astonishment her approximate age.

The change in the character of her work that led to her identi-fication with a school of much younger artists had nothing of the nature of the sudden 'conversion' to which academy painters are occasionally subject. Although not yet easy to trace in detail, it was beyond question a process of steady growth.[2]

During the First World War an observant spectator might have noticed, besides the dashing proficiency of her work, a note of intensity and a complicated but certain sense of colour. Both these are perceptible in her first oil painting, *Two Women with a Basket of*

[1] 23 April until 12 May.

[2] A chronological list of the artist's works is included in 'Frances Hodgkins: Four Vital Years', by Arthur R. Howell, 1951–2.

Flowers, of about 1915,[1] aesthetically a strange blend of vice and virtue. One of the women, for instance, but for a touch of robustness, resembles one of those arty masks in white china made for the decoration of suburban walls, yet the colour, suggested by Vuillard, one would suppose, has been subtly and personally transposed. (We know that she looked with attention not only at Bonnard and Vuillard, but at Cézanne, Derain, Dufy and other Parisian contemporaries, and even attended the opening of the first Futurist exhibition.) This picture was purchased by the Tate in 1944. The following summer I wrote to her to ask for certain facts regarding it. I give her reply in full, as it shows that she began to paint in oils some years earlier than is generally believed (according to Miss Evans, this was about 1919), and, more generally, gives an indication of the warmth and impulsiveness of her character:

STUDIO,
CORFE CASTLE,
DORSET.
Oct. 7th 1945.

*Belated reply to letter
dated July 13 1945.*

DEAR MR. ROTHENSTEIN, – This is the letter that should have been written 2 months or more ago, rather late, indeed *very* late and I am filled with remorse that such an important event for me as the acquisition of my earliest painting should go unacknowledged by the artist. My excuse must be for not replying earlier to your letter, is that I was in Wales painting at the time.

Please accept my apologies.

I was absolutely overcome by the high honour paid me – and I greatly appreciate the recognition of my worthiness as creative artist.

In reply to your request for the date when *Two Women with a Basket of Flowers* was painted I think 1915 St. Ives is sufficiently accurate – I remember Mr. Moffat Lindner liking it so much that he bought it as soon as it was finished and from then on it hung in his beautiful house among the Elite – Sickert, Steer, etc.

It would be interesting to know how it came to the Tate Gallery – and when.

(2) It gives me intense pleasure to know my picture is enshrined in glory at Millbank. I hope I shall soon see it. I was delighted with the copy of 'Windmill' and the excellent reproduction. It gave me a thrill – a nostalgic one. Will you convey my grateful thanks to the Editors from me – and the great pleasure it has given me.

[1] The Tate Gallery, London.

Thanking you for the warm sympathy and interest you have shown my work.

Yours sincerely,
FRANCES HODGKINS.

In reference to the Drawing of a Woman that you mention I believe it belongs to me. I shall verify this when I am next at the Lefevre Gallery. If this should be the case I would like to present it to the Gallery.[1]

The drawing mentioned in the postscript is a big half-length of a seated woman made probably during the 'twenties, which is so complete a statement in the formal sense that a sculptor could carve from it (indeed, it has the look of something carved out of a tree trunk). Its noble, clearly defined forms make it to my thinking one of the finest drawings of our time. But it is neither for such a painting, intriguing as it is, as *Two Women with a Basket of Flowers* or the somewhat similar *Portrait of Moffat Lindner*,[2] a tempera of 1916, or even the drawing I mentioned just now, that Frances Hodgkins is chiefly to be valued, but for the intimately personal poetry of her last years, when she had shed the last of her borrowed plumage. Writing in December 1929 to Mr. Arthur R. Howell from the South of France, she described the panoramic splendour of what she saw.

But let me tell you [she added] that in my humility I have not lifted up my eyes higher than the red earth or the broken earthenware strewn about making such lovely shapes in the pure clear light . . . you may hear them clink as you unroll the water-colours I am sending along to you by this same post.

To-day she has found favour with fashionable opinion: she is even spoken of as a great master. But of course she was not that: she lacks the scale, the range, the variety, the purposefulness. What Frances Hodgkins succeeded in doing, after twenty years of ceaseless experiment, was so to attune her eye and train her hand as to enable her to respond 'to the broken earthenware strewn about making such lovely shapes in the pure clear light', and to make out of such things

[1] It proved to be the property of Messrs. Reid and Lefevre, from whom it was purchased by the Tate Gallery in 1948.

[2] Privately owned.

fantasies intimate and lovely, yet so convincing that, in her own words, we can hear them clink. This, in picture after picture, was what she had succeeded in doing, when, on 13 May 1947, in Purbeck, where for the last fifteen years of her life she had made her home, she died. Neither her talents nor her industry, nor even the admiration of people of influence, enabled her to make more than a precarious living, and latterly not even that. In 1942 she was granted a Civil List pension.

WILLIAM ROTHENSTEIN

1872—1945

BIOGRAPHIES, memoirs and journals always fascinated my father, but he used to complain of the disproportionate attention often given to childhood. Yet I have never known anyone whose own childhood so manifestly and so decisively shaped his character. First and most potently the countryside around Bradford, Yorkshire, where he was born, at 2 Spring Bank, Horton, on 29 January 1872, the third of the six children of a wool merchant.

Above Saltaire, a couple of miles from home [he wrote fifty years afterwards] were the moors, and one could walk, I was told, as far as Scotland, without taking the road. In winter sometimes when the moors lay under snow, no footmarks were to be seen; one walked through a landscape strange, white and virginal, while above one's head the peewits wheeled and uttered their haunting cry. The low stone walls on the moor looked black against the snow ... the mill chimneys along the valley, rising up tall and slender out of the mist, would look beautiful in the light of the setting sun.

Again:

These old quarries had a great fascination for me; there was a haunting stillness and a wildness about them. . . . A deserted old quarry, not more than fifteen minutes' walk from our own house, was a favourite playground. It lay off a path, a hundred yards from a canal, among black and stunted trees; there hung about it that haunted atmosphere peculiar to places where men have once been quick and busy, but which, long deserted, are slowly re-adopted by the old earth.

And here and there over the stark and sombre earth stood the stone skeletons of the great medieval abbeys, in those days not restored and tidied up, but grass-tufted, masonry fallen, weed-choked, widely scattered over the surrounding land. Of these the nearest were Kirkstall and Bolton; beside this last was the famous 'Strid' across the Wharfe, which became a sacred place in my father's eyes when he knew that Wordsworth had written a poem about it. And at nearby Haworth the presiding genius of the region was still a living memory: my father heard old people there speak of 'Miss Charlotte'. The two sons of Mr. Brontë's successor were in his form at school, and he used on a Sunday to walk across the fields to the church where Mr. Brontë had lately ministered and spend the day with his friends at the Vicarage which had been the Brontë's home. 'The Vicarage, the church and churchyard, and the Black Bull close by', he noted, 'and the steep grey street with the austere stone-roofed houses were all much as they were in the Brontës' time.' Of all these places he made his first childish drawings.

A man of sensibility born and reared in this grim, twilight region is likely to respond in one of two ways: he may shudder and recoil and depart, as soon as may be, for some tamed, mellow place; or he may take the starkness and the grimness to his heart. In the material sense, my father did, at the age of sixteen, leave Yorkshire for ever, but it is my conviction that the Yorkshire landscape, its dour, smoke-blackened buildings, yes and the stubborn, unsmiling people, strong in their frankness, and in their conscious rectitude, nurtured the most fruitful as well as the most enduring element in his personality. There was in his bewilderingly many-sided personality much more than this; but it is my conviction that these made its core. And it was a core of unusual strength, ever predisposing him towards an assertive and an unyielding independence and against compromise of any kind.

The quality of the Liberalism which he imbibed at home, besides fostering in him a natural love of justice, a natural humanity, also sanctioned an openness of mind even sometimes in those spheres where decisions are imperatively called for. He would often observe, for instance, that it was possible for a man to lead a life of virtue, no matter what religion he professed, or even if he professed none at all, but from this truism he was disposed to draw the conclusion that all religions were therefore equally true. This disposition derived partly from his abiding sense of the unchanging nature of man, and of the identity of the predicaments in which in all ages he has found himself, of the need, for instance, for reconciling the desire of the artist for perfection with his needs and duties as a social being, while the problem whether the man who desires the perfection of his own soul ought to retire from the world or remain in it, to struggle with deadly and multifarious temptations was one which constantly preoccupied him. It derived no less directly from that indeterminate quality in the heart of Liberalism that declares itself in a shrinking from sharp-edged definitions. This is less noticeable in its operation in the political sphere, where the loosely but generously conceived principles which it prefers have often compared well with opportunism to the Right and pedantry to the Left, but in the quest for the absolute they are apt to prove equivocal guides. My father was apt to regard any precisely formulated principles with suspicion, and to discount them as arbitrary theories to which men must, in his own words, 'conform or be damned'; religious dogma he discounted with that bland incomprehension common among Englishmen. He never saw it as possibly an assertion, in its starkest, most enduring form, of objective truth, but, at the best, as a perhaps necessary but artificial construction. I remember how, as a schoolboy, when I contended that the doctrines of the Catholic Church were either (as I believed) true or else they were false, but that in either event they treated of realities, he insisted that 'the Church needs dogma as a garden needs walls to enclose it'.

Such, besides a passion for drawing, a responsiveness to beauty and an eagerness for experience, were, I think, the most important emotional and intellectual features of the sixteen-year-old boy who, in 1888, left Bradford for the Slade School and a year later for a four years' stay in Paris. In addition, he possessed immense energy and a power of concentration to match it. For the rest he was a striking combination of moral earnestness and high-spirited wit, of shyness and audacity.

The year he spent at the Slade was of value to him on account of the personality and methods of Alphonse Legros, the Professor. 'We really did *draw* at the Slade', my father used to say, 'at a time when everywhere else in England students were rubbing and tickling their paper with stump chalk, charcoal and indiarubber.' Legros, whose earliest exhibited work had attracted the favourable notice of Baudelaire, had settled in England on the advice of Whistler, where he became friendly with Rossetti. In the true but almost forgotten sense of the term, Legros, who had studied under Ingres, was a fine academic draughtsman, a disciple of Mantegna, Poussin and Rembrandt.

He taught us [said my father] to draw freely with the point, to build up our drawings by observing the broad planes of the model . . . he would insist that we study the relations of light and shade and half-tone . . . this was a severe and logical method of constructive drawing.

This method of drawing was one to which my father wholeheart-edly responded; thenceforward constructive drawing became for him both an incitement and a discipline. From Legros he had also an immediate sense of contact with the great succession of European draughtsmen: he listened rapt while he quoted sayings of his master, Ingres, and spoke of Millet and Courbet with a familiarity tempered with reverence. But by the late 'eighties Legros had grown tired of teaching, and my father, oppressed by the spiritless atmosphere of the Slade, was easily persuaded to go to Paris.

In Paris he who scarcely more than a year before had been a provincial schoolboy and who at the Slade had vainly longed to speak to one of the older students, aroused the benevolent interest first of his professors at the Académie Julian, and not long afterwards of Whistler, Pissarro, Lautrec and Degas. Whistler one day paid an unexpected early-morning call at his studio, and thereby began a close friendship and, on my father's side, an ardent discipleship, which continued for some years until the friendship was suddenly extinguished in one of the Butterfly's most envenomed quarrels. My father's drawing in those days was lighter in touch and feeling, more stylish, than it afterwards became, yet Whistler showed an almost prophetic insight into the underlying weight and intensity of his nature when he used to say of him that he carried out right to the end what with others was mere gesture. The effect of the friendship of Whistler was conspicuous, but not enduring. It is manifest in a series of portraits of men painted in the early 'nineties, such as *L'homme qui sort*,[1] of 1892 (a portrait of Conder, shown at the Salon du Champ de Mars), another portrait of *Conder*,[2] and portraits of *Gordon Craig*,[3] *Max Beerbohm*[3] *and Marcel Boulanger*,[4] in all of which the subject is represented as a tall frock-coated figure in elegant silhouette against a low-toned but slightly lighter background.

The friendship of my father with Degas and Pissarro resulted from

[1] Toledo Museum of Art, U.S.A.   [2] Musée d'Art Moderne, Paris.
[3] Privately owned.   [4] Lost.

11. JAMES PRYDE. *The Red Ruin* (*c.* 1916).
Oil, 60¾ × 55½ in. Privately owned.

12. FRANCES HODGKINS.
Two Plates (1940).
Water colour, 16 × 27 in.
Privately owned.

13. SIR WILLIAM ROTHENSTEIN. *Portrait of Augustus John* (*c.* 1900).
Oil, 29½ × 21½ in. The Walker Art Gallery, Liverpool.

14. SIR WILLIAM ROTHENSTEIN. *The Abbey Church of St. Seine* (1906).
Oil, 29½ × 21½ in. The City Art Gallery, Manchester.

16. HAROLD GILMAN.
Eating house (1914).
Oil, 17⅜ × 23⅜ in.
Privately owned.

17. HAROLD GILMAN. *Mrs. Mounter at the Breakfast Table* (1917).
Oil, 36×23 in. The Walker Art Gallery, Liverpool.

18. GWEN JOHN. *A Corner of the Artist's Room in Paris* (1900–05?).
Oil, 12½ × 10½ in. Privately owned.

his first exhibition, held with Conder in 1891 in a small gallery in the Boulevard Malesherbes which belonged to a courageous dealer named Thomas, whom Lautrec had interested in their work. Degas sent word by a model of his that my father might, if he cared, pay him a visit. Pissarro came to the exhibition with his son Lucien. With Degas my father's relations were never so intimate as they were with Whistler, but I think their effects, if less apparent, struck nevertheless a deeper chord. Creative powers of the highest order, united as they were in Degas with austerity and an uncompromising integrity, commanded his utmost admiration. That such a man should admit to his friendship a boy hardly nineteen years old aroused his gratitude. The long evenings in the Rue Victor Massé (where Degas lived in two flats, the walls of the lower hung with the French masters he collected and the upper with his own works), spent in detailed discussion and close examination of works of art, did more to broaden and sharpen my father's critical faculties than any other experience in his early life. He delighted in Degas's deadly wit, the phrases that deflated or drew blood; in his stories about his master, Ingres, and the great men of his age. For all his veneration he was unable, in one important respect, to profit by Degas's advice. Degas not only seldom painted direct from nature, but was apt to ridicule this practice as an odious outdoor sport, and he urged my father to paint only from studies, and showed him how to correct and simplify these by redrawing on tracing paper pinned over them. But my father's visual imagination was weak; he was dependent upon the immediate presence of nature, which alone incited his faculties to function at their highest pitch. In the course of his life he carried out a number of elaborate figure compositions. These called for the redrawing, often the radical modification, of studies made from nature, but it is true to say that everything most living in his work was done in the heat generated by direct contact with his subject. Degas's belligerent nationalism expressed itself in various ways, but in none so consistently as in his hatred of the cosmopolitanism that had already begun to supplant the culture of France, the disintegrating effects of which he continually deplored. In so speaking, he strengthened my father's own innate antipathy for cosmopolitanism, above all for its frequent concomitants, the exotic and the smart.

The effects of his contacts with Pissarro are difficult to isolate from those of Impressionism as a whole. For some years before my father's arrival in Paris, this movement had put a powerful spell upon students, especially upon English students. The influence of Whistler, with his insistence upon low tones and severely selective composition, and of Degas, with his insistence upon precise drawing and his continuous praise of Ingres, however, combined to postpone the day when my father had to reckon with Impressionism.

After he had lived for four years in Paris, chance, in the guise of two commissions, led him home to England. Lord Basil Blackwood, son of the British Ambassador, invited him to stay at Balliol to draw his portrait, and some drawings he did there attracted the attention of John Lane, the publisher, who commissioned him to make a set of twenty-four Oxford portraits. These commissions he interpreted as signs that his life in Paris was drawing to its close, and as good omens of a new life in his own country. He possessed the talent for applying himself with such passionate industry to any work he had in hand, and for experiencing any phase of life to the utmost, that when the call came to undertake something fresh he was able to make changes without regret. 'You have gathered in your sheaves', I remember MacColl saying to him, towards the end of both their lives. But when the time came to give up his studio he was troubled by doubts as to whether he was wise to leave Paris, for his four years there had been years of achievement and experience. His drawing had become expressive and elegant; his sense of character vivid and humane; his intellect had been enriched and sharpened in the quickest thinking, the most critical and creative society there was. He had won the respect and the friendship of those whom he most ardently admired, and all this by the age of twenty-one. Whistler, Wilde and Conder urged him to remain. Reflection confirmed his intention to return to England and, with a brief interlude painting landscape at Montigny, he went from the society of Lautrec and Verlaine to that of the Common Rooms of Balliol and Christ Church. At Oxford, and in London where he settled a year later, he added to the already extensive gallery of portraits, begun in Paris with Verlaine, Zola and Rodin, likenesses of Pater, Swinburne and Henry James.

Soon after the beginning of the new century a radical change, involving both loss and gain, began to be manifest in his work. It was a change due perhaps mainly to intellectual conviction, but it may be in part the consequence of some psychic disturbance possibly unconnected with painting. I know nothing of the cause of such a disturbance, but I offer it as a possible explanation of a change of outlook more radical than an intellectual re-orientation would be likely to effect. Before about the year 1900 his work was distinguished by an eager curious insight into character, whether of face, of figure, or of locality, which expressed itself, notwithstanding his obvious high spirits and irrepressible humour, with a grave, disciplined detachment. His drawing, elegant and tenuous though it often was, showed a surprisingly sure grasp of form. The intellectual motive for the change is clearly expressed in my father's own words. Of the years after his return to England he wrote:

> My sympathies were with the Realists; but I felt there was something accidental, a want of motive and of dignity, in contemporary painting. To achieve the vitality which results from direct contact with nature, with nature's final simplicity and radiance, how unattainable! Yet only by aiming at an impossible perfection is possible perfection to be reached.

A few lines later he expressed what was, I think, the central article of his own belief:

> . . . I was possessed with the faith that if I concerned myself wholly with appearance, something of the mystery of life might creep into my work. . . . Through devotion to appearance we may even interpret a reality which is beyond our conscious understanding.[1]

The Wordsworthian conviction that form is the discipline imposed by God upon the universe, and that by subjecting himself to it, the artist may approach the innermost realities, is one which again and again finds expression in his critical writings. Such reasoning was cogent enough, yet there is something mysterious about the transformation of my father's outlook. He had always been serious and always industrious, but in the course of the early nineteen-hundreds he became increasingly marked by an extraordinary earnestness and intensity, an almost fanatical industry and an increasing severity with

[1] 'Men and Memories', 1931, I, p. 325.

himself. This heightened earnestness showed itself in every one of his many activities. 'Your father is far more interested in religion than the average parson', Eric Gill said to me. There was an occasion when a French Benedictine, perceiving this preoccupation, tried to persuade him to enter the Order's house at Flavigny. He was strongly affected by the writings of Tolstoy. He was shocked at the impoverishment of English provincial life by the progressive concentration of civilization in London, and he struggled to arrest it. The revival of fine traditional craftsmanship and the recognition of the undervalued art of India were other active preoccupations. And for the recognition of the achievements of those artists whom he most admired, especially of his younger contemporaries, his efforts were unremitting. Of Steer, Augustus and Gwen John, Stanley Spencer, Paul Nash his praise was constant, and if occasion required it, no exertion on their behalf and on that of many others at different times was too great. I have never known an artist whose generosity towards his fellow artists was so positive and so unstinted. But it is with this heightened earnestness and intensity as it showed itself in his work that I am chiefly concerned. So far from wavering in his conviction that for him Realism was the inevitable means of interpreting nature, it seemed to him on the contrary that the defect of all but the greatest Realists, Rembrandt, Velazquez, Chardin and a handful of others, was that they were too easily satisfied, that they stopped complacently when they should have pressed audaciously forward to pierce the baffling complexity of the appearance of nature so as to approach more closely the innermost truth. So it was without illusions as to his own shortcomings that he attempted with the whole force of his own passionate nature to come to closer and closer grips with the world of appearance. The attempt resulted, broadly speaking, in a vast increase of power at the expense of grace. It seems to me that nothing he did after the change approached in noble elegance of style his lithographed drawings of *Henry James*, of 1898, of *Fantin-Latour* or of the big double portrait of *Ricketts and Shannon*, both of 1897, or even the pastel *The Model*,[1] made when he was eighteen years old. He renounced, or rather, the more exigent ideal which possessed him involved the renunciation of, certain felicities of style. The grimness of his determination to be faithful to this ideal

[1] Lost. Reproduced in 'L'Art français', 2 April 1892.

exposed him to serious temptation. First, on account of his conviction that he ought always to be ready to take advantage of every spark of inspiration, he worked too continuously and always under the highest pressure. This led to a species of recurrent imaginative exhaustion, a recurrent aridity; and this in its turn led, as he himself confessed, to much painting for the sake of painting. Second, his ardour to probe his subject to its very depths, to resolve its complexities and to achieve final simplification led him, as Sir Charles Holmes complained, to 'aim to put too much into each canvas'. What was still worse, there were occasions when, in his eagerness to 'intensify' (the term was continually on his lips) some aspect of his subject, he would take insufficient care with his composition.

About this time, another artist, some seven years his junior, a man infinitely remote from him in temperament and convictions, made an observation which was curiously relevant to my father's predicament.

I shall have to disappoint people at first [Paul Klee noted in his diary in 1903]. Things are expected of me which a clever fellow could easily simulate. But my consolation must be that I am more handicapped by the sincerity of my intentions than by any lack of talent or dispositions.

I have expressed my admiration for my father's earliest work: I have called attention to the principal defects of the later; but I do not suggest that the total effect of the change was for the worse. The change itself may be interpreted as the determination on his part to face all the risks of total failure in an attempt to paint greatly, rather than to continue as a minor artist; 'to aim,' in his own words, 'at what was beyond me rather than to achieve an easier and more attractive result'. To this attempt – to vary a famous naval order – to engage nature more closely, to wring the very utmost out of his subject, he brought an inflexible will and extraordinary powers of concentration, and an inability to compromise.

The effect of this rededication, daily – indeed, hourly – renewed, was by its very earnestness, by its very strenuousness, in part self-defeating. The grace and ease that distinguished the work of his boyhood and youth gave way to a dourness, an almost aggressive 'probity' (to use one of his own highest terms of approbation), even

I

on occasions when his subjects, young women, children, sunlit orchards or fields of ripe corn, would seem to call for lighter handling. But if dourness and aggressive probity dried up much of his later work, this passionate rededication was not in vain, for when inspiration came, there he was, alert and disciplined, with the pent-up energy of a coiled steel spring. At such times, as though in compensation for the months of humble and dutiful effort so grudgingly rewarded, he painted pictures which – it seems to me – possess qualities of greatness. I mean that they realized Baudelaire's artistic ideal ... 'The creation of a suggestive magic containing at one and the same time the object and the subject, the world outside the artist and the artist himself.' ... Of these I would name *The Quarry*,[1] of 1904, *Aliens at Prayer*,[2] of 1905, *Farm in Burgundy*,[3] of 1906, *St. Seine L'Abbaye* (Plate 14),[4] of 1906, *Cliffs at Vaucottes*,[5] of 1909, *Morning at Benares*,[6] of 1911, *St. Martin's Summer*,[7] of 1915, and *Portrait of Barnett Freedman*,[8] of 1925. There is at least one painting which anticipated the later attitude, *Vézélay*,[9] of 1896, while the earlier one persists in two of the best of his later paintings – namely, *Mother and Child*,[10] of 1903. *Portrait of Augustus John* (Plate 13)[11] and *The Doll's House*,[12] both of 1899, show him in happy transition.

The effects of his enhanced seriousness of purpose might have been oppressive had it not been for another but apparently unconnected change in his vision which also occurred in the early years of the century. This was a sudden preoccupation with full daylight, with a consequent intensification of his own palette. Its chief cause was probably his increasing interest in landscape. He worked, almost always, not from studies but in front of his subject, which brought him up at once against the problems of the representation of open-air light. Another cause was the delayed influence of Impressionism, from which he had been temporarily immunized by Whistler's

---

[1] The City Art Gallery, Bradford.
[2] The National Gallery, Melbourne.
[3] Privately owned.
[4] The City Art Gallery, Manchester.
[5] The Tate Gallery, London.
[6] The City Art Gallery, Manchester.
[7] The City Art Gallery, Manchester.
[8] The Tate Gallery, London.
[9] Privately owned.
[10] Privately owned.
[11] The Walker Art Gallery, Liverpool.
[12] The Tate Gallery, London.

advocacy of low tones. Rejection of Whistler's dandyism, I surmise, led naturally to the end of this immunity, and his eye was gradually filled forthwith by dazzling light. But the twentieth century had begun, and it was impossible for an artist of sensibility to respond, quite simply, to the original Impressionism of Monet. The emphasis on conscious design, on structure, and on poetry and drama, which crystallized in the Post-Impressionist movement, accorded too closely with my father's own predilections not to make it inevitable that the Impressionism that so richly coloured his vision should be an Impressionism transformed. Although the theories of Seurat attracted him as little as those of Monet, in so far as he attempted to unite hard structure with brilliant colour he may properly be regarded as something of a Post-Impressionist, but the appellation would have surprised him. For far from being associated with Post-Impressionism, he was widely regarded as hostile to it; but his positive alienation from it was due to a personal clash with Roger Fry, the promoter of the movement in England. Fry was a warm admirer of my father's work, and had written in forthright praise of it, and, perceiving, perhaps, the elements which it had in common with that of the avowed Post-Impressionists, he urged him to associate himself with them. Want of respect for the work of some of the Post-Impressionists, a certain mistrust of Fry's leadership and a sense of loyalty to the New English Art Club with which he had exhibited since 1894 impelled him to decline. His refusal eventually aroused in Fry an enmity which was as active as it was lasting. The critical opinions expressed by my father with regard to several aspects of Post-Impressionism, and the personal hostility towards him, within the movement, fomented by Fry, opened a breach between him and painters whose principal aims he shared. Certainly he showed no sympathy at all for one derivative of Post-Impressionism – namely, Abstraction – which he regarded as a cardinal heresy, because it seemed to him to involve nothing less than a new atheism: implying a denial of the material world, and the reliance of artists on their intellects rather than on their eyes. Nor had he any particular sympathy for the work of van Gogh or of Gauguin, yet he shared the sense these artists had of the inadequacy of the Impressionists' aims. He held that the urge to express form and colour was the first among the painters' impulses,

but the minds of artists [he wrote] are not so limited, so poorly furnished, that they cannot associate their sense of form with those touching
elements in man's pilgrimage through life which bring the arts within
the orbit of common experience.

It seems to me that there was a certain inconsistency that marked at
one point his attitude towards the subject of a work of art. Although
the subjects to which he responded most naturally were faces, figures,
buildings and the things fashioned by man for his use such as were
beautiful or interesting in themselves, he had a clear apprehension
that no object in itself is trivial, and that only trivial treatment can
make it so. He spoke often of Rembrandt's making so noble a work
of art out of the split-open carcase of an ox, and of Chardin's power
of representing a knife and a loaf and Cézanne a dish of apples with
similar breadth and force. Yet for all his own passionate preference
for subjects that pertained, as he put it, to 'man's pilgrimage through
life', and his indifference to subjects that were fortuitous or slight, he
showed, nevertheless, an odd reluctance to make due allowance for
the power of the noblest of all subjects – namely religion – to
inspire great works of art. Of the early Italians he wrote:

> The notion that these were great religious artists because all painters
> and sculptors believed in the stories they were hired to illustrate, is a
> fallacy . . . such . . . subjects . . . allowed the artist to paint the streets
> and buildings of the towns which they lived in. . . .

Granting the element of truth contained in this contention, the
suggestion that Giotto and Duccio, Piero della Francesca and Fra
Angelico were the Courbets and Manets of their times, drawing their
inspiration solely from the life around them, is to deny the main-
spring of their art. To regard the world as a complex of forms to be
æsthetically related to one another seems to me to imply a pitiably
impoverished vision, but at least a consistent one. But if subject
is to be regarded as significant, where is the logic of praising Chardin
and Cézanne for their belief in their loaves and apples, and calling in
question the belief of the great religious artist in the Incarnation? And
where the logic of extolling nobility of subject, if the noblest is not,
in fact, held to be inspiring at all? It is easy, however, to insist too
much upon this contradiction, for it arose from his deeply felt conviction that both the fundamental concern and the most vital

inspiration of the artist was the beauty of the visible world. Later in life, he experienced in altered form a renewal of the intermittent religious impulse of his childhood and youth, heightened later by his contacts with Indian mystics. But his sense of his obligation as an artist to interpret this beauty was so overwhelming as to confuse his vision of the religious life which nevertheless increasingly absorbed him. Towards the very end he drew near to the Catholic Church, but the final act of entry into her communion was inhibited by his abiding conviction that all of himself that was of any account had already been offered to God in the only way in which he certainly knew how to offer it – namely, to the praise of the world which God had created. Two priests of the Society of Jesus followed the inconclusive struggle with respectful sorrow. To the last there remained an inner recess of his consciousness where he still believed, like Dubedat, that the great artists were his saints, whose creative activities were the only activities of any abiding significance. Even the understanding of these, he used to maintain, was a mere social amenity – as though works of art are not created to be understood; as though they are not fulfilled by comprehension.

This habitual opinion did nothing to mitigate the recurrent bitterness that seared his later years, arising from the precipitous decline in his own reputation as an artist. That he did not suffer oblivion was due to the impossibility of ignoring so formidable a personality. To one who in youth won the admiration of Degas and Pissarro, who in middle age was regarded without question as one of the most representative English artists, who had exerted himself so continuously in the service of his fellow artists, who had been the teacher of so large a proportion of the ablest among his juniors, the neglect of his paintings was a grief – a grief sharpened, if anything, by the undiminished respect paid to him as a writer, as an authority, and as a person. There was something particularly ironical in his eyes in the praise which he continued to receive for everything except his painting, for almost all his other activities, with a single important exception, were then confined to those hours when the light was insufficient for painting. To his writings in particular no time was allowed which he could have given to his art. A grave illness, which made work impossible during the middle twenties, seemed to me to be aggravated by his

enforced inactivity. I therefore urged him to set down his recollections. He made a beginning during his convalescence, but after his
recovery he wrote the remainder of three large volumes of his 'Men
and Memories', amounting to about half a million words, before
rising in the mornings, and, rather less frequently, after nightfall.
During these hours he was also occupied with a vast correspondence.
The important exception was his teaching; the Principalship of the
Royal College of Art, which lasted from 1920 until 1935, inevitably
involved continual interruption of his painting. In the same way, his
passionate advocacy of the art of India and the formation of his own
collection of Indian paintings, of the revival of wall painting, of
local craftsmanship, farming, and many other activities at Far Oakridge, the Gloucestershire village which, apart from a brief interlude,
was his home from 1912 until his death, were all the occupations of
what, in another man, would have been his leisure hours. And as
though these and, at one time or another, many more were insufficient to absorb his energies, he used to rise with the sun at Far Oakridge, and, with axe and billhook, clear acre after acre of overgrown
woodland. And he possessed the capacity of experiencing, with an
extraordinary intensity, all his activities and his friendships; and
above all, the various phases of his own art. From each he extracted
all that he was capable of extracting. The sustained exaltation with
which he experienced a new subject is expressed most explicitly,
I think, in the chapter on India in the second volume of 'Men and
Memories'. During both World Wars, in the first, as an artist on the
Western Front, in the second with the Royal Air Force, his comrades,
bored, uncomfortable, exasperated, noted with incredulity the
entranced activity of a man for whom every instant of those dreadful
days was manifestly precious.

The bitterness of his last years must not be exaggerated: cheerfulness kept breaking in. At work, in spite of the almost inevitable
falling-short of the exacting standards he set himself, in spite of the
grimness of the struggle, his happiness was intense. It was not only
painting and drawing that he enjoyed to the end, but the various
incidental experiences which they involved. When the Second
World War broke out he was sixty-six years old. On account of his
age and of his unfashionable reputation, his chances, he rightly
considered, of official employment as a regular war artist were small,

and he resigned himself to serving, at the best, upon some appropriate committees. I persuaded him to offer his services as an artist directly to the Royal Air Force, which offered subjects as inspiring as they were novel. Neither he nor I was unaware of the dangers which would attend such a course of action, for he had suffered, for more than twenty years, from a heart gravely weakened by overwork.

So it was that he had the delight of working as an artist to the end. We did not meet often during the war, but I shall always carry with me the memory of the slight, straight-backed, energetic figure in a sky-blue uniform, carrying his portfolio of paper, setting eagerly off for some airfield, or else returning with a sheaf of drawings and innumerable stories of new-made friends. What a strange conjunction there was of two remote periods of time when this small figure, mentioned in the 'Goncourt Journals', the familiar of Verlaine, Pater and Oscar Wilde, was out over the North Sea in a Sunderland flying-boat, with a crew not a member of which was less than half a century his junior.

Want of success had reduced his income to minute proportions, yet he gave his services to the Royal Air Force, and presented all the work that he did on his own account while on active service to the nation. But he gave even more than his work. The ordeal of constant air flight, the draughty messes, the indifferent food imposed a strain upon his injured heart heavier than it could withstand; he became ill, and after a year or two of restricted activity he died.

Portraits had formed the largest part of his production, but when he sat on the terrace of his house at Far Oakridge knowing that he had only a little time to live, it was not faces, illustrious or beautiful, that occupied his thoughts; it was the Stroud Valley with its severely defined contours, its sonorous depths. It was as though he saw all the loveliness of nature gathered in between its steep, wooded declivities. As he sat and watched it with rapt attention hour after hour under the changing effects of light, marvelling at its beauty, more deeply than ever was he convinced that by yielding himself up humbly and absolutely to the attempt to represent this beauty the artist might reveal, here and there, a glimpse of the reality behind it. Strong in this faith, but able no longer to act in accordance with its dictates, he died on 14 March 1945.

When I learned of his death and looked back over his benevolent and industrious and amazingly full life, in the mass of memories one incident, trivial at first glance, disengaged itself from the rest, and stood forth as peculiarly typical of my father's daily conduct. Not many years before, he and I together visited an exhibition, where he was attracted by an example of the later work of Sickert, of which he was in general highly critical. Presently he was engaged in conversation with a lady, to whom I heard him say: 'That small study is absolutely enchanting, and it's delightful to be able to praise it. Certain of Walter's recent works have made it difficult for his old friends to look him in the face.' As we were leaving, I warned my father, whose often untimely candour provoked resentment, against speaking in such terms in public, 'How can you place,' I asked, 'the slightest reliance on that lady's discretion? Incidentally, who was she?' In sombre tones came the reply: 'Mrs. Sickert, John.'

WILLIAM NICHOLSON

1872—1949

WHEN William Nicholson was twenty-one years old he made a woodcut portrait of Queen Victoria which, published in 'The New Review', then edited by W. E. Henley, made him famous in a day. Among its numerous admirers was Whistler. 'A wonderful portrait, Mr. Nicholson', he said. 'Her Majesty is a wonderful subject', Nicholson modestly replied. 'You know,' rejoined Whistler, 'Her Majesty might say the same of you.'

Nicholson was a wonderful subject, but, in my estimation at least, for reasons different from those voiced by the friends who have written about him from the most intimate knowledge. In a biography[1] as vivacious in tone as it is pious in intention, Miss Marguerite Steen tacitly endorses the opinion of certain unnamed authorities whom she quotes that 'William Nicholson is the greatest master of Still-Life of his own or any other age'. In the most discerning appraisal[2] of his art that has yet appeared the late Robert Nichols asserts that 'a Nicholson, albeit surrounded by twenty other paintings, can be instantly recognized across a room on first entry to a gallery'. One has only to think of the still-lifes of Chardin, of Velazquez, of Manet, of a dozen others to see that Miss Steen's claim will not bear an instant's scrutiny. Nor is Nichols's claim justified. A dandy is rarely conspicuous, and William Nicholson, artist and man, was a dandy. He was not a great master, and as a painter he was as little original as a man of high gifts and undeviating independence could well be. (His originality showed itself in his woodcuts and to a lesser degree in the posters over which he collaborated with Pryde.) William Nicholson the painter seems to me to be something quite different; something rare, especially in England – namely, a little classical master. As a little master, he would in several periods of history have been acclaimed. But our own is not interested in modest perfection. To-day van Gogh is the most popular painter.

[1] 'William Nicholson', 1943.

[2] 'William Nicholson', Penguin Modern Painters, 1948.

The heroic failure is preferred to the completely achieved but minor success. The vehement, unstudied utterance is preferred, and infinitely preferred, to the polished epigram. (The very expression 'polished epigram' has become as incongruous with what is most admired in contemporary art as a frock-coat or a heavily tasselled malacca cane with contemporary fashion in dress.) The little master is, then, of all kinds of artist the least fashionable; to such an extent unfashionable that those who loved and admired William Nicholson will, I am afraid, regard this description of him as disparagement.

The dandy, as Baudelaire noted, has his special discipline to follow, his special sacrifices to make, and William Nicholson was no exception. He needed a measure of success to enable him to develop his small but perfect talent, sufficient to bring up a family early established and quickly increasing and thereby to place him beyond the caprices of patrons. In addition to his talent, he possessed three invaluable assets. First, a remarkable capacity for work – a capacity not so much the product of will power or of a sense of moral obligation as of a restless creative activity. He could never be idle. Second, an acute business sense, which brought him early and increasing material success. Third, and most important, an intimate understanding of the nature of his own talents. Many artists waste half a lifetime in the vain pursuit of objects unattainable through their particular gifts; Nicholson early understood what he should be about, so that, wasting no time, he took every opportunity of learning what he needed to learn. There is, in consequence, a close-knit coherence about his fastidious life-work.

Nicholson was born on 5 February 1872, at 12 London Road, Newark-on-Trent, and christened William Newzam Prior, the second son and third child of the second wife of William Newzam Nicholson, the proprietor of the Trent Ironworks and Member of Parliament. Exceptionally observant and continuously active, Nicholson was without any power of concentration upon anything which did not engage his interest, and at Magnus Grammar School, Newark-on-Trent, which he attended, nothing except drawing engaged his interest. His schooldays were unfruitful and unhappy and he attempted in after years to erase the memory of them. But now and then the nightmare would come seeping back through the doors he supposed he had bolted and barred upon it, and he would describe how he and the other boys scraped off their bread the loathsome grease they were given in place of butter, and pushed it through the iron grating which covered the heating pipes in the floor, and how the rats swarmed to eat the grease, and the deadly stench given off by the combination of grease and rat when the furnace was lighted. 'Greek before breakfast', he used to say, 'on an empty stomach, after breaking the ice in the washbowl, prevented me from ever wishing to visit Greece.' Yet these years were not utterly unfruitful, utterly unhappy. They were redeemed by the presence in the school of a drawing master named William H. Cubley.[1] This humane and perceptive man was a pupil of Sir William Beechey, who was a pupil of Reynolds. So it came about that in this malodorous wilderness was an old man giving precise but unheeded instruction in the technical methods of Sir Joshua. Cubley not only gave his pupil an insight into traditional methods of oil painting, but he persuaded his father to allow him to study art, and enabled him to escape from a school which offered him present misery and no prospect of success.

Herkomer's art school at Bushey, to which his father sent him at the age of sixteen, if less positively disagreeable to him, was hardly more profitable than the Magnus School. The instruction perfunctorily given in Herkomer's grandiose Bavarian castle was based upon no rational principles, and it was not long before Nicholson realized that he was learning nothing – nothing, at least, from Herkomer. One day the life-class was aroused from its apathy by the noisy intrusion of a flock of geese, driven in from an adjacent common by a student. This spirited and whimsical act, so incongruous with the portentous atmosphere of the school, attracted the attention of Nicholson to the boisterous, intractable girl responsible. Her name was Mabel Pryde; she was, as she proudly informed him, sister to James Pryde, who presently himself arrived at Bushey. The company of a brother and sister as original and exhilarating as Herkomer was dull made Nicholson more and more refractory to his teaching and intermittent in his attendance at the classes. Relations between master and student became tense. One day, it being Nicholson's turn to arrange the model, he brought in a woman from

[1] 1814–1896; twice Mayor of Newark-on-Trent.

the village and posed her with an open umbrella behind her head. Of her he made a lively sketch. This Herkomer described as 'a piece of Whistlerian impudence' and dismissed Nicholson from the school for 'bad attendance and bad work'. The displeasure of Herkomer put an end to his profitless pupillage, but an incident of a strangely similar kind a little later embittered his relations with his father. He painted a portrait of his mother, and his father, invited by his diffident son to look at it in the studio by himself, came out speechless with uncomprehending rage. There followed a short period of study in Paris at the Académie Julian. The particular problems which pre-occupied his French contemporaries had no special relevance to Nicholson, who made few intimate contacts, and remained, in fact, a somewhat solitary figure. A chance visit to Ridge's bookshop in Newark shortly after his return to England had consequences more important for his life as an artist than the sum of his Parisian experience, even though this included the copying of a painting by Velazquez, a master whose combination of the most searching realism with the most exquisite taste must have helped Nicholson to a knowledge of himself. Ridge's was an old-established firm which had published some of the early work of Byron, and possessed a large and interesting collection of old woodblocks. Excited by what he saw, Nicholson went home, secured a piece of wood, planed it down, and with nails and a penknife he cut a block from which he printed his first woodcut. Nicholson's work as a wood-cutter lies outside the scope of these pages, but it radically affected his work as a painter.

Not long after his return from Paris Nicholson's courtship of the girl who had driven the flock of geese into the life-class at Herkomer's culminated in marriage. The Prydes were a violently opinionated, quarrelsome and eccentric family, and Nicholson, sensible, shy, a hater of 'scenes', conducted his unobtrusive courtship of Mabel largely in the coal-cellar of the Prydes' house in Blooms-bury, where the family had migrated on Dr. Pryde's retirement. Mrs. Pryde, under the spell of one of her successive enthusiasms, had installed in the cellar a vapour bath, wherein the victim sat, the lid closed firmly over his head, while steam was raised by an interior lamp. So long as this enthusiasm lasted, the interior mechanism of this formidable apparatus was shown to the more privileged visitors to the house. One day, when William and Mabel were chattering among the coalsacks, Mrs. Pryde – whose disapproval of the court-ship was notorious – descended the steps followed by a body of visitors; embarrassed, he jumped into the vapour bath and held down the lid, to the disappointment of Mrs. Pryde when her utmost efforts failed to raise it.

The unpredictable temper of the Pryde household persuaded the young couple that it would be prudent to make their plans without consultation with the parents of either. They were accordingly married in secret at Ruislip on 25 April 1893.

Nicholson's marriage led immediately to an association more momentous for his work than his marriage itself. Within a few days of his settling with his wife into the first of their many houses – 'The Eight Bells', a small former public-house at Denham – James Pryde arrived for a week-end and remained with them for two years. The collaboration of the brothers-in-law as the Beggarstaffs, for the designing of posters, briefly treated earlier in these pages, was the chief consequence of this prolonged visit. The estrangement of Nicholson and Pryde in later life has led to a tendency on the part of the advocates of each to belittle the contribution of the other to the illustrious partnership. To assess with any degree of precision the contribution of these two would be, after so many years, as difficult as it would be unfruitful. Pryde's was the more mature and the more audacious personality. Edinburgh had not yet dwindled into a repertory of conventional formulae; memories of her high sombre buildings, her dark history, still haunted his dreams. If he was lazy and irresponsible, the reckoning was yet to come. Nicholson's personality had the greater potentiality for growth, but at this time he seemed no doubt, in comparison with Pryde, a diffident, pedestrian being, which no doubt accounted for the condescension discernible in Pryde's attitude towards him. But about Nicholson's industry, his manual dexterity and his business capacity there was no doubt. If the original conceptions were, perhaps, mostly Pryde's, their translation into finished designs was chiefly due to the skill and pertinacity – doubtless heightened by his responsibilities as a married man – of Nicholson. But if the assumption of Pryde's readier invention is justified, Nicholson's work of the immediately ensuing years as a wood-cutter proclaims him an apt pupil. Like

Pryde, Nicholson learnt two obvious but important lessons from their joint experience as designers of posters; clarity and economy of statement, and effective distribution of light and shadow.

The Beggarstaffs were so intimately identified – as collaborators and as brothers-in-law – that the radical differences between them have sometimes been overlooked. They had, indeed, very little in common. They were alike in possessing little of the humbleness of most serious artists. Pryde's pride, which proclaimed itself in grandiose talk, was obvious enough; Nicholson's was masked, but it went deeper. To boast, like Pryde, would have been repugnant to the dandyism which governed Nicholson's conduct of his life as well as of his art, but somewhere in his innermost being there was, I suspect, a hard core of spiritual complacency. But not the kind of complacency that ever excused him from the utmost exertion. He was never a facile artist: the suavity, the cool vivacity, the truth of tone, the buoyancy, the character in his portraits – all these were purchased at the price of an agony of effort, sustained throughout a lifetime. With Pryde there was little agony of effort, or none. So long as his Edinburgh memories were sufficiently fresh to stir his imagination, he exploited the consequent ferment. When they faded, he exploited his prestige, his dignified handsomeness, his odd engaging humour instead – in a word, he cadged. He trod the broad path as inevitably as Nicholson trod the narrow. Potentially, Pryde was, perhaps, the larger artist, as he was the larger human being; he was built upon a scale more ample and generous than Nicholson, but he lacked Nicholson's capacity for growth. Even the latter's most conspicuous qualities – his taste, his sense of perfection – were not 'gifts', but endowments painfully acquired and improved. Those who admire the work of Nicholson are apt to be impressed so deeply by his most perfect achievements that they can scarcely perceive his defects. Yet could anything show the tastelessness of art nouveau more clearly than the landscape backgrounds of his several paintings of Morris dancers, made during the first years of the century? Could anything be worse drawn than the obtrusive near thigh – too long, too flat and a ludicrous match for the far one – of *Carlina*,[1] of about 1909? Or a more ostentatious display of dexterity than the famous

[1] The Kelvingrove Art Gallery, Glasgow.

Hundred Jugs,[1] of 1916? I cite these examples of failure (which, incidentally, have found places in the principal exhibitions and publications devoted to the work of this artist) to support my contention that his perfection, like the perfection of the prose of George Moore's maturity, was the outcome (but at no time the certain outcome) of anguished effort. Yet than his best paintings none look more effortless. In these he shows a suave and assured perfection or an insight into character which will, I fancy, enable them to offer an effective resistance to the blind but mercilessly probing assaults of Time. Of the still-lifes for which I would claim the relative perfection possible in an age which cares little for perfection, I would name *The Lowestoft Bowl*,[2] of 1900, *The Marquis Wellington Jug*,[3] of 1920, *Glass Jug and Fruit*,[4] of 1938, and *Mushrooms* (Plate 15),[5] of 1940; of portraits *Miss Jekyll*,[6] of 1940, *Walter Greaves*,[7] of 1917, and *Professor Saintsbury*,[8] of 1925, and of intimate landscapes *Black Swans at Chartwell*,[9] of 1932.

Nicholson was at his best when he responded directly to a simple subject (in so far as any subject might retain its simplicity under the subtle scrutiny of this being whom Robert Nichols aptly compared to a sophisticated child), for he seems to have been little interested in the deeper implications of the appearance of things. His mind, like his eye, was preoccupied wholly with the intimate segments of the surface of the world that came under his minute and affectionate observation (with foreign or unfamiliar subjects he had no success). Never was there a less enquiring or reflecting, or, in the best sense, a more *superficial* mind. Very occasionally he did probe beneath the surface. For instance, in the amusingly contrasted double portraits of *Mr. and Mrs. Sidney Webb*,[10] of about 1927, and *The Earl and Countess of Strafford*,[11] of 1940, he has made, in the words of Miss Steen,

an almost Hogarthian commentary on the new and the old aristocracy. In the one [she notes] with its ugly modern fireplace of a suburban villa, its litter of documents, the earnest shapelessness of Lord Passfield's

[1] The Walker Art Gallery, Liverpool.   [2] The Tate Gallery, London.
[3] Privately owned.
[4] The National Gallery of Canada, Ottawa. (Massey Collection.)
[5] The Tate Gallery, London.   [6] The National Portrait Gallery, London.
[7] The City Art Gallery, Manchester.   [8] Merton College, Oxford.
[9] Privately owned.   [10] The London School of Economics.
[11] Privately owned.

trousers, his carpet slippers, his wife's hand clawing absently towards an economical fire, epitomizes low living and high thinking as thoroughly as the other epitomizes high living and as little thinking as possible. . . . Lady Strafford changing one of the cards of her Patience, Lord Strafford dangling 'The Times' from one drowsy hand.

Miss Steen's claim is justified: the artist has summed up and contrasted two ways of life and thought with extraordinary acuteness. But ordinarily he is content with an almost wholly visual regard – a regard not simply retinal, as Monet's sometimes was, but a vision disciplined by his sense of style and amplified by knowledge. 'Painting isn't only sight', he observed to Nichols; 'it's knowledge. In addition it's capacity to remember.' Nicholson's intimate, civilized vision is a highly traditional vision, for it perceives clearly defined objects, and has little in common with that newer vision evolved by Rembrandt, Turner, Constable and Delacroix, according to which appearances are composed of planes and contours which change continually under the influence of light. Now and then not only in his landscapes, but even in such a still-life, for example, as the *Glass Jug and Fruit* referred to above, he was conspicuously affected by it, but he was most himself among objects which existed tangibly, so to speak, in their own right. This remained essentially though less emphatically the case, it seems to me, until the end, even though he moved steadily from the umbrageous glossiness of *The Lowestoft Bowl*, *The Marquis Wellington Jug*, to the light-suffused *Gold Jug*,[1] of 1937.

The relation between the art and the personality of William Nicholson was not complementary or in any sense paradoxical: the one was, quite simply, an extension of the other. There was about this personality, as both Miss Steen and Nichols have observed, something childlike: he lived in the present, without much troubling himself about past or future. He delighted in what was civilized – for preference, in the intimate, the highly finished, the whimsical – he was alienated by anything which might be regarded as pretentious, but he occasionally condemned as pretentious persons and achievements authentically great. When he served as a Trustee of the Tate Gallery, he was sparing in his praise of his contemporaries, but when he praised, he praised with an endearing conviction and pugnacity,

[1] Coll. H.M. Queen Elizabeth the Queen Mother.

and I recall with gratitude his advocacy of two painters, favourites of mine, whose art had nothing in common with his own, Walter Greaves and Edward Burra. Dandyism, in his case a desire for an unobtrusive yet original elegance, was, I believe, the strongest and most enduring motive of his actions: such elegance he also aspired to achieve, though with less passion, in his clothes, in his houses – in fact, in everything with which he was intimately concerned. He would wear white duck trousers and patent leather shoes in his studio. He was the pioneer, I believe, of the spotted collar worn with the spotted shirt. When collars were worn high, he, 'seeking glory', he admitted, 'even in the cannon's mouth', wore higher collars than anyone else. I cannot recall his appearance in such early days, but I well remember the small, neat figure in the olive-green coat and white trousers, and the 'ivory-coloured, enquiring little face, with a hat cocked at a knowing angle' which impressed Miss Steen when she first met him in the middle nineteen-thirties. No. 11 Apple Tree Yard, St. James's, the stable which he took in 1917, he gradually transformed into a studio that was efficient, a delight to live in, and a monument – a miniature monument – to his taste, filled with the whimsical precious accumulation of years: lustre jugs, sporting prints, caricatures by Max Beerbohm, Callot maps, military drums, a top-hat to hold his brushes. . . .

About 1947, following a stroke, he experienced a sudden failure of his mental powers. Miss Steen, with whom he lived since shortly after their first meeting in 1934, took him to Blewbury, the Berkshire village where she had a house, and devoted herself to a vain attempt to restore him to health. It was suggested that he should continue to paint, on account of the tranquillizing effect of this occupation. Rather than fall below the severe standards which he had always set himself, he renounced the possibility of recovery and the greatest pleasure which life had to offer him. His health continued to decline, and he died on 16 May 1949.

HAROLD GILMAN
1876—1919

MENTION has been made earlier in these pages of the co-operative activities of a group of friends radiating from 19 Fitzroy Street, one of Sickert's accumulation of odd painting rooms. Sickert, whose opinions underwent frequent changes, never changed his prejudice against the selection by jury of works of art for exhibition – a prejudice shared by his Fitzroy Street friends. There was no no-jury exhibition in London in those days. In 1907 the art critic Frank Rutter undertook to organize one. The Allied Artists' Association, a body similar in organization to the Société des Artistes Indépendants in Paris, was consequently formed. The new Association gained enthusiastic support in Fitzroy Street. At the General Meeting held in the spring of 1908, in response to a plaintive proposal by an obscure member that 'the best works by the best artists' should be given the best places in the exhibition, Sickert thus voiced the prevailing sentiment: 'in this society there are no good works or bad works: there are only works by share-holders'. The Association's first exhibition – a huge assembly of pictures by some 600 members – was opened in the Albert Hall in the July of the same year. The Association, although open to anybody who cared to join, in fact replaced the New English Art Club as the rallying point for adventurous talent, and as the most effective rival to the Royal Academy. The attitude which members of the new society maintained towards the old was exemplified in the reply of a member of the hanging committee, Theodore Roussel, to a lady who asked him how he could hang such dreadful pictures. 'Madam', he said, 'we have the same privilege, as at the Royal Academy, of hanging bad pictures; only here *we have not the right to refuse the good.*' But there was in general a geniality about their disapprobation. 'You're going to tell me', said Walter Bayes to Rutter, who had invited him to become a member, 'that your exhibition will be better than the Royal Academy.' 'I'm not', Rutter said. 'It's going to be bigger and worse.' 'In that case', Bayes said, 'I'll join with pleasure.'

In accordance with the democratic constitution of the Association, all members were eligible to serve on the hanging committee, and invitations were sent out in alphabetical order. By the third year, 1910, it was the turn of the Gs. This system brought together Harold Gilman, Charles Ginner and Spencer Frederick Gore. The result of this fortuitous meeting was to give a new impetus and a new direction to English painting. Not since the earlier years of the New English Art Club had there been so quickening a centre of energy and enquiry as was presently provided by the intimate association of these three painters. The outlook of the New English, though ferociously attacked in academic circles, was, in fact, sufficiently temperate to remain content to develop the ideas which had animated the Barbizon painters and the Impressionists – ideas which, for Paris at least, had long since ceased to be a novel focus of interest. It was not, however, the principles of its most articulate members, nor even the brilliant performance of its most gifted, that enabled the Club to play so singularly fructifying a part in the history of English painting. This part it was enabled to sustain for more than two decades by the discriminating liberality of its management, and the resulting interaction of temperaments issued in a widely diffused impulse to creativity.

The movement generated by Gilman and his friends was more firmly anchored to principle, and its impact, though sharper, was necessarily more limited both in duration and extent.

Gilman was a massive, confident figure, tenacious and fond of argument, with the kind of presence suggested by a contemporary journalist, who wrote of his 'bald head and regal mouth'. Ginner, one of the most consistent painters of the time, possessed a knowledge of Parisian theory and practice approached by very few of his English contemporaries. Gore fostered a wonderful talent for reconciling all honourably reconcilable attitudes.

Gilman and Gore were already old friends who had studied together at the Slade and were also friends of Sickert and Lucien Pissarro, and frequenters of 19 Fitzroy Street. Gore had admired the paintings that Ginner sent over from Paris to the first exhibition of the Allied Artists' Association two years before and asked Rutter who he was. Rutter knew nothing of him except that he lived in Paris. In 1910 Ginner came over especially to serve on the hanging committee. Gilman and Gore introduced themselves, and told him they liked his work.

Harold Gilman was the second son of the Rev. John Gilman, Rector of Snargate with Snave, Kent, a son of Ellis Gilman, head of the firm of Hamilton, Gray & Co., of Singapore. He was born at Rode, Somerset, on 11 February 1876, and educated at Abingdon, Rochester and Tonbridge schools. In 1894 he went up to Brasenose College, Oxford, but ill-health compelled him to terminate his studies before he could take his degree. The year 1895 he spent in Odessa. In 1896 he decided to become a painter, spending a year at the Hastings Art School and the four following years at the Slade, working under Brown, Steer and Tonks. The year 1904 he spent in Spain, he visited the United States in 1905 and Norway shortly before the First World War. At the Slade he seems to have learnt little and made no mark. The important event in his early life as a painter was his study of Velazquez at the Prado, of several of whose works he made careful copies.

I have seen few of the paintings which resulted from his attempts to apply the principles of Velazquez, but they appear to have been mostly portraits, often life-size, low-keyed harmonies of greys and browns, and smooth in texture and in general somewhat Whistlerian in intention, with something about them of Manet and the Belgian Stevens. I recently saw a landscape, a crepuscular, weakly drawn Whistlerian essay, _The Thames at Hammersmith,_[1] of, perhaps, 1909, which is, though far from undistinguished, a tidy compendium of the very qualities which, but a few years later, he was most fiercely to abjure. The real significance of his discipleship of the Spanish master was not, however, apparent in these paintings, but in the insight he gained into the mind of one of the supreme realistic painters. Gilman's was one of those powerful temperaments which mature slowly, but however unconvincing its first-fruits, it is clear that prolonged contact with Velazquez strengthened his own innate realism. It is reasonable to suppose that it was from him that he learnt that the pursuit of nature could not be too close. Next he came into the orbit of 19 Fitzroy Street. At this time he was still preoccupied with tone values, but his admiration for Lucien Pissarro, and through him for the Impressionists, led him to an enhanced sense of the attrac-

[1] Privately owned.

tions of pure and brilliant colour. At the same time, Sickert opened his eyes to the poetry of popular subjects, of public-houses, of Camden Town 'interiors' with their chests-of-drawers and iron bedsteads, and showed him how to extract poetry from the near and the familiar. Camden Town, for Gilman, was, of course, the near and the familiar, for he spent the greater part of his life as a painter in this neighbourhood, first in the Hampstead Road by the railway bridge, later at 47 Maple Street, Tottenham Court Road. (The last time I saw this square Georgian house, the rooms of which Gilman depicted in such brilliant colours, it had become a blackened ruin, and the wooden shutters were being furiously banged by the cold night wind.) From Sickert he also adopted the broken brush stroke but he used rather lighter tones than this friends, and his touch was already more deliberate. It was at this point in his development that he and Gore met Ginner. Immediately afterwards, Ginner called on him, and found him painting the portrait of the wife of his friend, R. P. Bevan. Gilman, although he was very much aware that there had been momentous movements on the Continent since Impressionism had passed its climax, had no precise idea of their nature.[1] The discovery that his new friend Ginner was familiar with the work of those fascinating but, so far as London was concerned, mysterious leaders of the younger generation, Gauguin, Cézanne and van Gogh, still further enhanced in Gilman's eyes the value of his friendship.

There took place at this time an event that provoked differences more radical and widespread, perhaps, than any single event in the history of art in England. This was the exhibition 'Manet and the Post-Impressionists' – generally known as 'The first Post-Impressionist Exhibition' to distinguish it from the 'Second Post-Impressionist Exhibition' held in the same place from 5 October until 31 December 1912 – organized by Roger Fry, and held at the Grafton Galleries, Grafton Street, from 8 November 1910 until 15 January 1911. For it was through this exhibition that the British

[1] Works by contemporary Continental masters had occasionally been shown in London before 1910: Sixty paintings and twenty drawings and lithographs by Lautrec at the Goupil Gallery in May 1898. Cézanne was represented (with Boudin, Degas, Manet, Monet, Morisot, Pissarro, Renoir and Sisley) at the International Society's first exhibition in the same year, and by ten works in a Durand-Ruel Exhibition at the Grafton Galleries in 1905, and again with Rodin in 1906, and Matisse and Gauguin at the New Gallery in 1908.

public (including almost the entire body of British artists) first received the full impact of Cézanne, van Gogh and Matisse – and a shattering impact it was. When the ensuing controversy died down, it was seen that this exhibition had changed the face of the art world of London. Here, as everywhere else, there had always been conflict between 'progressive' and 'conservative' opinion. 'Progressive' opinion upheld, while 'conservative' opinion condemned, for instance, Benjamin West's use of contemporary, in place of the traditional classical, costume in the painting of 'history', Pre-Raphaelitism, and the 'Impressionism' of the New English Art Club. Yet it was also the case that 'progressive' and 'conservative' had always merged by insensible degrees one into the other. One of the principal consequences of the first Post-Impressionist Exhibition was to sharpen the differences between the opposing factions. Thenceforward one had to be for or against 'modern art', without qualification. Another was that British painting assumed a less insular character. A third was the emergence of Fry[1] as the most influential English art critic and politician in the place of D. S. MacColl,[1] the severe and eloquent theorist, champion and chastener of the New English and scourge of the Royal Academy.

Gilman and Ginner visited this momentous exhibition together. At first sight Gilman was captivated by Gauguin, in particular by the richness of his colour and his variety as a designer, but he was unable to accept van Gogh as an entirely serious painter. What he saw at the Grafton Galleries impressed him so deeply as to call for a complete examination of his own fundamental convictions. For a nature so scrupulous, so deliberate, so confident in the validity of ideas as Gilman, this was a serious process. Ginner took him to Paris, where they saw everything that could be seen: the room decorated by van Gogh at Bernheim's; Pellerin's fabulous assembly of Cézannes; the great collection of Impressionists at Durand-Ruel's, and the work of painters of more recent growth, the Douanier Rousseau, Bonnard, Vuillard and Picasso at the galleries of Vollard and Sagot. On his return, his judgements were compared, in the course of innumerable discussions, with the maturer judgements of Ginner. As Gilman reflected and talked, his original enthusiasm for

[1] Some account of whose life and opinions will be given in an Appendix to the second volume of this work.

Gauguin cooled into respect. Cézanne he deeply admired, but it was van Gogh who in the end emerged for him as the greatest of modern masters, and as the master who could teach him most of what he wished to learn. ('Letters of a Post-Impressionist, being the familiar correspondence of Vincent van Gogh', which was constantly in his hands, might be termed his Bible.) These discussions, in which Gore often joined, and assiduous experiment, crystallized in a distinctive aesthetic, to which all three artists subscribed.[1] Ginner eventually formulated the general idea which formed the heart of it when he declared:

All great painters by direct intercourse with Nature have extracted from her facts which others have not observed, and interpreted them by methods which are personal and expressive of themselves – this is the great tradition of Realism. . . . Greco, Rembrandt, Millet, Courbet, Cézanne – all the great painters of the world have known that great art can only be created out of continued intercourse with Nature.

The arch-menace to the great tradition of Realism, he contended, is always

the adoption by weaker commercial painters of the creative artist's personal methods of interpreting nature and the consequent creation of a formula, it is this which constitutes Academism. . . . It has resulted in the decadence of every Art movement . . . until it finally ended in the 'debacle' of Bouguereau, Gérôme, of the British Royal Academy. . . .

He then proceeded to the analysis of the form which the arch-menace had assumed at the time at which he wrote. Although

the old Academic movement which reigned at Burlington House and the Paris Salon counts no more . . . there is a new Academic movement full of dangers. Full of dangers, because it is disguised under a false cloak. It cries that it is going to save Art, while, in reality, it will destroy it. What in England is known as Post-Impressionism – Voilà l'ennemi! It is all the more dangerous since it is enveloped in a rose-pink halo of interest. Take away the rose-pink and you find the Academic skeleton.

[1] This was set forth by Ginner on various occasions, most comprehensively in an article entitled 'Neo-Realism', which first appeared in 'The New Age' and was reprinted as the foreword to the catalogue of an exhibition of paintings by Gilman and Ginner at the Goupil Gallery, held in 18 April–9 May, 1914.

Those who adopted the superficial aspects of the work or the teaching of Cézanne, whether straightforward imitators or Cubists, were singled out for particular condemnation. A sharp distinction was drawn between the Romantic Realism of Gauguin, who himself went to the South Seas, and his personal interpretation, and the formula created by Matisse and Co., 'to be worked quietly at home in some snug Paris studio. . . .' He attacked the idea that Decoration is the unique aim of art, and spoke of the importance of subject to the realist:

> Each age has its landscape, its atmosphere, its cities, its people. Realism, loving Life, loving its Age, interprets its Epoch by extracting from it the very essence of all it contains of great or weak, of beautiful or of sordid, according to the individual temperament.

Impressionism in France, he concluded, was beyond question the latest and most important realistic movement, for 'the Impressionists, by their searching study of light, purified the muddy palettes by exchanging colour values for tone values'. The Neo-Impressionists neglected, in their scientific preoccupations,

> to keep themselves in relationship with Nature. . . . On the other hand, we find Cézanne, Gauguin and van Gogh, all three children of Impressionism, learning from it, as a wholesome source, all that it had to teach, and with their eyes fixed on the only true spring of Art: Life itself.

I have quoted from Ginner's essay at some length not because it adumbrates a theory – albeit at points somewhat summarily – to which I can subscribe, but because it provided a basis for the practice of three serious and gifted painters and general guidance for a number of others.

The close association of Gilman, Gore and Ginner affected Ginner relatively little, as his own highly personal style was already mature when he came to England in 1910, but it resulted in the formation of something approaching a common style. This left the widest latitude to the individual eye and hand: it would hardly be possible, that is to say, to mistake any single canvas by any of these three for one by either of the others. The most noticeable consequence of their study of the Impressionists, of Cézanne and of their two great successors was their adoption of a brighter palette. This involved, for Gilman and Gore, an end of their discipleship of Sickert, who continued to use the sombre colours which they came to regard as anathema. Wyndham Lewis has described how Gilman

> would look over in the direction of Sickert's studio, and a slight shudder would convulse him as he thought of the little brown worm of paint that was possibly, even at that moment, wriggling out on to the palette that held no golden chromes, emerald greens, vermilions, *only,* as it, of course, should do.[1]

Equally important was their repudiation – most emphatic with Gilman and least with Gore – of the Impressionist conception of a painting as having something of the character of a sketch, of something begun and completed under the same ephemeral effect, or of having that appearance. Gilman was determined to give his work the qualities of permanence and dignity. To this end he broadened his planes, simplified his masses and gave his designs firmness to the point of rigidity. And he rejected the light brush strokes of the Impressionists and Sickert: he painted with slow deliberation, putting the utmost thought into every touch. And his colour assumed a splendid and forthright brilliance. In the course of his struggle to obtain these qualities, and on the advice of Sickert and Ginner, he worked less from life and relied more upon his admirable pen-and-ink drawings. Ardently as he rejoiced in broad planes, firm designs and deliberate brush strokes, which made mosaics of brilliant colour, he never painted for painting's sake, nor was he moved solely by the aesthetic impulse. On the contrary, he was intensely moved by the human significance of the spectacle of surrounding life: he did not paint his mother, and Mrs. Mounter, the landlady whom he has made immortal, or his rooms in Maple Street, or even his massive teapots, as Cézanne painted apples, because they were accessible and they stayed still. He painted them because he loved them. Discussing Daumier's series of Don Quixotes, Gilman confided to his friend Sir Louis Fergusson that one of his greatest ambitions was to create a character, or rather to seize the essence of a character in real life and exhibit it on canvas in all its bearings. His love for the persons and things nearest to him grew with his growth as a painter.

[1] 'Harold Gilman: An Appreciation', by Wyndham Lewis and Louis F. Fergusson, 1919, p. 13.

The consistent growth of his powers of heart and eye and hand can be traced by comparing four paintings of different periods of his maturity: *The Little French Girl*,[1] of about 1909, a delicate work, beautifully true in tone, in greys and pinks plainly derived from his study of Velazquez. The girl herself is affectionately portrayed; so too is the furniture. When we set this beside *The Artist's Mother*,[2] of 1917, it seems to lack personality and candour: we become aware that the touch of pathos in the little girl is a consequence of the expedient of placing her, by herself, in a big room. The dignity and repose of his mother are obtained, as Americans put it, 'the hard way', by the most direct rendering in deeply pondered, immediately arrested, brush strokes. But next to *Mrs. Mounter* (Plate 17),[3] of 1917, even his mother, splendid painting though it is, looks small in form and confused in colour. *Mrs. Mounter*, with its majestic design in broad planes, its intensely brilliant colour and its tender insight, in my opinion is one of the great English portraits of the century, one among perhaps a dozen. I do not think that Gilman ever surpassed this portrait, but his last big painting, of a subject panoramic and entirely unfamiliar, which called for a composition infinitely more complex, showed that he had not reached the limit of his development. This picture was the radiant and stately *Halifax Harbour after the Explosion*,[4] of 1918, which, when I last saw it, shed an incongruous lustre in a dark, neo-Gothic gallery in the New World, above the door of which, unless my memory is playing tricks, was carved the word FOSSILS. Although this must take a place among his finest paintings, he did not require, in order to obtain grandeur of form, a subject grand, as Halifax Harbour is, in any ordinary sense. A picture which it is instructive to compare with this great work is one scarcely inferior to it which represents the interior of a small *Eating-House* (Plate 16),[5] of about 1914. Here, three wooden partitions against walls of pitch-pine and wallpaper and casual glimpses of nondescript diners have been transformed by Gilman's robust affection into a noble design in which harshly glowing colour is fused with closely knit form.

[1] The Tate Gallery, London.   [2] The Tate Gallery, London.

[3] The Walker Art Gallery, Liverpool. There is a smaller version, of 1916, in the Tate Gallery.

[4] The National Gallery of Canada, Ottawa.   [5] Privately owned.

By 1914, when he was thirty-eight years old, Gilman had evolved a way of seeing and a way of drawing and painting which enabled him, when circumstances were propitious, to produce masterpieces. Five years later he and Ginner caught Spanish influenza in the great epidemic of 1919 and were taken to the French Hospital, where he died on 12 February.

The death of Gilman was a grave loss to English painting. He was the acknowledged leader of a group of friends who had infused a new vigour into a great modern tradition. His character, in particular the union of intense seriousness with exuberant goodwill, endeared him to a wide circle of friends. Something of the flavour of this character is caught in this description by Wyndham Lewis:

The Gilman tic was a thing prized by his friends next to the sternness of his painting. He was proud of a pompous drollery, which he flavoured with every resource of an abundantly nourished country rectory, as he was proud of his parsonic stock. He was proud of his reverberating pulpit voice: he was proud of the eccentricities of his figure. He was also proud of a certain fleeting resemblance, observed by the ribald, to George Robey, the priceless ape. But, above all, he was proud to be a man who could sometimes hang his pictures in the neighbourhood of a picture postcard of the great modern master, van Gogh.[1]

Unlike many, possibly the majority of artists, Gilman was deeply concerned for the wellbeing of the art of painting in general. He favoured working with a small, cohesive group of other painters, partly because he believed that new methods are evolved not by individuals, but, as Sickert used to say, by gangs, partly because he regarded such a group as an effective means of propagating sound methods. He was also an able and earnest teacher.

The Allied Artists' Association was recognized by Gilman and his friends as a valuable means of enabling artists, especially independent and lesser-known artists, to show their work, but its exhibitions were on altogether too vast a scale to exert influence in any particular direction. The more clearly their opinions crystallized, the more aware did they become of their need for a platform from which to proclaim them. The question as to how they were to obtain one was the occasion of numerous discussions among them. This question

[2] 'Harold Gilman: An Appreciation', pp. 13-14.

quickly resolved itself into a simple issue: whether to try to capture the New English Art Club or to form a new society.

> . . . I doubt if any unprejudiced student of modern painting will deny [wrote Sickert in 1910] that the New English Art Club at the present day sets the standard of painting in England. He may regret it or resent it, but he will hardly deny it.[1]

This estimate of the Club's importance was shared by Gilman and his friends, but of recent years his own work and that of the painters whom he most admired had been rejected by its juries. Sickert was of the decided opinion that they stood no chance of obtaining control of the New English, and Gore (who had become a member the previous year) was reluctantly convinced that it had tacitly renounced the pioneering policy for which it had earlier been conspicuous, and had become, in fact although not in profession, an academic force, and that its capture was therefore not even to be desired. Augustus John firmly maintained the view that the New English stood for the highest prevailing standards, and it would be wrong to secede, especially for him who owed everything to it. The climax of these discussions came early in 1911 when, over dinner at Gatti's, it was decided to form a new society. Gilman, innately uncompromising, who had favoured this course from the first, was jubilant, and Sickert, leaving the restaurant ahead of the others, grandiloquently exclaimed, 'We have just made history.' A meeting to settle details was held at 19 Fitzroy Street. There were further meetings at the Criterion Restaurant, and, finally, in May, at a restaurant long since demolished, off Golden Square, the new society was formed and appropriately christened by Sickert 'The Camden Town Group'.[2] Gore was elected President. The Group held only three exhibitions, in June and December 1911 and December 1912, all at the Carfax Gallery in Bury Street, St. James's. None of these was a financial success, and Arthur Clifton, the director of the Carfax Gallery, was not prepared to continue them. Members of

[1] 'The Allied Artists' Association', *The Art News*, 14 July.

[2] The original members were: Walter Bayes, R. P. Bevan, Malcolm Drummond, Harold Gilman, Charles Ginner, Spencer Gore, J. D. Innes, Augustus John, Henry Lamb, Wyndham Lewis, M. G. Lightfoot, J. B. Manson (Secretary), Lucien Pissarro, W. Ratcliffe, W. R. Sickert, Doman Turner. Duncan Grant joined after the first exhibition.

19. GWEN JOHN. *Self-portrait* (*c.* 1900?).
Oil, 17⅝ × 13¾ in. The Tate Gallery, London.

20. GWEN JOHN. *The Convalescent* (1925–30?).
Oil, 16 × 12¾ in. Privately owned.

21. AUGUSTUS JOHN. *Robin* (c. 1909?).
Oil, 18×14 in. The Tate Gallery, London.

22. AUGUSTUS JOHN. *Lyric Fantasy* (c. 1911–15).
Oil, 92 × 185 in. The Tate Gallery, London.

23. AUGUSTUS JOHN. *Portrait of Joseph Hone* (c. 1926).
Oil, 20 × 16 in. The Tate Gallery, London.

24. CHARLES GINNER. *Flask Walk, Hampstead, under Snow (c.* 1930).
Oil, 26 × 16 in. Privately owned.

25. SPENCER GORE. *North London Girl* (1911).
Oil, 30 × 24 in. The Tate Gallery, London.

26. AMBROSE McEVOY. *The Hon. Daphne Baring* (1916).
Oil, 42½ × 32½ in. Privately owned.

the Group then approached William Marchant, proprietor of the Goupil Gallery, with the view of transferring their exhibitions to his premises. He was sympathetically disposed, but he objected to the title of the Group for the very reason that had led Sickert to choose it – namely, that a sensational murder had given Camden Town an ominous reputation. He also favoured an enlarged society in order to ensure that his more capacious galleries should be filled.

By 1913 there was a spirit of fusion abroad. Of the various groups active in the region about Tottenham Court Road – of which the membership was largely identical – each had its particular difficulty. All suffered from insufficient resources and the consciousness of being too small to be effective. The Camden Town Group fused with 19 Fitzroy Street, and successfully sought the adherence of the Vorticist Group led by Wyndham Lewis, of which Frederick Etchells,[1] William Roberts and Edward Wadsworth were the principal members. After protracted negotiations, a meeting was held on 15 November 1913 at 19 Fitzroy Street, with Sickert presiding, at which it was decided to form yet another and more comprehensive society, and to call it the London Group. Gilman was elected President, and continued in office until his death. The new group represented a fusion not only of the three groups already mentioned, but also of the Cumberland Market Group which came into being on the initiative of Gilman and Bevan[2] as a successor to 19 Fitzroy Street. Shortly afterwards Spencer Gore died, and with his death the tensions within the London Group, latent in the presence of his disinterested benevolence, his tact and his charm, caused dangerous rifts. The outbreak of the First World War brought further confusion, and when it cleared away, the Group fell under the control of Fry whose aims were totally opposed to those of its founders.

More satisfying to Gilman than all this formation and amalgamation of groups – for he lacked the adaptability, the guile, the

[1] After the First World War he devoted himself mainly to architecture.

[2] Robert Polhill Bevan, painter of horses, market scenes and landscapes. Born in Hove, Sussex, 5 August 1865. Studied for a short time at the Westminster School under Brown, then in Paris at Julian's. Met Gauguin 1894 at Pont Aven. Married S. de Karlowska 1897. An original member of the Camden Town Group 1911, and of the London Group 1913; member of the New English Art Club 1923. Died 8 July 1925 in London.

ambition and the talent for intrigue, all, indeed, of the political talents except clarity of aim, persistence and the more doubtful asset of courage – was his teaching. For a time he taught an evening life-class at the Westminster School. The class had for some time been taught by Sickert, who resigned shortly after the outbreak of war, and Gore was appointed in his place. On the death of Gore, or possibly earlier, the class was taken over by Gilman. Before long Sickert, wishing to resume his teaching at Westminster, secured Gilman's dismissal. This caused a breach between him and his friend and teacher that was never healed. Gilman's evening classes, both at the Westminster and at the small school at 16 Little Pulteney Street, Soho, that he afterwards ran with Ginner, were attended by admirers of his painting who, in the words of one of them, 'wished to learn to see colour as he saw it'. The usual subjects were nudes and charwomen. Gilman, who shared Sickert's disapproval of the painting of figures in isolation from their environment, used to fit up a screen with a boldly patterned wallpaper for a background. The method of painting he taught was, of course, that which he had himself evolved. In accordance with this method his students made no under-painting or anything of the nature of a preliminary sketch, but instead they built up their pictures in separate brush strokes, each carefully considered and rightly related to the rest. They began with the highest lights and worked downwards to the darker passages, looking rather for colour than tone relations, for he did not subscribe to the widely held belief that if tone relations were right, right colour relations would inevitably follow. They were taught that there was no such thing as a uniform surface that could be represented by a wide sweep of the brush; that all surfaces that presented this appearance at first glance proved under scrutiny to have infinite subtle variations. Although they were enjoined to aim at finality with each brush stroke and never to be content with less, it was recognized that this was a counsel of perfection, and they were bound to err, especially at first, but it was infinitely preferable to err on the side of overstatement of a colour's strength and purity, and the grossest error was to take refuge, when in doubt, in some indeterminate colour such as brown. Colours inclined to be neutral must be forced to confess a tendency to a positive colour, and this intensified. The colours of the spectrum and white were the colours they used. Gilman said one day, after some deliberation, that an occasion *might* arise when, say, raw sienna was the proper colour to use, for one touch, but this he thought most unlikely, and he advised them (for the hundredth time) to avoid, if they were to escape the danger of muddiness, all earth colours. The scraping off of any paint from their canvases he never favoured, but advised them instead to add fresh touches on top of the old, nor did he mind how thick, in consequence, they painted, observing that some of Rembrandt's canvases must originally have been very heavily loaded.

Gilman gave his students the strong impression of *seeing* the clear, pure greens, lilacs and yellows he used in painting flesh, and of being unable to see in any other way. Inevitably they themselves came to see nature in terms of pure colour relationships. Certain of his methods evidently derived from Signac and Seurat, but his aims, unlike theirs, were in no way affected by their scientific preoccupations: with him the emphasis was always on the *beauty* of the colour in the subject. He shared Sickert's opinion that even a knowledge of perspective and anatomy was superfluous to someone able to render tone and the direction of lines with sensibility and precision. He surprised one of his students by telling him to begin the drawing of a nude with an outline silhouette. So confident was he that he tempered his own dogmatic approach by taking any observations a student ventured to make with the utmost seriousness, and by an openness to new ideas. This combination of certainty and modesty made him an admirable teacher. He did not work on his students' canvases, and their familiarity with his own work made 'demonstration' unnecessary. His criticism generally took the form of a searching analysis of the subject in terms of colour relations.

In spite of the brevity of his professional life and of his restricted scope as a teacher, and of the prompt diversion to ends with which he could have had no sympathy of the organization that represented the culmination of his political activity, there are signs that the reputation and influence of this single-minded and uncompromising painter stand higher than at any time since his death. Higher, certainly, in one particular: during his lifetime scarcely anybody except his friends bought his modestly priced pictures; now they are year by year more difficult to acquire.

GWEN JOHN
1876—1939

GWEN JOHN was in almost every respect the opposite of her brother Augustus. He is an improviser; she developed methodicity, as he has told us, to a point of elaboration undreamed of by her master, Whistler. He is expansive; she was concentrated. He is exuberant; she was chaste, subdued and sad. He is Dionysian; she was a devoted Catholic. He enhanced or troubled the lives of those whom he touched; she stole through life and out of it almost unnoticed.

Neither in France, where she mostly lived, nor in her own country, did her work arouse sufficient interest during her lifetime to inspire, so far as I am aware, a single article. In 1946, seven years after her death, a Memorial Exhibition, consisting of 217 works in various mediums, was held in London.[1] This was received with marked respect, but a few months later, if she was not quite forgotten, she occupied only a tiny niche in the public memory. Its most memorable consequence was the arresting evocation of his sister's memory in Augustus John's foreword to the catalogue.

Yet few of those privileged to know her work fail to receive from it a lasting impression. Many of them are moved to compare it with that of her brother, to his disadvantage. The expressions of personalities so opposite as Gwen and Augustus John are hardly comparable; we can only note the contrasts between them. About this there would be nothing invidious, for he is his sister's most ardent advocate. The very extremity of the contrasts between these two children of the same parents has always seemed to fascinate Augustus John: I have seen him peer fixedly, almost obsessively, at pictures by Gwen as though he could discern in them his own temperament in reverse; as though he could derive from the act satisfaction in his own wider range, greater natural endowment, tempestuous energy, and at the same time be reproached by her single-mindedness, her steadiness

---

[1] At the Matthiesen Gallery, from 17 September until 12 October; a selection was shown under the auspices of the Arts Council in several other cities.

of focus, above all by the sureness with which she attained her simpler aims.

The case of Gwen John provides a melancholy illustration of the neglect of English painting. I am not expressing an original opinion in saying that I believe her to be one of the finest painters of our time and country, yet – apart from her brother's eulogy and a discerning article on the Memorial Exhibition by Wyndham Lewis[1] – her work has received no serious consideration whatever; indeed, it can scarcely be said to have been noticed at all. Outside the Tate, which possesses a dozen of her paintings and drawings, she is insignificantly represented in public collections and there are relatively few of her works in private hands. Gwen John is, in fact, in danger of oblivion. It would be unjust to her contemporaries to suggest that they are solely to blame. She herself deliberately chose a life of seclusion. After her death a number of her paintings disappeared from the little room she occupied. No work by her later than 1932 is known, and so withdrawn was her life during the closing years of it that it is uncertain whether she ceased to paint or whether the paintings she made were lost. Not many of her friends survive, and those who do recollect curiously little about her. One of them invited me to his house not long ago, telling me that he saw her often during that last obscure decade. When I arrived he confessed that his memory retained nothing precise. Even her family's recollections are meagre. So it is an elusive personality that I am trying to reconstruct.

Fortunately, thanks to the kindness of Mr. Edwin John, her favourite nephew, I have had access to a number of important documents. During her last years she possessed a little shack on a piece of waste land where she lived and worked, and an attic room in a neighbouring house, which she had previously occupied but used latterly for the storage of her effects, both at Meudon. After her death her nephew, who is also her heir, went to Meudon, where he found in the attic room, besides a number of pictures, a mass of papers, covered with dust, that had lain for years there undisturbed. These include a few letters from Rilke, a number from her father, and a long series of intimate brief letters from Rodin. The letters addressed to her are largely complemented by

[1] 'The Listener', 10 October 1946.

copies that she made of others of which the originals are missing (several evidently from M. Jacques Maritain, for example), by numerous drafts or copies of her own letters to Rodin and others, and copies of prayers and meditations and extracts from the writings of the saints and other Catholic writers, as well as from Bertrand Russell, Baudelaire, Dostoievski, Oscar Wilde and Diderot. There is something puzzling about these copies. It is understandable that she should wish to preserve copies of such of her letters as she valued and make drafts of letters difficult to compose, but this does not account entirely for the number of such copies. There is one meditation of which there are seven, several of them identical. From all these papers I have had permission, through the kindness of her brother and her nephew, to quote, but in view of the most intimate character of many of them and of Gwen John's extreme reticence about her own life, I shall avail myself of it as sparingly as the requirements of my narrative allow.

Gwendolen Mary John was born on 22 June 1876 at Haverfordwest, Pembrokeshire, the second of the four children of Edwin William John, a solicitor, and his wife Augusta, born Smith, of a Brighton family. Not long after her birth the family moved to 5 Lexden Terrace, Tenby. Here, in an attic, Gwen and Augustus, in both of whom their vocation early declared itself, had their first studio. An extraordinary capacity for devotion was also early evident in Gwen, who was always, her brother relates, 'picking up beautiful children to draw and adore'. In 1895 she followed Augustus to the Slade and they shared a series of rooms together, which they constantly changed, living solely on fruit and nuts. The intensity of Gwen's friendships at times made the atmosphere of the group of which the two of them were the focus 'almost unbearable', according to her brother, 'with its frightful tension, its terrifying excursions and alarms'. The break in one such friendship brought a threat of suicide. But the excursions and alarms did not interrupt the progress of her art. How beautifully she drew while she was still a student is apparent from her *Self-portrait at the Age of About Twenty*[1] (in which she looks considerably younger). One of her passionate attachments, in fact, was invaluable in fostering her technical knowledge of painting, for Ambrose McEvoy imparted to her the results of his

[1] Privately owned. No. 57 in the Matthiesen Exhibition.

researches into the methods of the old masters. Without his help, she could hardly have painted the *Self-portrait*[1] (Plate 19) in a red sealing-wax coloured blouse, which, although I am unable to date it precisely, was probably done soon after she left the Slade. This portrait – to my thinking, one of the finest portraits of the time, excelling in insight into character and in purity of form and delicacy of tone any portrait of McEvoy's – owes the technical perfection of its glazes to his knowledge, as generously imparted as it was laboriously acquired.

On leaving the Slade in 1898 she lived in a little room over a mortuary in the Euston Road, and later in a cellar in Howland Street, where she made water-colour drawings of cats. After leaving Howland Street, she lodged for a time with a family, father, mother and two sons, one of whom became a celebrated painter, in a house where the shutters were always closed, for they paid no rates. Before long she left England and settled in France, returning only for occasional visits. How bleak the interlude was between the Slade and Whistler's school in Paris to which she presently attached herself is clear from a letter to her brother.

I told you in a letter long ago that I am happy [she wrote]. Where illness or death do not interfere, I am. Not many people can say as much. I do not lead a subterranean life (my subterranean life was in Howland Street) . . . If to 'return to life' is to live as I did in London – *Merci, Monsieur*! . . . There are people like plants who cannot flourish in the cold, and I want to flourish. . . .

At Whistler's school, taking to heart her master's saying, 'Art is the science of beauty', she proceeded, her brother has told us, to cultivate her painting in a scientific spirit. She used to prepare her canvases according to a recipe of her own, and invented a system of numbering her colour mixtures which, however helpful to her, makes her notes on painting and schemes for pictures unintelligible to anyone else.

. . . She had [he added] no competitive spirit and rarely went out of her way to study her contemporaries, but was familiar with the National Gallery and the Louvre.

[1] The Tate Gallery, London.

When asked her opinion of an exhibition of Cézanne water-colours, her reply, scarcely audible, was 'These are very good, but I prefer my own.'[1]

Whistler's school was not a school at all in the current sense, but a class, managed by a former model named Carmen, which Whistler visited once a week. A comment by Whistler on the work of Gwen John is related by her brother, who met him in the Louvre and introduced himself as the brother of one of his pupils:

> Mr. Whistler with great politeness asked me to make Gwen his compliments. I ventured to enquire if he thought well of her progress, adding that I thought her drawings showed a feeling for character. 'Character?' replied Whistler, 'Character? What's that? It's the tone that matters. Your sister has a fine sense of *tone*.'

Her attendance at Whistler's school was confined to the afternoons. She lived in a top flat in the Rue Froidveau, which she shared with two fellow students, Ida Nettleship, who was shortly to become the wife of Augustus John, and Gwen Salmond, some years later the wife of Matthew Smith. The three girls practised the most rigorous economy, and, although Gwen John outdid her companions in this respect, she was not able, out of her tiny allowance, to save sufficient to pay the small fees required to attend Whistler's school. By a benevolent act of intrigue, Gwen Salmond secured her admission as an afternoon pupil. 'I've written home', Gwen John delightedly exclaimed, 'that I've got a *scholarship*.' In spite of her dedication to painting and drawing, she seems to have done little of either at this time. An incident related by a friend who was a witness of it may explain this singular circumstance. Some time after she had gone to Paris, her father arrived on a short visit. By way of welcome, she arranged a small supper to which she invited several of her friends, at which she wore a dress copied from one in a picture by Manet. It was a dress to the making of which she had given infinite trouble; it had been purchased at the price of many frugal meals foregone. 'You look like a prostitute in that dress', was her father's opening observation. 'I could never accept anything from someone capable of thinking so', she answered, and my informant believes that in order to replace the rejected small allowance she posed regularly

[1] Introduction to the Catalogue of the Memorial Exhibition.

as an artist's model. For this she was qualified by a grave dignity and a beautiful, slender figure, 'un corps admirable', as Rodin, an authority on the subject, called it some years later. The incident left no bitterness, to judge from the long series of unintimate but prosily friendly letters from her father which she preserved.

Dates are difficult to establish, but it was probably in the autumn of 1898 that she first settled in Paris. A year or so later she was in London again. For a time she shared what my father described as 'comfortless' quarters with her brother in Fitzroy Street; then they moved into a house lent to them by my parents. My father, having to return to London for a night in the middle of the following winter, telegraphed to the Johns to warn them of his arrival, which he thus described:

> When I reached Kensington I found the house empty and no fire burning. In front of a cold grate choked with cinders lay a collection of muddy boots. . . . Late in the evening John appeared, having climbed through a window; he rarely, he explained, remembered to take the house-key with him.[1]

(In this house, 1 Pembroke Cottages, Edwardes Square, I was born eighteen months later.) Recalling, in the winter of the present year (1951) the events of that earlier winter, Augustus John observed confidentially: 'I'm afraid Will did not find Gwen and me very satisfactory tenants. . . .' He married in 1900, and Gwen must have remained in England for a while, for Ida, his first wife, wrote to my mother many months later saying: 'I long for Gwen; have you seen her lately?'

One autumn early in the new century, probably in 1902, she returned to France in circumstances which should enable me to fill in a little the tenuous outlines of the portrait that I am trying to draw – a portrait which nevertheless I shall find it difficult to bring clearly into focus. She was accompanied on a journey to Paris, by way of Bordeaux and Toulouse, by Dorelia, whom her brother married shortly after the death of his first wife, and to whom I am indebted for some details about both the journey and her companion. The two girls travelled by boat to Bordeaux, whence they walked to Toulouse. Their first night in France they spent in a field on a bank of the Garonne, and they were wakened in the morning by a

[1] 'Men and Memories', Vol. I, 1931, p. 352.

boar. They intended to walk on to Italy, but after spending three months or so in Toulouse and visiting Montauban they went to Paris instead. Here Gwen stayed for the rest of her life, apart from a few brief visits to England and to the French coast, for she loved the sea, and from time to time she needed, with a curious urgency, the refreshment she was able to draw from no other source. On their journey they lived spartanly. In Toulouse they lodged in two bare rooms which they rented for two francs a week; they subsisted upon bread, cheese and figs, which cost them fifty centimes a meal, and which they ate in the fields; and they bathed in the river, maintaining themselves meanwhile by making portrait sketches in cafés for three francs each. The person who emerges from Mrs. John's description was attractive to men and susceptible to their admiration; reserved and quiet-voiced; pale and oval-faced, her hair something in colour between mouse and honey, done with a big bow on top; with a slender figure, and tiny, delicate hands and feet, yet of exceptional strength, able to carry heavy burdens over long distances at speeds which her companion found excessive. 'I shouldn't like to carry *that*', shouted a sturdy Montauban workman, indicating the big bundle on her back. While not unsociable, she loved solitude; indifferent to mankind as a whole, she was passionately attached to her few friends, and apt to form other strong attachments that quickly cooled. Beneath a reserved friendliness occasionally varied by moodiness, Mrs. John was aware of a strain of censorious puritanism. She disapproved, for instance, of the theatre; she spoke angrily of the 'vulgar red lips' of a beautiful girl whom they used as a model. She rarely spoke of painting or other serious matters, but when they became subjects of conversation she was able to express herself with ease and conviction.

A few days after Mrs. John had given me the foregoing information, I received from her the following note, evidently intended to correct the rather too austere impression she thought she had given:

FRYERN COURT,
FORDINGBRIDGE, HANTS.
Jan. 19th/51.

DEAR JOHN,
    . . . You asked me how Gwen dressed and though I cannot remember what she wore she always managed to look elegant, and

though I cannot remember what we talked about I do remember some very light-hearted evenings over a bottle of wine and a bowl of soup. She wasn't at all careless of her appearance; in fact, rather vain. She also much appreciated the good food and wine to be had in that part of France, though we mostly lived on stolen grapes and bread.

Yours sincerely,

DORELIA.

During her three months in Toulouse, Gwen John worked steadily. She painted at least two portraits of her companion, the lamplit *Dorelia at Toulouse*[1] and *Dorelia in a Black Dress*,[2] both from life, directly on to the canvas without preliminary studies. She both drew and painted quickly, her brother told me, 'with an intensity you could scarcely believe'. *Dorelia at Toulouse* is one of her best portraits. The beautiful young woman reading at night, facing the full lamplight that casts her shadow big on the wall behind, is painted with extraordinary tenderness, as though in pity for a being trustfully unaware of the scarring realities of life. Yet it is not with a sentimental, but a serenely detached, an almost impersonal pity that the beautiful reader is portrayed.

By 1902, when she was twenty-six, the art of Gwen John had reached maturity. It may indeed have matured still earlier, but I am unable to assign a definite date to any painting done before *Dorelia at Toulouse* (my surmise that the Tate *Self-portrait* was painted some three years earlier is based upon slender evidence). I have examined a number of her paintings with her brother, her nephew Edwin, Mrs. Matthew Smith and others who knew her, but I was able to elicit, with regard to dates, few opinions and no facts. *A Lady Reading*,[3] *Nude Girl*[4] and other paintings of the same character would seem to be among the earliest that survive, but what of the lovely *A Corner of the Artist's Room in Paris*[5] (Plate 18). This picture, an ultimate expression, surely, of the Intimiste spirit, by its tiny perfection reminds us not of any other picture so much as of the song of a bird. When was it painted?

The art of Gwen John shows throughout an extraordinary consistency and independence. There are few painters whose origins do

[1] Privately owned. [2] The Tate Gallery, London.
[3] The Tate Gallery, London. [4] The Tate Gallery, London.
[5] Privately owned.

not appear, or, rather, obtrude themselves, in their early works (if not their later). But where outside her own imagination are the sources of this artist's inspiration? There are artists wider in range (indeed, there are few narrower), but I can think of none in our time to whom the term 'original' can more properly be applied. Nothing could be more restricted than her subjects: a handful of women: her sister-in-law Dorelia, a girl called Fanella, a few nuns, a few orphan children, herself; some cats; but beyond these – except for an occasional empty room or view from a window – she scarcely ever went. Nor was her treatment of them various: all are represented singly and in simple poses; all (except the cats) are chaste and sad.

So deep were the roots of her art that it seems hardly to have been affected by two events, one of which whirled her, she said, like a little leaf carried by the wind, and the other eventually transformed her life. The first of these events was her long intimacy with Rodin; the second her adoption of the Catholic faith. The circumstance that they were to some extent coincidental made the years of her life affected by them a time of extraordinary anguish.

Their correspondence suggests that she met Rodin in 1906. At their first encounters at all events there was no trembling of the leaf. In an early letter she even alluded to her lack of respect for his work. In another undated but evidently later letter she wrote with bitter reproach: 'Quel vie vous me donnez maintenant! Qu'est-ce que je vous ai fait mon Maitre. Vous savez toujours que mon cœur est profonde. . . .' We may surmise that Rodin quickly overcame her indifference and tapped the deep wells of her adoration, and, having reduced her to a condition of helpless dependence upon him, found her single-hearted devotion, when the first excitement ebbed away, an added complication that his already complicated life could hardly sustain. In 1906 he was already sixty-six years old and con- stantly, he complained, 'enrhumé' or 'grippé'; he was the most illustrious sculptor of the modern world, and deeply involved in a wide complex of relationships, professional, social, amorous and financial. But it would be unjust to depict him as a man who under the spell of a superficial attraction recklessly established an intimacy that he soon regretted. The numerous brief letters he wrote to her testify to a friendship that was close and enduring, and that certain of them should be evasive in the circumstances need be no matter for surprise. They speak of his appreciation of her painting and drawing, but above all of his concern at her neglect of her health. In one of the earliest, written in 1906, he says. 'Il faudrait changer de chambre [her room at 7 Rue Ste. Placide] qui est trop humide et n'a pas de soleil.' Continually he urges her to eat well, to take exercise. There is a sentence in a later letter that sums up their relations: 'Moi je suis fatigué et vieux. Vous me demandez plus que je peux mais j'aime votre petit cœur si devoué, patience et moins de violence.' A singular, if unimportant, fact about their friendship is Rodin's continuing vagueness about her name. He addressed her letters 'Mademoiselle John Mary', 'John Marie', sometimes simply 'Mary'. Anguishing though Gwen John's friendship with Rodin evidently became, it was incomparably the largest and most deeply felt friendship of her life.

Not comparable in its intensity or indeed in its character with her relationship with Rodin was that which she formed with Rilke, probably the most enduring friendship she had. There is a letter from him dated 17 July 1908, in which he offered to lend her books, and expressed regret that since the previous year she had not wished to remember him, and there is a brief, cool reply from her, written in the third person. But their friendship grew, and a letter from her dated April 1927 shows how much she came to rely upon his guidance and affection:

I accept to suffer always [it runs], but Rilke! hold my hand! you must hold me by the hand! Teach me, inspire me, make me know what to do. Take care of me when my mind is asleep. You began to help me. You must continue.

It was her concern for Rilke's soul that caused her, the day after his death, to call on the Maritains (who also lived at Meudon) to ask whether she should pray for it there or at the place where he died.

Precisely when Gwen John was received into the Catholic Church I have been unable to discover, but it must have been early in 1913. On 10 October 1912 she wrote to the Curé of Meudon to excuse herself for not attending an instruction, and on 12 February of the following year she noted: 'On Saturday I shall receive the Sacrament for the 5th time'; but it would seem that her relations with Rodin had not changed. Her religious life therefore began in circumstances of extraordinary difficulty, but the courage and the implacable clearsightedness with which she faced them made her will, already exceptionally strong, into an instrument of formidable power. But the process was one of prolonged, unmitigated anguish. 'A beautiful life', she wrote, 'is one led, perhaps, in the shadow, but ordered, regular, harmonious.'

The many prayers and meditations she left do not reveal an aptitude for speculation, or an intellect of exceptional interest, but she possessed, in a high degree, the quality of *immediacy* by which we are constantly arrested in the writings of Newman and Pascal. 'Do not think', runs one of her notes, 'that you must wait for years. In to-night's meditation God may reveal himself to you.' She was relentless with herself in her determination to transform her life.

> I have felt momentarily [she wrote] a fear of leaving the world I know, as if I should be loosing [*sic*] something of value, but I cannot tell what there is of value in it that I should be loosing [*sic*]. It is because I cannot criticise the world I know, because I have not been able to criticise it that it appears to have a value [she wrote in English or French according to her fancy; inaccurately in both].

In the notice of her Memorial Exhibition from which I have quoted, Wyndham Lewis asked how she could have isolated herself so successfully from the influences of her age. 'Part of the answer', he wrote, 'is that one of her great friends was Jacques Maritain: she belonged to the Catholic Revival in France.' Apart from the question whether the friendship of M. Maritain would be likely to isolate an artist from contemporary influences, the fact is that neither of the scorching and exalting experiences she underwent appears to have had any immediate effect on her art; they would seem to have neither hastened nor retarded its serene progress. She was protected from the effects of current modes of feeling and expression, just as she was protected from the unsettlement that such experiences bring to shallower natures, by her extraordinary, though wholly unassertive, originality and independence. I do not mean that her painting did not change; in its unhurried fashion, it changed greatly. In her early paintings, the Tate *Self-portrait* and the other probably rather later and equally fine *Self-portrait* belonging to her brother, she used glazes or else thin fluid paint, gradually and delicately correcting until the picture corresponded with her vision of her subject. In her later painting her method was the opposite of this: she used thick paint, and was reluctant to touch her canvas more than once in the same place, preferring, in the event of failure, to begin again. She gradually abandoned the use of dark shadows – shadows sometimes almost black – and kept her tones light and very close together. As with advancing years her tones grew lighter, so her austerely simplified forms attained still greater breadth. But these changes were never accompanied, as they have been sometimes, even in the work of as considerable a painter as Monet, by diffuseness. Her later work, on the contrary, is distinguished by a heightened intensity. And the delicate colours – they look as though they were mixed with wood-ash – applied with touches so modest but so sure, and the firm draughtsmanship beneath produce an impression of extraordinary grandeur, no matter on how small a scale she worked. The wisdom she gained from her emotional and spiritual ordeals was little by little embodied in her deeply rooted art. In the later years her goodness, which had earlier been instinctive and unfocused, became radiantly manifest.

The last twenty-five years of her life or thereabouts were spent at Meudon, whither she had no doubt followed Rodin not long before her reception into the Church. For some years she occupied the attic room in which her pictures and her papers were found after her death at 29 Rue Terre Neuve, but in the summer of 1927 she acquired a small piece of ground in the Rue Babie, at the back of which stood a garage. In this secluded and rather dilapidated structure, the trees and shrubs growing up to shield it, she lived and painted. Without any of the domestic arts (she could scarcely cook the simplest dishes), she existed in what to an ordinary mortal would have been un-endurable discomfort, eating scarcely anything (although never neglecting to feed her cats), sleeping in summer in the open in her flowering wilderness. Cats were her constant companions, and she experienced in their acutest form the anxieties from which those who have animals for friends are never immune. 'Fearful anguish because of the cat', runs one of her little notes. 'All equilibre lost.' It was on their account that she so rarely revisited England during these years. 'The cats more than my work make it too difficult for me to come over', she wrote to a friend. 'I've had so many tragedies

[*sic*] with them, now I'm afraid to leave the two I have now.' Nor
was she easily persuaded to send her pictures for exhibition in
London or New York, where, in spite of her indifference to the
opinions of anyone except her friends, she had a few deeply convinced admirers. My father was one of the few whose praise she
valued. In an undated letter to my mother she wrote: 'You say my
pictures were admired. I tell myself since reading that, that Will
admired them. I do not care for the opinions of others.'

The innumerable pieces of paper upon which she wrote down her
drafts and copies of letter, prayers, meditations, notes on painting
tell the story of her later life. The notes on painting are the rarest.
Some of them are indecipherable, others unintelligible, but a few
vividly evoke her palette. 'Smoky corn and wild rose', runs one of
them, 'faded roses (3 reds), nuts and nettles faded roses and vermi-
lion roses in a yellow basket . . . cyclamen and straw and earth. . . .'
Another, in a draft of a letter to a friend, recalls her loving intimacy
with nature: 'At night I used to pluck the leaves and grasses in the
hedges all dark and misty and when I took them home I sometimes
found my hands were full of flowers.' But most of these random
notes concern the religion which shared her life with painting:
'Ma religion et mon art, c'est toute ma vie', she said to her neighbour in the Rue Babie. She took Holy Communion daily, but when
she reached a point in the painting of a picture when her undivided
attention was demanded she would work continuously and absent
herself from Mass for as long, sometimes, as a month. Reproached
gently by her neighbour about these absences, she consulted the
Curé:

. . . un prêtre en qui elle avait la plus entière confiance, très éclairé et
de grande largeur d'idées. [I quote from an unpublished account[1] of
Gwen John written by her neighbour.] Il savait qu'il avait à faire à une
artiste, qu'il ne pouvait traiter comme tout le monde, aussi, elle revînt
toute joyeuse: 'il ne m'a rien dit, il ne m'a pas dit que j'avais fait un
péché'. Je compris a mon tour, et je ne lui en parlai plus.

Although she lived a devout, even a saintly life, Gwen John
preserved, in all the spheres where it was appropriate, her independence unimpaired, and never felt, like many others, in

[1] Written in 1947.

particular, perhaps, English converts to the Church, the need to make excessive demonstrations of piety.

Sous un certain angle, elle était restée protestante [as her neighbour quaintly put it]; j'en eus un bel échantillon le jour de la mort du Pape PIE XI. Outre qu'il était le chef des catholiques, c'était un ami de la France, et nous avions été tres émus de sa disparition. Je l'apprends à Mlle. John qui me répond 'qu'est-ce que vous voulez que ça me fasse', et à son tour, elle m'apprend la mort d'une vieille voisine, assez peu sympathique que nous connaissions à peine l'une l'autre. Vexée de la réponse je lui dis : 'mais vous semblez plus fâchée par la mort de Mme. M. que par de celle du Pape.' Elle part d'un éclat de rire franc, prolongé, qui m'interloque 'Bien sûr que je suis plus fâchée par la mort de Mme. M. . . . un million de fois plus. Elle je la connaissais, je passais tous les jours devant sa porte, mais le Pape ! Il y en aura un autre, et puis voilà ?' C'est tout le regret que j'en pus tirer.

During her last years her passion for solitude grew more imperious than ever, but she was friendly with the several orders of nuns in Meudon, in particular the Dominican Sisters of the Presentation. The Sisters, and the orphans who were their care, became her principal subjects. She did nothing better than her best portraits of these nuns, *Mère Poussepin*[1] (the Mother Superior, and her special friend), for example, and *Portrait of a Nun*,[2] in which her uncompromising search for visual truth is beautifully balanced by her affection for her friends.

But her way of life was one that could not last for long. For a person of her temperament the price of such entire independence and solitude as she demanded was increasing ill health. The self-neglect against which Rodin had ceaselessly protested ended her life.

To go to a doctor inconvenienced her [her friendly neighbour complained], to take solid nourishment inconvenienced her also, and without comfort, without ease, treating her body as though she were its executioner, she allowed herself to die.

In the early autumn of 1939 she became ill, and too late felt a sudden longing for the sea. She took train for Dieppe, but on arrival she collapsed, and was taken to the hospital of a religious house, where she died on 13 September. She neglected to take any baggage with

[1] Privately owned.　　　　　　[2] The Tate Gallery, London.

her, but she had not forgotten to make provision for her cats in her absence. 'This retiring person in black', as her brother once described her, 'with her tiny hands and feet, and soft, almost inaudible voice', died as unobtrusively as she had lived. He has also related how narrowly she missed having a part in a great public monument:

> Commissioned by the Society of Painters, Sculptors and Engravers to execute a memorial to Whistler, Rodin produced a colossal figure for which my sister posed, holding a medallion of the painter. This was rejected by the Society, following the advice of the late Derwent Wood, on the grounds of an unfinished arm, and instead a replica of the *Bourgeois de Calais* took its place on the Embankment.[1]

Her brother came upon it years later, he told me, neglected in a shed in the grounds of the Musée Rodin.

[1] Catalogue of the Memorial Exhibition.

AUGUSTUS JOHN
1878—1961

NOT long ago I was discussing the relative merits of contemporary English painters with one of the most serious and
influential of English art critics. 'I suppose', he said, gazing
into the distance, and speaking with the conscious open-mindedness
of a man to whom no field of speculation is closed, 'I suppose there
are people who would place John among the best.' Future ages, I am
convinced, will marvel at the puny character of an age when even
the most highly regarded critical opinion is so little able to
distinguish between average and outstanding stature.

There are, of course, obvious reasons why John should not, for the
time being, greatly excite the curiosity of the young. His aims are not
theirs, and in any case he has been illustrious for so long as to provoke
their impatience. So to-day, so far as critical opinion is concerned, he
is on the way to become 'the forgotten man' of English painting,
and his fanciers are the old and the ageing for whom his work was
the inspiration of their formative years, or else 'outsiders', intelligent
stockbrokers and the like, with the wit to consult their eyes rather
than their ears when buying pictures. The withdrawal of the aura of
fashionable approval leaves a man's faults exposed, and many of
John's paintings and drawings expose him to legitimate criticism.
There are paintings which, owing, perhaps, to some want of constructive power, he is unable to finish and compelled to abandon,
wastes of paint which his utmost efforts have failed to bring to life.
And there are paintings in which, under the spell of El Greco, he has
coerced his own robust forms into a kind of parody of the gaunt and
rhetorical forms of the great Cretan. There are paintings which
manifest a vulgarity unredeemed by any positive merit, such, for
instance, as *Rachel*.[1] Nor are his drawings always beyond criticism.
It is not difficult to discover instances of a figure's being marred by a
forced or a purposeless posture, or a face 'improved' into conformity
with a type which momentarily monopolizes his admiration. The

[1] The Tate Gallery, London.

occasions for criticism offered by such defects are genuine enough, and it would be wrong to discount them, but considered in relation to the magnificence of the life's work of Augustus John they furnish material for, if not a negligible, at least a comparatively tame indictment.

Contemporary critics, from a nice aversion from dwelling upon the obvious, end by ignoring the obvious altogether. It is therefore necessary to say that, according to the accepted canons whereby an artist can be judged, elusive though these admittedly are, Augustus John – to make no higher claim – is a considerable painter. He has been able, not sometimes but again and again, to fuse, by the intensity of his imaginative heat, the four ingredients of painting so well and simply defined by Allan Gwynne-Jones as drawing, design, colour and a sense of space.[1] And he has done this, not only often, but with an audacity and a majestic sweep that I believe to justify my use just now of the term 'magnificence' to describe the sum of his achievement.

I propose to say little about the landmarks of the painter's life. I have not had the advantage of seeing his as yet unpublished autobiography, and the extracts that appeared in 'Horizon', he tells me, have been radically revised. Furthermore, although I expect this book to be of absorbing interest and written in the evocative and poetic prose of which he possesses the secret, I shall be surprised if it contains very many of those basic facts that must form the framework of any biography, even of the briefest sketch. This supposition I base upon the knowledge that, although the memory of the artist retains innumerable images of rare interest and beauty, it does not so easily retain the sequence of events, their dates, or even their causes. Nor does he preserve, except by accident, letters or documents of any kind. I remember a few years ago, when I was engaged upon my 'Phaidon' monograph on this artist, I called at his studio in the faint hope of his dating certain of his paintings. There was one in particular, a portrait of one of his sons, of which I required the date. 'Dodo will be able to help you', he suggested, and we consulted his wife forthwith. 'It oughtn't', I said, 'to be so difficult. He might, mightn't he, be about six in the portrait? When was he born?' His parents, so eager to help me, looked at each

[1] 'Portrait Painters', 1950, p. xiii.

other with abysmal blankness. They could not remember. This would be no great matter had the artist's life been an uneventful affair, a life of uninterrupted toil in a garret, say, or a quiet pastoral life. It has, however, been a many-sided life, deeply implicated in many other lives, adventurous, bold, robust and long: in fact, a saga. Like the life of Sickert, it is too vast a subject to be attempted, however briefly, in these pages. Nor is it likely to suffer neglect. John, like Sickert, will be lucky if he escapes his Thornbury.

Augustus Edwin John was born at 5 Lexden Terrace, Tenby, Pembrokeshire, on 4 January 1878, the third of the four children of Edwin William John. In the combination of powerful impulses which form his temperament, the chief is a passion for personal liberty and entire independence. To judge from a letter,[1] written on revisiting his birthplace, to my father more than forty years after he had left it, John was from very early days painfully aware of his temperamental incongruity with the constricted life of Tenby. 'I am ... suffering again from the same condition of frantic boredom and revolt', runs the letter, 'from which I escaped so long ago.' But he and his sister Gwen formed a close alliance to make their escape into the world of art of which they knew themselves citizens. First Augustus, and shortly afterwards Gwen, entered the Slade School, where Augustus remained from 1894 until 1898. The phenomenal mastery of John's drawing at the Slade has been generally acclaimed. Before he was twenty he had become the first draughtsman in England. The admiration his drawings evoked among his fellow students is described by Spencer Gore in an unpublished letter to Doman Turner:[2]

> I think [he wrote] that John when he first went to the Slade started making the very slightest drawings; when I went there he was making hundreds of the most elaborate and careful drawings as well. I have seen sketch-books full of the drawings of people's arms and feet, of guitars and pieces of furniture, copies of old masters, etc. He used at that time to shift his rooms occasionally, and people used to go and collect the torn-up scraps on the floor which was always littered with them and piece them together. I know people who got many wonderful drawings in that way.

The best of his student drawings can hang without dishonour in any company. In the expression of form and movement, they are not

[1] 6 May 1939.　　　　[2] 25 January 1909.

inferior to the drawings of Keene, nor in energy to those of Hogarth, while their combination of lyricism, robustness and strangeness make even the poetry of Gainsborough's drawings a little tame and expected. Palmer could at his rare best draw with a greater imaginative intensity, but how very rare that best was. With John the power of drawing splendidly endured for decades, changing its character, flickering, faltering and slowly sinking, but always present, and even in old age apt to blaze suddenly up.

The moment when he seems first to have shown his extraordinary talent was attended by a singular circumstance. My father used to relate a story which also finds a place in his memoirs, which he heard, he said, from Tonks, according to which John was 'quiet, methodical and by no means remarkable' when he first came to the Slade, but while diving at Tenby struck his head on a rock, and emerged from the water 'a genius'. This story he occasionally told, not, I fancy, because he thought that it had any basis in fact (he was inclined to be severely sceptical about occurrences that appeared to involve the suspension of natural laws), but because it seemed to him amusingly in keeping with the fabulous personality of his friend. Not long ago I happened to read some memoirs in MS. by John Everett, a close friend of John's and his contemporary at the Slade. In this MS. – an extremely candid and detailed record – the same story is related by someone who believed in its literal truth, and who, although not a witness of the dive, was a witness of the transformation of John, after the visit to Tenby, from a plodding student into a commanding personality with a genius for drawing. The Gore letter just quoted also suggests that his early Slade drawings were unimpressive.

Though at the Slade he drew like a master, he painted like a gifted student. He had studied the painting of Rembrandt and Rubens at the National Gallery, and on his first visit to the Louvre, in 1899, in company with my father, he received from Puvis de Chavannes impressions of an idealized humanity, and of the beauty of the relation between figures and landscape, so strong that they never left him. The inspiration of this painter is manifest in many of his own figures in landscape, whether in big compositions, such as the *Lyric Fantasy*[1] (Plate 22), of 1911, or the small, brilliantly coloured paint-

[1] The Tate Gallery, London.

ings he made in company with Innes in the years preceding the First World War. One other painter on this first visit to the Louvre made an impression upon him which, though perhaps more powerful still, was less enduring. This was Daumier, who reinforced with immense authority the lesson he had begun to learn from Rembrandt, of seeing broadly and simply, and who taught him to interpret human personality boldly, without fearing to pass, if need be, the arbitrary line commonly held to divide objective representation from caricature. The Rustic Idyll,[1] a notable pastel of about 1903, was made under the immediate inspiration of Daumier.

Whatever its effect upon his draughtsmanship and his personality, John's dive at Tenby did not make him a painter. The Portrait of an Old Lady,[2] of 1899, the year after he left the Slade – which the artist told me was his first commissioned portrait – is probably a fair example of his painting of this time. In grasp of character as well as in drawing it is far inferior to the best of the drawings he did at the Slade. The hands, for instance, are without form or the power to move. When, having found his hesitant essay in a dealer's gallery in 1941, I brought it to his studio for identification, he did not at first recognize it as his own.

Only three years later, however, his Portrait of Estella Dolores Cerutti[3] proclaimed him a master in the art of painting. Certainly he has not often surpassed it, but then neither have most of his contemporaries. A comparison between these two portraits gives the measure of his progress. The earlier is niggling in form; the later is clearly stamped with that indefinable largeness of form characteristic of major painters, but, except for occasional youthful accidents, scarcely ever of minor. The paint of the earlier laboured almost in vain; that of the later powerfully radiates a cool light. The old lady is modelled hardly at all; the young lady as plastically and as surely as a piece of sculpture. The earlier can be taken in at a long glance; the later indefinitely holds the spectator's interest, without, however, yielding up the secret of the artist's power.

From the time when he painted the Cerutti portrait John must be accounted a masterly painter as well as draughtsman, but his painting is most masterly when it approximates most closely to drawing. Most

---

[1] Privately owned.   [2] The Tate Gallery, London.
[3] The City Art Gallery, Manchester.

of his finest paintings have the strong contours and the clearly defined forms that belong particularly to drawing. Especially is this true of his early and middle years. The vision of painters tends to grow broader and more comprehensive with age. One need only compare the later with the earlier work of those who in other respects have so little in common as Titian, Rembrandt, Turner and Corot to see how pronounced this tendency is. Of recent years John's vision has undergone a similar change. Not only his painting but his drawing has grown broader, more comprehensive, more 'painterly', though he has remained essentially a draughtsman.

During the past century there has been a widespread decline in technical accomplishment, and the wisest painters have felt obliged to try to compensate for this loss of manual skill with greater thoughtfulness, above all by giving their utmost attention to design.

Almost from the beginning of his life as an artist, John has commanded immense technical resources; never, therefore, has he been aware of any need for a compensatory concern with composition (still less for the cultivation of an esoteric taste or – in spite of possessing an intellect of exceptional range and power – of protective aesthetic theories). Little hampered by technical obstacles, his art has grown freely, and it reveals with an extreme directness the personality of the artist. For the style of the man who is able to set down his emotions, his intuitions, his ideas, without greatly troubling about the means he employs, reveals more than that of the man who organizes, minutely qualifies, polishes; in fact, a style of such a kind may hide almost as much as it reveals. 'Do not be troubled for a language', said Delacroix; 'cultivate your soul and she will show herself.' Confidently trusting in his preternaturally gifted eye and hand, John has implicitly followed this injunction. Like the periods of a great natural orator, John's designs are improvisations. Organization and theory would stultify John's vision and the flow and flicker of his wonderfully expressive natural 'handwriting', just as the classical conventions so integral to the drama of Corneille and Racine would have stultified the poetic impulse of Hugo, Lamartine, Baudelaire or Whitman. There is, of course, a weakness inherent in the very nature of the improviser. Spontaneous invention depends upon intense emotion; and intense emotion notoriously fluctuates. In a work of art that has been meticulously planned, and its every detail worked out in advance, the conversion, at a critical moment, of failure into success may be achieved by some slight adjustment; but in an improvisation a mistake can be redeemed as a rule only by a painful struggle of which the outcome is uncertain. Often John carries all before him in a first impetuous assault, and produces masterpieces almost without effort, but there are times when no efforts, however tenacious or prolonged, suffice to avert the results of some apparently insignificant error.

Later in these pages I say something of the contrast between two categories of artist: between him whose work is an obvious extension of the man, and him whose work is a compensation for what the man is not. John belongs unequivocally to the former class: the people whom he represents (with the inevitable exception of the subjects of many commissioned portraits) are the people who attract or interest him as human beings, and the landscapes are the places where he most enjoys living. His work, that is to say, is in the most intimate sense an extension of himself.

> Nature is for him like a tremendous carnival [Wyndham Lewis once wrote in 'The Listener'] in the midst of which he finds himself. But there is nothing of the spectator about Mr. John. He is very much a part of the saturnalia. It is only because he enjoys it so much that he is moved to report upon it – in a fever of optical emotion, before the selected object passes on and is lost in the crowd.

The love of liberty that is John's strongest passion is not a remote, political concept (although in so far as he is interested in politics he is libertarian enough), but personal liberty. The almost physical urge from which it springs is expressed in an undated but very early letter to my father:

> . . . You know the grinding see-saw [he wrote] under a studio light cold formal meaningless – a studio – what is it? a habitation – no – not even a cow-shed – 'tis a box wherein miserable painters hide themselves and shut the door on nature. I have imprisoned myself in my particular dungeon all day to-day, for example all day on my sitters' faces nought but the shifting light of reminiscence and that harrowed and distorted by an atrocious 'skylight' . . . this evening at sun down I escaped at last to the open to the free air of space, where things have their proportion and place and are articulate. . . .

It was thus neither chance nor casual romanticism that drew John to the gipsies – those nomads in whom the spirit of personal liberty burns most obstinately – but his apprehension of a community of outlook between himself and them. 'The absolute isolation of the gipsies seemed to me the rarest and most unattainable thing in the world', he wrote.

The early part of John's life was devoted mainly to the subjects in which this spirit was plainly manifest. At the Slade he used to discover, among tramps and costers, as well as gipsies, strange characters whom he took for models. In summer holidays in remote parts of Wales he sought out primitive peasants, the unconscious purveyors of strains of wild poetry that come singing out in his drawings of them. In Liverpool, where in 1901 he spent about a year as a teacher of art, it was the homeless wanderers by the docks, wayward old men, in whom he discovered a novel and expressive magic. In his early days he discovered people such as these, but later he has had mostly to content himself with emphasizing such aspects of the gipsies' spirit of 'absolute isolation' as he is able to discern in the faces of the sitters who have knocked at his studio door. For in England to-day every painter without means who wishes to make a living by the practice of his art must paint portraits. If John had been able to continue to devote himself to the portrayal of the types of men and women who have resisted the pressure of urban civilization and preserved their primitive way of life, we should possess a dramatic and unique portrait of an aspect of England and Wales that has almost vanished from our sight. But life is not kind to artists, and John will never complete this portrait, but we must be thankful that with brush, pencil and etching-needle he has enabled us to share his haunting vision of a freer, braver and more abundant way of life than that which most of us know.

The art of John has always been marked by an audacious and independent but not with a revolutionary character. His own debt to the past he has always readily admitted. 'I am', he wrote in an early letter[1] to my father 'about to become a *mother*. The question of paternity must be left to the future. I suspect at least four old masters.' His chosen masters, besides Puvis de Chavannes and Daumier, are Rembrandt, Goya, Gauguin; among his contemporaries, the two from whom he learnt most were Conder and Innes. At all times, however, he has taken freely according to his needs, but

[1] 4 May 1901.

there has been little danger of the integrity of a personality so positive and so robust being impaired by what it assimilates. There is one master, however, from whom he has taken much that has resisted assimilation. This, as I have already noted, is El Greco; working under the spell of whose ecstatic rhetoric John is not entirely himself.

'Advanced' movements in painting he is inclined to regard with sympathetic curiosity, but also with detachment. A sentence in an early undated letter to my father, evidently written from Paris early in the century, gives an indication of his attitude. 'The Independents', he wrote, 'are effroyable – and yet one feels sometimes these chaps have blundered on something alive without being able to master it.'

The introductory chapter of this book deals at some length with the diminished attraction exercised by the visible world over the minds of artists of the Post-Impressionist era, which has led to the virtual abandonment of the traditional European ideal of representing in something of its fulness the world to which the senses bear witness. This disinterest, although it has affected at one time or another many, even perhaps the greater part, of the most original painters of our time, has never touched John. Every one of his paintings and drawings, be it failure or success, testifies to his passionate response to the world that his eyes see, but it may nevertheless be of interest to quote a passage from a letter that also speaks, as vividly, I think, as any of these, of the quality of his vision, with its combination of frank enchantment with the nearest and most obvious material realities and of a mysterious apprehension of deeper realities beneath. The passage comes from the letter, already quoted, about studios:

Never have the beauties of the world [it runs] moved me as of late. Our poultry run I see to be the most wonderful thing – so remote, so paradisaic, so unaccountable it seems, under the slanting beams of the Sun, and loud with the afflatus of a long day's chant of love. The birds move automatically, like elaborate toys, but with a strange note from the East (subdued now, their wild flight forgotten on the long journey) amidst dappled gold under gilded elders, old medicine bottles, broken pots and pans and cans; the unseemly debris – the poor uncatalogued treasures – of a midden.

Three short sentences in a letter written many years later succinctly sum up his confidence in his preoccupation with what is at hand, with what he likes and, above all, with what is alive:

I find the country better to live in than the town [he wrote to my father]. One comes across thrilling things which don't take place in the studio. In art one should always follow one's nose, don't you think?[1]

John's small figures in landscape, his pure landscape, his still-lifes and above all his portraits, however boldly idiosyncratic, however romanticized, are firmly based upon what he sees, but he engages in one kind of painting which primarily depends not upon observation but on invention. This is the big composition. No kind of painting interests him so deeply. I remember his saying when he opened the exhibition of photographs of contemporary British wall paintings at the Tate Gallery in 1939, 'When one thinks of painting on great expanses of wall, painting of other kinds seems hardly worth doing', and shortly afterwards, in a restaurant: 'I suppose they'd charge a lot to let Matt Smith and me paint decorations on these walls.' In a monograph[2] on the artist published some years ago, I spoke with some indignation of the neglect of his powers of painting upon a great scale. Although the world would beyond doubt be a more beautiful and inspiring place if there were a number of public buildings embellished by big completed wall paintings by John, I now think that I a little overestimated his capacities as a painter on a monumental scale. Certain important qualities he does possess: a rich and abundant creative impulse, extraordinary powers as a draughtsman, and above all a noble largeness of style. In all his essays in painting on such a scale, these are luminously apparent. I spoke earlier in this study of the weakness inherent in the improviser's temperament: it follows that the larger the scale of operations the greater the likelihood of their being frustrated by this weakness.

The small improvisation can be abandoned without regret and started afresh. How many thousands of failures Guys or Rowlandson must have crumpled up! But in a large picture too much is at stake from the first; such a work can be brought to a successful conclusion by the science and intellectual discipline that alone can compensate for the inevitable fluctuations of intense emotion. Genius is rightly held to be the capacity for taking infinite pains, but there is a kind of genius capable of taking infinite pains only while it is, as it were, in action. In fact, a special kind of genius is required to

[1] 6 May 1939. [2] 'Augustus John' (Phaidon British Artists), 1945.

take infinite pains by way of preparation. John belongs to the first order: he enjoys painting pictures rather than planning them, and while no effort is too strenuous while he has his brush in hand, he lacks all those qualities that go to make a great organizer. I doubt whether any human achievement on a monumental scale is possible without a pre-eminent capacity for organization. And so it is that John's monumental paintings, even the finest of them, remain unfinished, dazzling sketches abandoned with their difficulties unresolved. The *Study for a Canadian War Memorial*,[1] of 1918, an immense and complex composition in charcoal, peopled by scores of figures, was never carried out. *Galway*,[2] of 1916, for all its brilliance is no more than a gigantic sketch. (Its 400 square feet were covered, the artist told me, in a single week.) The vivid and animated *Mumpers*[3] (of about 1914?) could have been carried further. So also the *Lyric Fantasy*, of about 1911, which is more highly charged with a mysterious poetry than any of his other works of this order. The subject is a group of wild, lovely girls, to whom he has given something of the fierce and lofty isolation that he envied in the gipsies, and some ravishing children in an arid, Piero-haunted landscape. John is acutely regretful of its unfinished state. Their incompleteness is not, of course, due solely to the want of this capacity in the artist. The times are uniquely unpropitious. Artists cannot be expected to undertake works that call for great expenditure of time and energy without any assurance of being able to sell them, and neither governments nor private corporations give painters or sculptors opportunities remotely comparable with those which their predecessors enjoyed of working on a heroic scale.

Perhaps the most notable quality of the monumental paintings – in particular, the *Lyric Fantasy* – is the poetic relation between figures and landscape. This he developed, less magnificently but with more completeness, in a whole series of paintings on a relatively miniature scale. As a young man he became friends with Innes, a painter with an original and lyrical vision. In him a passion for mountains – those of his native Wales and the South of France, for preference – and for pure, vivid colours burned with a heat particular to men conscious of having a short time to live, for he was

---

[1] The National Gallery of Canada, Ottawa.

[2] The Tate Gallery, London.   [3] The Detroit Institute of Arts.

consumptive, and he died at the age of twenty-seven. Innes's intense and romantic vision of mountain country was an inspiration to John, who assimilated and enhanced it, for among glowing, exotic Innes-conceived mountains he placed brilliant and evocative but summarily painted figures in peculiar harmony with their surroundings. When Innes died and the focus of John's interest shifted, something went out of English painting that left it colder and more prosaic. The importance of the group of poetic paintings inspired by the association of John, Innes and the delightful but much less gifted Derwent Lees has yet to receive full recognition.

During the course of his immensely productive life he has been attracted by a wide range of subjects, but portraiture has remained his principal concern. England is the portrait-painter's paradise: from the sixteenth century onwards she has given not only to native portrait-painters, but to a long succession of foreigners also, full scope for their talent. The death of Lawrence seems to mark a singular change in the history of portrait-painting. Until about 1830 the best exponents of this art were professionals. No amateurs rivalled Holbein, Van Dyck, Lely, Kneller, Gainsborough, Reynolds or Lawrence himself, but since then amateurs have painted the outstanding portraits. Few portraits by professionals are comparable with Stevens's *Mrs. Collmann,* Watts's gallery of great Victorians, Whistler's *Miss Cecily Alexander*, Sickert's *George Moore*, Steer's *Mrs. Raynes*, Wyndham Lewis's *Miss Edith Sitwell* and *Ezra Pound*, or Stanley Spencer's early *Self-portrait*. Like his contemporaries McEvoy and Orpen (who began as genre painters and turned professional portrait-painters later on) John, especially during the latter part of his life, has painted great numbers of portraits, but, unlike these two, he may be said (though the distinction is a fine one) to have remained something of an amateur, for he is constantly at work on compositions large and small, flower-pieces, landscapes and drawings of the figure, and from time to time he loses interest in commissioned portraits and abandons them, a course which a professional would be unlikely to adopt. Change of subject preserves the spontaneity of his response to the drama of faces.

The portrait-painters of the epoch which Lawrence brought to an end were sustained, during spells of lassitude and indifference (to which most artists are subject), by the momentum of a workmanlike and dignified tradition: but the waning of that tradition left the painter face to face with his sitter, dependent, to an extent which his predecessors never were, on his personal response to the features before him, on his power to peer deeply into the character which they mask or reveal. Very rarely is a man's response to faces, or his understanding of them, sufficiently powerful and sustained as to enable him to make it his whole profession, and he who paints little or nothing except portraits deadens by exploiting this response. To paint portraits supremely well, it would seem to be wise to refrain from painting them too often. A passionate preoccupation with portraiture has only occasionally tempted John to over-indulge it, or to exploit it for the benefit of those who are eager to purchase the immortality which at certain moments it lies in his power to confer. At such auspicious moments he gives splendid expression to the qualities of nobility, strength, courage, wisdom, candour and pride in his sitters, but should they happen to possess none of these, he is able to make little of them. But his portraits are not therefore merely romantic tributes to the elements of greatness which he discerns; they rarely suffer from the absence of the critical spirit; they are free from the touch of personal approbation that marks Watts's portrait of his great contemporaries. John's portraits are the products of a more sceptical nature and a less reverent age. Watts portrayed select spirits, as almost wholly noble; John, whose sitters are more arbitrarily chosen, portrays the noble qualities in men and women whose natures on balance are as often base as noble. And where Watts brought a grave and exalted mind to bear upon his sitters, John comprehends his with a flame-like intuition, as in the miraculous *Joseph Hone*[1] (Plate 23), of about 1926, *Robin*[2] (Plate 21), of about 1909, and *David*,[3] of about 1918.

Genius which is intuitive and spontaneous is of necessity uneven in its achievement. If John's crowded annals have failures to record, in his inspired moments no living British painter so nearly approaches the grandeur and radiance of vision, the understanding of the human drama, or the power of hand and eye of the great masters of the past.

[1] The Tate Gallery, London.   [2] The Tate Gallery, London.
[3] Privately owned.

CHARLES GINNER
1878—1952

GILMAN and Gore I had not the privilege of knowing. I always climbed the stairs that led to Ginner's little painting room at 66 Claverton Street with the pleasurable anticipation, not only of seeing a friend, but of entering a presence for whom these two others were living memories. They have been dead for more than thirty years, and Claverton Street is miles away from Camden Town, yet something of the way of life which all three lived in intimacy together in North London was still gently sensible in these rooms in Pimlico: the way the landlady loomed large, the way the landlady's choice in wallpapers was accepted, and the way the streets outside receded in long, grey, symmetrical vistas, down which, on certain auspicious evenings, one made one's way with Ginner to some 'eating-house' with shabby, comfortable red-plush seats. I live only a few minutes' walk away, but I mostly see chromium and neon lighting, except when I walked with Ginner along streets which are, or seem in recollection to be, gas-lit. Sickert used to say that English artists live like gentlemen, but Ginner lived with a simplicity that put one in mind of a Continental artist: two small (meticulously tidy) rooms, adorned by half a dozen studies given to him by friends, a small library consisting of a few score well read classics, half English and half French, an annual 'painting holiday' – that represented about the extent of my friend's needs.

No biography has been written of Ginner, nor has there been published a collection of reproductions of his work. So far as I am aware, he is not even the subject of an informative article.[1] I propose therefore to preface this brief study of his art by giving the principal landmarks of his life.

Charles Ginner was born on 4 March 1878 in Cannes, the second

---

[1] The nearest approach is the generous tribute in Frank Rutter's 'Some Contemporary Artists', but this very slight sketch – which contains a number of inaccuracies – was published as long ago as 1922.

27. AMBROSE McEVOY. *Portrait in Black and Green*. (1923).
Water colour, 26 × 18 in. (sight). Privately owned.

28. Sir William Orpen.
The Play Scene from 'Hamlet'
(1899).
Oil, 69¼ × 87½ in.
Privately owned.

29. Sir William Orpen. *Hommage à Manet* (1909).
Oil, 62×51 in. Privately owned.

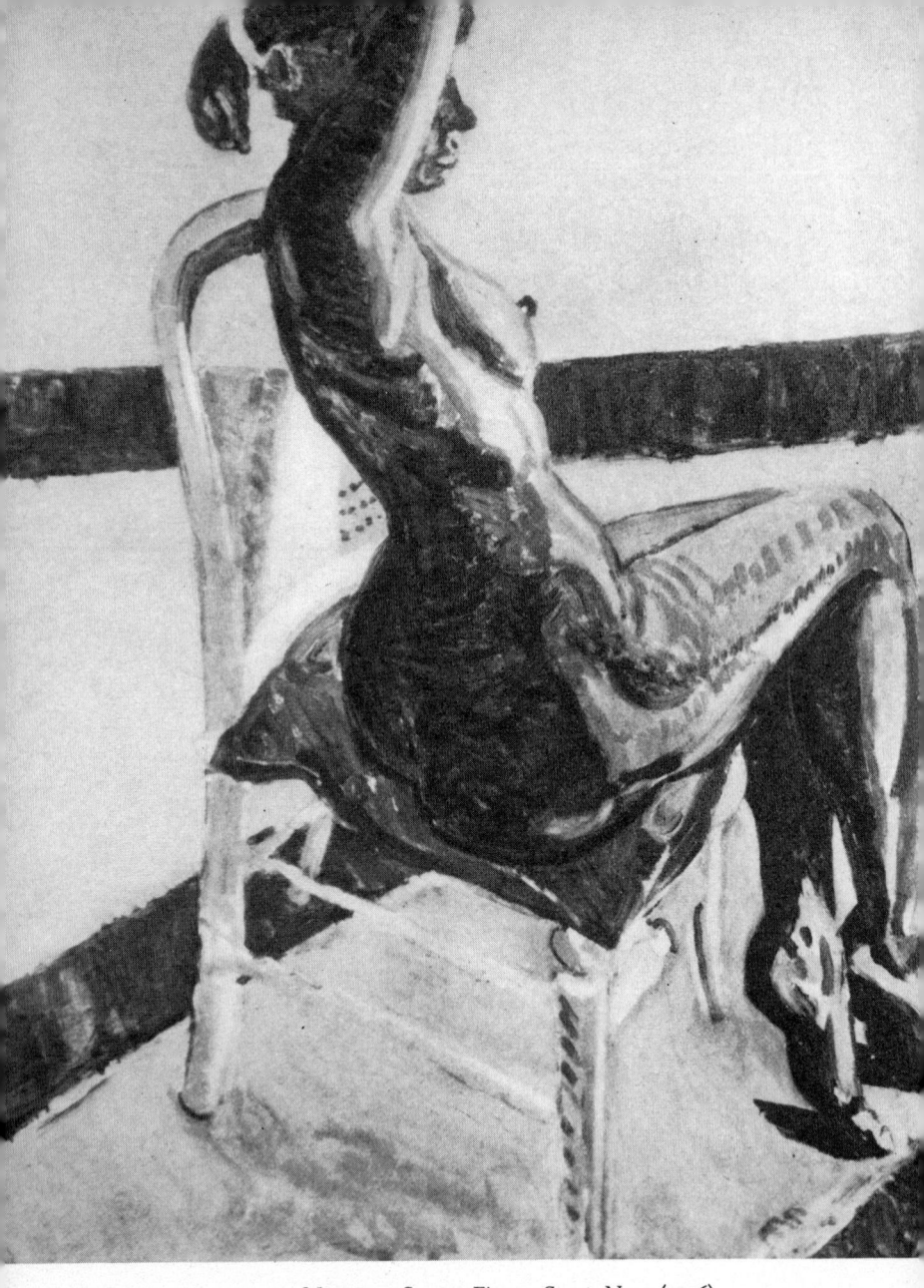

30. MATTHEW SMITH. *Fitzroy Street No. 1* (1916).
Oil, 34 × 30 in. The Tate Gallery, London.

son of Isaac Benjamin Ginner, an English physician practising on the Riviera. Dr. Ginner came originally from Hastings; his wife was a Londoner of Scottish descent. Ginner's grandfather was a mysterious figure: meagre vestiges of legend attribute to him a propensity for smuggling and a detailed knowledge of the Bible. Of his grandfather's six sons, all left England, and one was murdered in China. Ginner attended the Collège Stanislas at Cannes. For as long as he could remember he wished to be a painter, but he had to overcome the opposition of his family. At the age of sixteen his health broke under the combined assault of typhoid and double pneumonia. For almost a year, in a successful attempt to restore it, he sailed the South Atlantic and the Mediterranean in a tramp steamer belonging to an uncle. On his return he spent some time in an engineer's office, and when he was twenty-one he left Cannes for an architect's office in Paris. In 1904 his family withdrew their opposition to his becoming a painter and he entered the Académie Vitti, where Henri Martin was teaching, but he worked mostly under Gervais. From the first he used bright colours; Gervais expressed sharp disapproval and used to hide them beneath coats of umber. The year following he entered the Ecole des Beaux-Arts, but in 1906, after Gervais had left, he returned to Vitti's, where his principal teacher was the Spanish painter Hermens Anglada y Camarasa. At that time the art schools of Paris were being slowly permeated by Impressionism, but the Post-Impressionists were still officially regarded with contempt. When Ginner confessed his admiration for van Gogh, Anglada replied, 'A man who'd paint his boots can't be an artist.' He left Vitti's in 1908 and worked on his own for two years in Paris, where he took van Gogh, Gauguin and Cézanne for his guides. In April 1909 he visited Buenos Aires, where he held an exhibition, thus introducing Post-Impressionism into the Argentine. In January 1910 he came to London to serve, as already noted, on the Hanging Committee of the Allied Artists' Association's third exhibition. It was owing to his friendship with Gilman and Gore, and to their urgent persuasion, that he decided to settle in London. At first his mother kept house for him at Prince of Wales Mansions, Battersea, and he had a studio in Tadema Street, Chelsea, near the World's End, but later he took rooms on his own in Chesterfield Street, by King's Cross Station, in the heart of the 'Camden Town Country', where Gilman and Gore were near neighbours. These three met constantly in one another's studios, at the Etoile Restaurant, at the Café Royal and at the Saturday afternoons at 19 Fitzroy Street, which were also regularly attended by R. P. Bevan, John Nash, Albert Rothenstein, C. R. W. Nevinson, Jacob Epstein and Walter Bayes, Sickert and Pissarro presiding.

The four years between his arrival in London and the two events that brought this period to a melancholy close – namely, Gore's death and the outbreak of the First World War – were the happiest of his life. Although he had neither the authority of Gilman nor the charm of Gore, he enjoyed affection, influence and respect. He had many qualities to warm the hearts of his friends, among which modesty, benevolence, generosity and candour were conspicuous. His own work, which was at first more mature than that of his two friends, showed qualities that they were eager to emulate. He was, furthermore, familiar with the work of Continental masters who for almost all his English contemporaries were distant demigods. This made him something of an oracle among them, although Bevan had worked with Gauguin at Pont Aven. And he possessed the capacity – too rarely exercised – for expressing himself in lucid, energetic prose.

The essay on Neo-Realism, for instance, quoted at length in the chapter on Gilman, aroused considerable interest and was the subject of a long review by Sickert.[1] All these circumstances combined to give Ginner during these years the exhilarating consciousness of playing an honourable part in one of the chief artistic movements of his time and country.

War, however, brought about the disruption of their circle, and with it their intimate and delightful collaboration, and presently the death of Gilman intensified for Ginner the sense of loneliness that had followed the death of Gore.

Ginner was called up about 1916, serving first as a private in the Royal Army Ordnance Corps, but his knowledge of French (he was completely bilingual) resulted in his transfer to the Intelligence Corps. He was promoted sergeant and stationed at Marseilles, and later recalled to England to work for Canadian War Records, with the honorary rank of Lieutenant. This involved an eight weeks'

[1] 'Mr. Ginner's Preface', *The New Age*, 30 April 1914.

visit to Hereford, to make drawings of a powder-filling factory for
an elaborate painting. Back in London, he took studios in the
Camden Road and at 51 High Street, Hampstead, living meanwhile
above the Etoile. In 1937 he moved to 66 Claverton Street, where he
lived until his death on 6 January 1952. In the Second World War
he served as an official artist, specializing in harbour scenes and
bomb-damaged buildings in London.

Ginner's faith in the value of friendly co-operation between artists
had been expressed by membership of many societies. Soon after he
settled in London, he was invited to become a member of 19 Fitzroy Street; he was a foundation member of the Camden Town, the
Cumberland Market and the London Groups. The New English
Art Club he joined in 1920, and he was elected an Associate of
the Royal Academy in 1942, where he consistently advocated the
admission of younger contemporaries of talent.

The most conspicuous attribute of Ginner as an artist is the
stability of his vision. Such an attribute, in itself, of course, affords
little indication either of high qualities in an artist or of their absence. It may accompany deep convictions, or mere laziness, sterility
or the determination to exploit a market. Ginner's achievement as
a whole offers no evidence of laziness or of sterility, and in the
changeable circumstances which prevail to-day a market is more
readily exploited by politic change than by stability. In fact, stability
has become as much the exception as it was the rule in, for example,
fourteenth-century Siena. Constant changes in aesthetic fashion –
the result of the absence of an authoritative tradition and of prevalent curiosity, restlessness, and the unprecedented accessibility of
examples of the art of other civilizations – in fact conspire to make
stability difficult to maintain. Therefore it may fairly be taken to-day
as a sign of a convinced and independent mind. The stability of
Ginner's vision, at all events, is so pronounced as to be phenomenal.
I have never seen a painting of Ginner's Paris period, but those he
sent over to the first Allied Artists' Association Exhibition in 1910
seem to have resembled those of later date. (According to Rutter,
they were a nuisance to handle because the wet paint stood out in
high ridges.) The practice of painting thick was at this time fairly
general, both on the Continent and in England. 'We have evolved
a method of painting with a clean and solid mosaic of thick paint

in a light key', Sickert wrote of the New English Art Club in 1910.[1] Ginner's practice in this respect was, however, based upon that of van Gogh: he applied the paint in strips. (It was from Ginner that Gilman learnt this method of painting.) In other and more fundamental respects his style was already what it has remained since. In *The Café Royal*,[2] of 1911, there is, for instance, the extremely complex yet entirely firm and logical construction, the mass of detail severely disciplined to the requirements of the design as a whole, that mark, though still more emphatically, the work of his later years. There are also the same defects. His pictures lack atmosphere, and they often, in consequence, have an archaic look, as though they were conceived before Constable and Turner showed that the accepted distinction between the solid objects of nature and the atmosphere through which they were seen, between, say, tree-tops and clouds, from the point of view of the painter, is not invariably a real distinction. There is an evident want of interest in, and an incapacity to represent, the human figure, weaknesses the more felt in view of the artist's unvarying preoccupation with the environment of man, usually, indeed, his own actual habitation. And his touch is without either subtlety or variety. But these weaknesses are far outweighed by his qualities. If he largely ignores atmosphere, few of his contemporaries have represented urban landscape or individual buildings with such intimate insight. The shabbiest of them, under his minute but tender scrutiny, reveals beauties at a casual glance scarcely conceivable. His representation of even so apparently monotonous a structure as a brick wall or a tiled roof – which are among his most favoured subjects – will be seen to present surfaces of astonishing variety, and each brick or tile to have its own identity. If, like Turner, he has little aptitude for portraying men and women, he creates an ineffable impression of their unseen presence: his steps are worn by their tread, his walls are blackened by the smoke of their fires, his flags are put out to declare their rejoicing or their mourning; there is little indeed in his pictures that does not refer, and always with an implicit affection and respect, to his fellow men. And if his touch inclines to monotony, is there not adequate compensation in what Sickert called his 'burning patience'?

[1] 'The New English and After', *The New Age*, 2 June.
[2] The Tate Gallery, London.

His earlier paintings were all done from oil sketches made in front of his subject. During a visit to Dieppe in 1911, Sickert showed him how to work from squared-up drawings. After 1914 he relied entirely upon detailed drawings of this character, accompanied by elaborate written colour notes. I am inclined to think that the words 'burning patience' go to the heart of his achievement. Ginner did not possess a tithe of the genius of his master, van Gogh, or even a tithe of the natural capacity of his exact contemporary, Orpen, yet this 'burning patience' enabled him to create, both in oil and pen and ink and water-colour, a long series of pictures which reflect the continuous growth of a personality entirely humane, honourable and modest.

N

SPENCER GORE
1878—1914

S PENCER GORE died at the early age of thirty-five, and
only a few months before the outbreak of the First World
War, an event that obliterated the memory of many
merely delicate talents. His paintings might be mistaken by an
inattentive observer for essays, tentative and lacking in decided
character, in the manner of the French Impressionists. And Gore
himself might have been discounted, too, by a casual acquaintance,
as a cultivated genial person, a shade too genial, perhaps, to be an
entirely serious person. Yet after his death Sickert, in an article
entitled 'A Perfect Modern',[1] paid a tribute to his work and character
in terms of higher praise than I recall his using in respect of any other
English painter of the time. Gore's obituary in 'The Morning Post'
expressed the opinion that 'his personal character was so exceptional
as to give him a unique influence in the artistic affairs of London in
the last dozen years'. Those who meditate to-day upon the achievements of those last years of the Indian summer of European civilization, if they do not entirely subscribe to the opinions of Sickert and
the unknown obituarist, weigh them, at any rate, with sympathetic
comprehension.

Spencer Frederick Gore was born on 26 May 1878 at Epsom, the
youngest of the four children of Spencer Walter Gore, Surveyor to
the Ecclesiastical Commissioners and holder of the first Lawn Tennis
Championship held at Wimbledon in 1877 (and brother of Charles
Gore, Bishop of Oxford), and his wife, Amy Smith, daughter of a
member of the firm of solicitors who acted for the Ecclesiastical
Commissioners in Yorkshire. Spencer Gore's boyhood was spent at
Holywell, his parents' house in Kent. He went to Harrow, where his
vocation declared itself, and he won the Yates Thompson Prize for
drawing. After leaving school he entered the Slade, where he worked
for three years under Brown and Steer and Tonks, whose teaching
he always recalled with gratitude, and he formed a lifelong friend-

[1] 'The New Age', 9 April 1914.

ship with Gilman. About the time of his leaving the Slade his parents suffered a financial reverse, and after his father's death his widow took Garth House, a much smaller place, at Hertingfordbury in Hertfordshire, where then and later he painted many landscapes.

At the beginning of the new century there was not much to distinguish Gore from other Slade students. Certainly the few Steer-like landscapes of about 1905 that I have seen give no indications of special promise, nor do the landscapes of the following years, which show that Corot and Sisley had displaced Steer as the principal objects of his study. It was in the summer of 1904 that he first met Sickert. The meeting was effected by my father's younger brother Albert, who was a fellow student of Gore's at the Slade. The two of them went to Dieppe and spent two days continuously in Sickert's company. So began an intimate friendship that was to end only with Gore's death. The meeting had other consequences. After years of wandering abroad, Sickert, always disposed for change, always interested in what his friends were about, had begun to grow tired of his self-imposed exile. In London the New English Art Club had entered upon the most brilliant and influential period of its history. The illustrious painters of mature talent – with two exceptions, every one of those treated in these pages was associated with the Club, most of them as members, a few as exhibitors only – were being joined by the most talented of the younger generation. The enthusiasm of his two visitors for what was happening at the New English, and at the Slade, from which its membership was so largely drawn, focused the interest of Sickert upon London and sharpened his desire to return there. As already noted, he settled in Camden Town in 1905. That year Sickert lent his house at Neuville to Gore, where he stayed from May until October. Of the paintings he did there – the Corot-Sisley inspired essays already mentioned – none of those that I have seen reflects a personal vision, but what they convincingly show is a deepened understanding of the science of painting, and, in particular, of the methods of the French Impressionists. His sympathies with Impressionism were not only, nor, perhaps, even principally aroused by his six months' intensive painting in France, for it was about this time that he formed an intimate friendship with Lucien Pissarro. This friendship was of cardinal importance for Gore, however, not for what it enabled him to learn about Impressionism

– by this time the movement, even in England, was widely known among the intelligent – but for the insight it gave him into Impressionism's ultimate development. Reference has already been made in these pages to the double part played by the younger Pissarro in substituting knowledge of Impressionism among English painters for rumour, and often alarmist rumour at that, and in explaining the activities of those, of whom Cézanne and Seurat were the chief, by whom Impressionism had been 'remade'. By none of the younger painters was this body of knowledge more intelligently assimilated than by Gore. His knowledge of Continental painting – like that of many of his generation – was notably enlarged by the first Post-Impressionist Exhibition. It is significant of the temperamental difference between Gore and Gilman that Gore was most attracted by Matisse, whose impact, coming after that of Gauguin, excited him to bolder experiments in colour and pattern, while Gilman received an impetus that lasted to the end of his life from the burning realism of van Gogh. During his time at Neuville he visited Paris and saw the big Gauguin exhibition at the Salon d'Automne. The Renoirs he saw at the Durand-Ruel exhibition at the Grafton Gallery that year had particularly impressed him, and after studying the Cézannes, the first probably that he had seen, he observed to a friend that 'there was something in them'. It was not until three or four years later that he arrived at a full understanding of the art of Cézanne.

It was in 1905, too, that the results of his always grateful yet independent discipleship of Sickert and Pissarro, and his own meditations upon the nature of painting and his assiduous practice, revealed themselves in a series of paintings of music-hall and ballet subjects that were both personal and mature. These subjects continued to occupy him until about 1911. It may be presumed that Sickert first drew his attention to the beauties of the theatre, but his treatment of them derives from Lucien Pissarro. Gore used to spend every Monday and Tuesday night, over long periods, at the Alhambra Ballet. After seeing the Russian ballets produced for the first time in London by Fokine, with Nijinsky and Karsavina in the leading parts, he turned to a friend and said, 'I've dreamt of things like this, but I never thought I should see them'. His method was to visit the theatre, always occupying the same seat, equipped with a small note-book, conté chalk and a fountain-pen. Thus stationed and equipped, he would add a stroke or two, at the relevant moment, to a study of a transient pose or relationship of figures. A tight-rope walker involved a succession of visits to capture a pose held only for an instant. 'Every time she got to a certain spot', he wrote, 'I had my pencil on the spot where I left off and added a little. It took some time.'[1] From the numerous resulting studies oil paintings were built up. Gore, like Gilman and Ginner, observed a strict distinction between paintings and drawings made in front of the subject and those made in the studio.

> I think [he wrote] that when in front of nature what you produce should be exactly what you see and not touched except out of doors. If you set out to arrange or compose, it should be done entirely away from the subject, making of course as many studies from nature as you want.[2]

Gore painted few portraits, but in one of them, *North London Girl*[3] (Plate 25), of 1912, his sense of colour and tone, as well as a strong sense of character, are happily combined. (The subject is the girl who served tea at the 19 Fitzroy Street 'at homes'.)

In 1907 he visited Yorkshire, where he painted several landscapes which showed that he was able to handle outdoor subjects maturely also. Although it was, for technical reasons, impossible to paint directly in the theatre, Gore did not share Sickert's belligerently held conviction that to paint in front of the subject was a cardinal error, and that pictures ought to be painted from studies. He always worked as directly from nature as circumstances allowed. His method was to draw his subject on the canvas in paint, next putting in the cool and the warm colours, keeping the range both of tones and values as narrow as possible, for he believed that fine distinctions were more 'telling' than violent contrasts. Upon this foundation he slowly built up a mosaic of paint unmixed with medium. It was his aim to define form in terms of colour. To Sickert's warnings against the dangers of overstatement he found it easy to pay attention, for overstatement was foreign to his nature and contrary to his upbringing: his statements about the form and colours and relations

[1] Unpublished letter to Doman Turner, July 1909.   [2] Ibid.

[3] The Tate Gallery, London.

of things were never, like those of his friend Gilman, challenges.

Up to about 1906 Gore was scarcely more than a serious and gifted student, but he had already begun to exert 'the unique influence in the artistic affairs of London' noted by 'The Morning Post'. Of the several qualities that combined to give him special authority among his fellow artists the chief was a combination of disinterestedness and charm. Disinterestedness without charm might have provoked exasperation, and charm without disinterestedness liking without esteem. It was the spectacle of this tall, young man of distinguished bearing, whose extreme carelessness of his personal appearance seemed to symbolize a carelessness of his personal interests, devoting himself wholeheartedly to the general good, in particular to the reconciling of differences that could honourably be reconciled, that won him this special degree of authority and affection. In addition he possessed an integrity that was not questioned and an unassertive assurance. Sickert wrote: 'I never heard him complain of anything.' No one was more emphatic in his recognition of Gore's qualities than Sickert. In reply to those who spoke of Gore's indebtedness to him, he used to insist upon what he had learnt from Gore, and after Gore's death he wrote of his career as 'the most complete object-lesson on the conduct of a life and of a talent that it is possible to have experienced'.[1] Gore had a quality which only reveals itself in his work upon the closest scrutiny – namely, extreme intelligence. By the kindness of the artist's widow, I have had the privilege of access to a remarkable series of letters written by Gore at odd moments snatched from his own laborious hours of work or from those of exertion on behalf of his friends, at moments, often, when he was too tired to paint or draw or organize, which shows how concentrated, supple, uncompromising, and above all how lucid his intelligence was. These letters were addressed to Doman Turner, a deaf fellow artist to whom Gore undertook to teach drawing. The first of them is dated 8 June 1908 and the last 24 November 1913. They give a clear insight into Gore's beliefs and his practice as a painter and draughtsman, and although they are impersonal in tone, they reveal almost as much of the character of him to whom they are addressed as of the writer's. They show

[1] Introduction to the catalogue of an exhibition of thirty-six of Gore's works held in February 1916 at the Carfax Gallery.

that, while he was satisfied with his pupil's technical progress, he is
dismayed to discover that he did not value his own talent as a serious
artist must, and that he suffered from a radical apathy. 'From your
letters', wrote Gore, 'I always have a kind of suspicion that the
things you do interest me more than they do you.'[1] The correspondence therefore lost its didactic character. I hope that one day it
will be published in full. Here in the meanwhile are a few characteristic extracts:

> Don't think about making patterns but of drawing objects in such a
> way that a sculptor could model from them. . . . Contours and light
> and shade have no value of themselves, it does not matter whether the
> lines are clumsy and the shadow ragged so long as they both help to
> explain the size or shape of some form in relation to the other forms
> which go to make up the object or objects you are drawing. What one
> asks of a draughtsman is What is your personal view of this head or figure
> or landscape? not how neatly or how smoothly you can cover up so
> much paper with lines and shading making up a pattern, even to imitate
> fairly accurately the general features of the thing seen.[2]
> In drawing, everything must grow out of something else – be in
> relation to it and everything else be referred back to it. . . . The interest
> is in what you see not what you know.[3]
> Drawing deals with the forms of things alone. Directly you go outside
> this you get to painting. That is to say, relations of tone or colour.
> And I think that drawings of effects are absolutely uninteresting or only
> interesting on account of the form and not of the effect. . . . Drawing
> from memory always leads to some kind of mannerism which may
> be good if it has enormous knowledge and purpose behind it as in
> J. F. Millet or Lionardo [sic], but it is interesting to notice in Millet and in
> Daumier and others who did not always get their facts first hand, that
> such things as the folds of a coat are never very interesting however
> magnificent the whole figure may be. . . . Whistler was a great artist
> . . . but he made the great mistake of setting up a standard of beauty
> derived from other painters. . . . If you compare this attitude with that
> of Renoir Degas Manet Monet Pizzarro [sic] Siseley [sic] . . . or Courbet
> . . . who all went to nature like children to find new beauty and whose
> work points to the fact that beauty exists everywhere; then you will
> find that Whistler like a backwater leads you nowhere while they are
> like a river carrying you wherever you want to go.[4]
> A drawing is an explanation of an observation. If you observe nothing
> special your drawings will have nothing to them. . . .[5]

[1] 9 September 1910.　　[2] 26 June 1908.　　[3] 28 August 1908.
[4] 8 September 1908.　　[5] undated.

These brief extracts from Gore's notes for his pupil will give, I think, an indication of one reason at least for the fruitful character of his influence – namely, his capacity for giving lucid and practical expression to the convictions that formed in his mind as a consequence of continuous practice and long meditation. They also show how firmly his own art was rooted in the visual world. It has been a disposition among those who, especially of recent years, have mentioned Gore to suggest that he began as an Impressionist and ended as a Neo-Impressionist. This would be an overstatement altogether. His vision underwent no transformation; there was only a change of emphasis. Gore was a close and perceptive observer of the work of the masters whose art was so radically affecting most of his generation, fully aware of the contributions of Cézanne and Seurat to European painting, and interested in Cubism from its beginnings. (There exist several of his own paintings which may be regarded as essays in a modified Cubism.) All these interests served to stimulate his preoccupation with design and with the structure of things. But with what detachment he regarded Neo-Impressionism years after he had become familiar with the movement from Lucien Pissarro and others is clear from an allusion to one aspect of it in a letter to Doman Turner.

Neo-Impressionism [he wrote] was the name given to people who tried to reduce the system of divided colour to a science. . . . The two chief exponents were Signac and Seurat. . . . Lucien Pissarro learnt to paint in this manner. It was not a great success because it made a painting very mechanical. . . .[1]

Gore was in fact nearer to this movement in his ballet and music-hall scenes – the *Inez and Taki*,[2] of 1910, than in his last Richmond landscapes. His Post-Impressionist sympathies showed themselves in an enhanced awareness of the structural elements in nature, and of the designs they formed, hidden from the inattentive eye. To the end his procedure was one of discovery, a seeking out of the design already there, never the imposition of a design upon nature. Gore's evolution has been succinctly described by his friend Ginner:

I have a fine example of a broad-minded artist who was ready to learn from the various modern schools. Spencer F. Gore, who was first

[1] 11 June 1910.   [2] The Tate Gallery, London.

influenced by Mr. Walter Sickert, corrected in himself his master's degraded colour by absorbing the influence of the Impressionists through Mr. Lucien Pissarro. Later on he did not close his eyes to the Cubist and Vorticist movements, but learned much from them while remaining a realist in his outlook on life. He had received from these schools of painting a stronger sense of design [and] saw it in nature. . . .[1]

From the time, about 1906, when he may be said to have reached maturity until his death was a span of only eight years. These he devoted first of all to painting, but he was constantly concerned with the welfare of the art of painting, and the service of his painter friends. 'He discovered and encouraged', wrote Sickert, 'any talent that came his way with devotion and sequence. . . .'[2] He was a founder-member of the Allied Artists' Association, of 19 Fitzroy Street, the unanimously elected President of the Camden Town Group (he selected and arranged the Group's comprehensive exhibition at Brighton[3]), a member, from 1909, of the New English Art Club (on its juries, Sickert has also told us, 'he exerted a salutary influence') and an active founder of the London Group.

Nothing as a rule can be less interesting than the small politics of the formation and conduct of artistic societies [wrote the obituarist already quoted]. Mr. Gore saw the necessity for these activities. . . . It was often asked . . . what was the bond of union which enabled the Camden Town and London Groups to hold together. . . . It is hardly an exaggeration to say that it was simply the character of Gore, so liberal in his enthusiasms, so incapable of petty jealousy. . . .

I never had the privilege of knowing Gore, but everything that I have heard from those who had confirms the justice of this tribute. His year of teaching, in 1914, at the Westminster School has already been noted, and in 1912 he supervised and carried out decorations at a highly intellectual night-club, the Cabaret Theatre Club, at 9 Haddon Street. Among the collaborators he secured were Wyndham Lewis, whose large panel won for Cubism its first success in England, and Eric Gill. At the height of his activity, at the moment when his work was showing a new breadth and firmness of structure, without sacrifice of the delicacy that had earlier

[1] 'Modern Painting and Teaching', *Art and Letters*, July 1917.
[2] Introduction to catalogue of Memorial Exhibition at the Carfax Gallery, 1916.
[3] At the Public Art Galleries from 16 December 1913 to 14 January 1914.

distinguished it, he died. In the early summer of 1913 he left Camden Town – where he had spent the greater part of his working life, first at 31 Mornington Crescent, now demolished, and later at 2 Houghton Place – for Richmond, where he settled at 6 Cambrian Road, in order to be near the Park. On 25 March 1914 he got wet while out painting, contracted pneumonia and forty-eight hours later, on the 27th, he was dead.

Small memorial exhibitions were held in February 1916 at the Carfax Gallery and in October 1920 at the Paterson Carfax Gallery, and in April 1928 a fully representative one at the Leicester Galleries.

He drilled himself [Sickert wrote] to be the passive and enchanted conduit for whatever of loveliness his eyes might rest upon. . . . But it is not only out of scenes obviously beautiful in themselves, and of delightful suggestions, that the modern painter can conjure a piece of encrusted enamel. Gore had the digestion of an ostrich. A scene, the drearyness and hopelessness of which would strike terror into most of us, was for him a matter for lyrical and exhilarated improvisation. I have a picture by him of a place that looks like Hell, with a distant iron bridge in the middle distance, and a bad classic façade like the façade of a kinema, and two new municipal trees like brooms, and the stiff curve of a new pavement in front, and on which stalks and looms a lout in a lounge suit. The artist is he who can take a flint and wring out attar of roses.[1]

[1] 'A Perfect Modern,'
The New Age, 9 April 1914.

AMBROSE McEVOY

1878—1927

THE branch of the McEvoy family to which the painter Ambrose belonged has no history. His father, a man as gifted as himself, emerged suddenly on a dark night in the eighteen-fifties from a turbulent sea upon the coast of one of the southern states of North America. After a quarrel with his parents, two shadowy Irish emigrants to New England, Charles Ambrose McEvoy ran away from home and embarked with a few companions in a small sailing ship. Overwhelmed by the waves, the vessel broke up, and he and two Negroes succeeded in reaching a small lighthouse. They were the only survivors. After being cared for for a short time by the lighthouse keeper, he was adopted by a cotton millionaire. A few years later, the War between the States broke out. Young McEvoy, who seems to have sympathized with the emancipation of the Negroes, assisted, nevertheless, in the capture of John Brown and fought for the state of his adoption. He served first in the Army of the Confederacy, but was disabled from further service by a wound received at the Battle of Bull Run, which was tended by Dr. Whistler, brother of the illustrious artist. He next placed at the service of the Confederacy his audacious resourcefulness as an inventor. Certain of his ideas were embodied in the construction of the primitive ironclad, the *Merrimac*, others in the fantastic *David*, a submarine vessel consisting of two immense concentric iron balls, which, setting out to raise the blockade of Charleston, moved out along the sea-bed with a 25-foot spar bearing a torpedo projecting from her bows. The Federal sloop, *Housatonic*, was marked out for destruction. The *David*, submerged, rammed her with her torpedo. There was a devastating explosion. The blockader and the *David* both sank. From this disaster to his own vessel, he evolved the principle of the depth-charge, with which, with extra-ordinary prescience, he predicted that the submarine would eventually be fought.

After the defeat of the Confederacy, Captain McEvoy and Dr.

Whistler both settled in England. Here he evolved and sold to the British Admiralty his principal invention, the first submarine-detector, the hydrophone. Science and engineering did not, however, absorb the entire energies of this prodigiously ingenious and versatile man, for he was interested in music and the visual arts. He was the first to discover the unusual talent for drawing of his elder son, Ambrose. Instead of treating it as an effeminate propensity, after the fashion of the usual prosperous Victorian parent, he had nothing but joy in watching its development.

Ambrose McEvoy was born on 12 August 1878 at Crudwell, Wiltshire. Shortly before the birth, a year later, of his brother Charles, the future playwright, the family moved to London, and settled at 51 Westwick Gardens, West Kensington. Both brothers attended, without notable results, a long-defunct school known as Elgin House.

Through the friendship between his father and Dr. Whistler, Ambrose McEvoy enjoyed the privilege of knowing Whistler, who showed a sympathetic confidence in his talent. He used, in after life, to recall how Whistler took him as a boy to Hampton Court, and, stopping before Tintoretto's *Five Muses of Olympus,* enjoined him to 'drink it in,' and how they stood in front of it for a long time in silence. It was on the advice of Whistler that his father sent him, in 1893, to the Slade School, where he remained for three years.

Those for whom the name McEvoy evokes the dashing creator of fashionable beauty in a nimbus of rainbow-coloured light may be surprised to know that at the Slade he was a slow and laborious worker and an impassioned student of the technical methods of the old masters. Upon this subject, at this time and later, he kept copious and detailed notes.

At the Slade he became engaged to be married. A fellow student, Mary Spencer Edwards, had watched him at the National Gallery while he was making a copy of Titian's *Noli me tangere,* and had been so moved by the tall young man with the poetic and gentle expression that marriage to the man to whom she was engaged became impossible any longer to contemplate. She wrote to him to break their engagement. A few days later, in front of the Titian, she and Ambrose McEvoy were introduced by Augustus John. A few days later she saw him again, at John's Fitzroy Street studio, and she watched him attentively, as, talking to a group of fellow students, he pushed with long fingers his hair out of his eyes. She was too shy to speak to him, but that day, he told her afterwards, he loved her also. Immediately afterwards they became secretly engaged. Marriage for the time being was a remote prospect. Captain McEvoy had met with financial disaster the year his son entered the Slade, and Colonel Edwards, her father, would have regarded marriage to an artist with repugnance.

When McEvoy left the Slade, he lived for several years in extreme poverty, continuing at the National Gallery and the Soane Museum his intensive study of the methods of the old masters, in particular of Titian, Rubens, Rembrandt, Claude, Gainsborough and Hogarth. In order to give the requisite time to his studies, he produced little. He was determined to give his painting the soundest possible technical basis, whatever the sacrifice of present comfort or reputation. In the course of his studies, he pondered his findings and slowly discovered the methods best suited to the fulfilment of his own aims. In the several notebooks in which, mostly between 1898 and 1902, he wrote down his miscellaneous observations upon the methods of the old masters, his æsthetic philosophical reflections, his injunctions to himself with regard to his procedures over a given painting or painting generally, there is nothing to suggest that he evolved either a consistent system of painting or a comprehensive æsthetic outlook. How deficient he was in the necessary intellectual power his dull disjointed writings clearly show. But they show also a habit of close, first-hand observation, especially of the various methods of glazing, and constant preoccupation with the capturing upon his canvas of the utmost that was possible of the harmony which he saw everywhere in nature. 'Harmony produced by all the means at our disposal,' he wrote, 'is the most interesting subject of thought to me. . . .' But he was a painter and not a writer, and if his notebooks suggest that as a thinker he was pedestrian and incoherent, his paintings and drawings of those early years proclaim him to be an artist of exceptional sensibility and insight.

His principal works were figures in interiors, low in tone, tranquil in mood. In spite of their beautiful, pensive quietness, McEvoy did not emerge as a quite distinct personality. Frederick Brown, his

master, in *Hard Times,* and other members of the New English
Art Club had painted pictures which contained, in a somewhat
robuster form, most of the elements of McEvoy's. In method
McEvoy's were based, more deliberately than theirs, upon his studies
of Rembrandt and Rubens: that is to say, the composition was
put in black and white and the local colour added to it. They are,
in other words, not original pictures, but there is a quality in their
mood of shadowy, pensive quietness, and in the delicate deliberation
with which each form is defined precisely without impairing in the
slightest the total unity, that raises them above mere school pieces.
The most characteristic of them, *The Engraving*,[1] of 1900, was bought
the following year by Frederick Brown for £25. The sale of two
other pictures in the same year, *The Thunder-Storm*,[2] a not very
successful attempt at a dramatic subject, and a landscape, enabled
him on 16 January 1901 to marry Mary Spencer Edwards. For a
time they lived in Jubilee Place, Chelsea, but he developed an almost
obsessive desire to acquire 107 Grosvenor Road, a house overlooking
the river, which he bought in 1906 and which remained his home for
the rest of his life and provided the background for many of his
pictures. Others he began elsewhere, often in his studio in Trafalgar
(now Chelsea) Square; they were mostly finished in the big studio
he built at the back of his riverside house.

The years immediately following his marriage were industrious,
penurious years. He worked almost continuously, and, though he
gave more time to painting than he had as a student, he still spent
two evenings a week at the South Kensington Museum in the study
of the methods of the masters. Before long the self-discipline, which
enabled him to resist the temptation to hurry in the face of actual
want, was rewarded by the appearance of a discriminating patron in
the person of Sir Cyril Kendall Butler. From him McEvoy received
very small prices, but he and his wife were maintained for more
than a year in a cottage near their patron's house at Bourton, near
Shrivenham. Gradually he received a more valuable reward: the
laboriousness so irksome to sitters was transformed into an extraordinary facility. Confident in having evolved methods whereby
his pictures would last, this slowest of painters became the most
rapid. Mrs. Archibald Douglas, the wife of his most generous and

[1] Privately owned.   [2] Privately owned.

constant patron, told me that his *Portrait of Lady Tredegar*,[1] of 1919, was completed in twenty minutes.

The absence of a clearly defined personality, of deeply felt convictions, is apparent upon close scrutiny of the subdued and tranquil interiors of McEvoy's first decade. How impressionable he was is shown by an incident which occurred in 1909. At the annual exhibition of the New English Art Club, there was a painting of a favourite Dieppe subject of Sickert's, painted in that artist's highly personal style. This painting brought Sickert much commendation. 'Better than anything you've ever done', remarked a brother artist with a fulsome smile. 'I'm afraid', Sickert answered, 'it is', and referred him to the catalogue. The painting was the work of McEvoy, done in the course of a visit to Sickert at Neuville. Nothing could be more different than this picture from his interiors, or from his own earlier landscapes, *The Orchard*,[2] of 1904, a highly artificial fusion of memories of Gainsborough and Claude, or the more closely observed and genuinely poetic *Winter*,[3] of 1905. During the few years following the painting of the Dieppe picture, changes in the character of his art proclaimed even more plainly that his interiors and his landscapes offered inadequate means of expressing what became his most passionate, his almost exclusive preoccupation, beautiful women. Such in all probability had always been the case, for such passionate and exclusive preoccupations, although they may show themselves suddenly, are rarely of sudden growth. This hypothesis would account for the element of reserve which prevents McEvoy's early interiors and landscapes – distinguished and poetic as they are – from carrying complete conviction. In painting them McEvoy was making beautiful pictures as a craftsman makes a beautiful object, but one look at any of the fashionable beauties of the later years – sometimes, by comparison, ill-considered and even vulgar – makes it clear that his interest was fully engaged. Although fashionable women came at last to absorb his energies entirely, and although his portraits of them could be, indeed, what his *Portrait of Lady Tredegar* so unabashedly is, examples of the vulgarest display, his habitual attitude towards his subjects was far removed from vulgarity.

The radical change in his outlook became apparent in 1913. Two

[1] Privately owned.　　　　　　　　[2] Privately owned.

[3] Whereabouts unknown.

years earlier he had painted the best of his interiors, *The Ear-ring*,[1]
which, in so far as it is, in essence, a study of a woman and only
formally an interior at all, foreshadows the change to come. In
1912 he painted what I believe to be the last of his interiors, *La
Reprise*.[2] This is an elegant and tender but listless work; for comparison between it and *The Engraving* or *The Book*,[3] of 1902, shows
how far his interest in the representation of rooms was exhausted.
It was the model for *The Ear-ring* and *La Reprise* – a Basque
governess who came in 1911 to look after the two McEvoy children
and who subsequently married the portrait-painter, Gerald Brock-
hurst – who provided the occasion for the change. In 1913 he painted
a portrait of her which he called *La Basquaise*.[4] This, shown at the
New English Art Club's autumn exhibition that year, brought him
popular success, which two other portraits shortly confirmed. These
were *Madame*, of 1914, an un-noteworthy portrait of his wife,
purchased by the French Government for the Luxembourg, and
Lydia,[5] of the same year, an entirely wretched portrait of the wife of
the painter Walter Russell. The success of these three pictures was
such that by 1916 this laborious and almost starving painter of
reticent interiors was besieged by fashionable ladies determined to
have their portraits painted.

McEvoy made a reputation as a fashionable portrait painter with
three inferior works, but it was abundantly justified by others.

The opinion has been for many years pretty widely accepted that
McEvoy began as a serious and sensitive painter of interiors and landscapes and that, dazzled by the glamour of fashionable women, he
degenerated into an audacious, even a flashy sycophant. I have
already intimated that this is an opinion from which I dissent. Even
were the early works still more distinguished and the later more
frequently as bad as the artist's detractors claim they are, I would
be reluctant to rate orthodox variants of existing works, however
impeccable in taste and however sensitive, which reveal the fundamental dullness from which all such works must suffer by their
nature, more highly than original works called into existence by an
ardent emotion. These last are the creations of Ambrose McEvoy;

[1] The Tate Gallery, London.   [2] The City Art Gallery, Aberdeen.
[3] Privately owned.   [4] Privately owned.
[5] Privately owned.

the earlier, in the last analysis, of his teachers and his older contemporaries. He suffered, let it be conceded without delay, a number of egregious, indefensible failures of method, failures of taste, but no more, I think, than might be expected of any artist working in an audacious manner beset by the many trials – capricious and unpunctual sitters, exacting social obligations, the frequent necessity of working in unfamiliar environments and the like – to which the fashionable portrait-painter is always subject. But there are other and, it seems to me, most notable works to McEvoy's credit.

In McEvoy's miscellaneous writings the expression 'beauty' is of frequent occurrence, in contexts which suggest that his conception of this attribute was strictly confined to things pleasing in themselves, a conception remote, for instance, from that of Sickert or Stanley Spencer, artists largely concerned with the discovery of beauty in things – iron bedsteads and amorous octogenarians – not in themselves beautiful. Among things in themselves most eminently pleasing – especially to men – are, quite obviously, women. Upon them, in his interiors of the very early 1900s, he fixed a scrutiny searching but reticent. After the passage of some years, this had grown franker: in an unconvincing *Interior*,[1] of 1910, one of them, for instance, is represented nude. After 1912 his interest in the women he paints was undisguised: the rooms in which in former times he had so carefully placed them, withered away, and they emerged as the sole subject of his pictures. On the comparatively rare occasions when he painted portraits of men, it is reasonable to suppose that his successes – as in *Viscount d'Abernon*,[2] of 1916, and more notably *The Rt. Hon. Augustine Birrell*,[3] of 1918 – owed much to the enhancement of his sensibilities in the face of a subject of a different kind. The last ten years of his life were devoted, almost exclusively, to painting beautiful and fashionable women. Had he been unconscious, had he not been, indeed, acutely perceptive, of their desirability as women and scarcely less of the distinction of the positions they occupied in the social system, he could have had no success as a painter of fashionable portraits. These two qualities must always be emphasized by the successful portrait-painter, whether his

[1] Privately owned.   [2] Privately owned.

[3] The National Gallery of Canada, Ottawa.

O

subjects are hieratic and remote infantas or princesses pretending to be milkmaids.

For McEvoy his sitters' allurements as women and as fashionable women never included overt sensuality, anything remotely corresponding to the wet, sensual mouths and the bare bosoms of Lely's ladies, or any traditional aristocratic symbolism, the vista of park, the fluted column. McEvoy's intention was, in fact, an extremely subtle one and the allurements and the social distinction of his sitters merely formed part of the raw material to be transmuted into an ethereal likeness in which direct allusion to such qualities would be intrusive and entirely destructive of the effect at which he aimed. This was to paint a beautiful woman as a man in love with her would see her : to paint her transformed into an unearthly being, her most exquisite qualities of body and mind projected in a radiant, many-coloured nimbus. (He could not bear to hear, his daughter Anna told me, the slightest disparagement of any sitter while her portrait was in progress, lest the spell which he wove about her should be broken.) Such an aim, impossible to realize in terms of the muted tones and the meticulously rendered detail of the early works, called for technical methods of an entirely different kind. The change in the focus of his interest was accompanied by reliance upon brilliant lighting, often from below, besides the very loose, very rapid way of painting already noted. In a book entitled 'The Technique of Portrait Painting', the author, the portrait-painter Harrington Mann, in the course of a eulogistic comparison between McEvoy and Botticelli, tells us that in the work of the former 'the design and the drawing are unimportant'. His brother artist had evidently looked with insufficient care at McEvoy's later portraits – for instance, at *The Hon. Daphne Baring* (Plate 26),[1] of 1917. McEvoy's design and drawing were relatively unimportant, except at the principal point of focus. Here – and it is precisely this that gives the poetry and the delicate distinction to the best of his portraits – the features, or certain of them, are drawn with extreme sensibility and precision. Without this point of lucid definition, a late portrait by McEvoy would be a mere iridescent chaos; and that, in fact, is just what his failures are. But *Daphne Baring* is far from being a failure. It is one of the best portraits he ever painted. The drawing of the face, the mouth in

[1] Privately owned.

particular, and even, at certain points, the Botticelli-inspired dress, is beautiful and exact. The farther removed, however, from such delicately wrought points of intrinsic interest, the broader, the less decisive, was the artist's touch, until, as he approached the margin of his canvas – or of his paper – the scarcely defined forms dissolve entirely.

In one respect, McEvoy's procedure in his later portraits was similar to that in the early interiors. Both were painted, not 'directly', in opaque colour, but usually in thin glazes over an almost mono-chrome sketch of yellow ochre, black and white, a procedure used by few of his contemporaries, and the result of his studies of his chosen masters of the seventeenth and eighteenth centuries, among .whom it was general.

It was inevitable that a painter who sought for such elusive aims should suffer failures, and a number of McEvoy's society portraits, for all his taste and all his application, are garish and in the worst sense 'dated' things. But there are his successes. Besides *Daphne Baring*, these include *Mrs. Charles McEvoy*,[1] of 1913, *Lady Gwendoline Churchill*,[2] of 1917, *Viscountess Wimborne*,[3] also of 1917, and *Miss Violet Henry*,[4] of 1918. But in none of his paintings in oils has he achieved so high a degree of perfection as in his water-colours. In this medium, so much more readily adapted to realize his particular aims, he did his finest work. Unfortunately for him, the painter of society portraits must carry these out in oils. But he has left *Black and Green*[5] (Plate 27), a magical portrait of a young girl in which he realized his highest aims, that could hold its own beside a Gains-borough; the only slightly less lovely *The Artist's Wife*[6] and two *Portraits of Zita*,[7] all of 1923. In the early 1920s he began to use the lighter medium more and more often, but he had by then only a few years left to live. Pneumonia cut short his life as Big Ben struck four on the morning of 4 January 1927.

[1] Whereabouts unknown.   [2] Whereabouts unknown.
[3] Privately owned.   [4] Privately owned.
[5] Privately owned.   [6] Whereabouts unknown.
                       [7] One, privately owned.

WILLIAM ORPEN

1878—1931

THE story of Orpen's life is a story of material success more spectacular and continuous than attended that of any of the other subjects of these pages. In terms of material success he is to be ranked, in fact, with the most successful painters who have ever worked in England – that is to say with Van Dyck, Kneller, Reynolds, Lawrence and Sargent.

In my own early memories (he was my uncle by marriage), he survives clearly as a small man with a pale, high-cheek-boned face, light grey eyes that observed much and revealed little, a figure without a trace of the atrophied staidness that marks most adults, but slim and active as a boy's. I remember an occasional sense of embarrassment when, having missed something he said on account of the rapidity of his speech, I had to ask him to repeat it. He was always ready to join in any game or sport, always as an equal – that is to say, without making facetious references to his age or arrogating to himself any authority as an adult – and he always excelled. One night we were playing table tennis at his house in Chelsea; he said: 'I'm going to ask one of the best players I know to come round.' Presently we were joined by a pale, small, old man in his middle twenties, whose name I did not hear, who beat us all without exertion. Many years later, when I met Ben Nicholson, I recognized him as the masterly player.

Orpen seemed to enjoy discussing, sometimes long afterwards, games we had played, which he was able to recall with surprising minuteness. Not long ago I came upon a copy of his book, 'An Onlooker in France', which he gave me inscribed 'In memory of a bathe at Groom's Farm, March 1921' – an occasion when we had played water-polo at a house in Buckinghamshire where the Orpen family spent a summer.

As a painter I was at first aware of him as a member of an as yet not sharply differentiated group of members of the New English Art Club which included Sickert, Steer – all the painters, in fact, about whom I have been writing. I can just remember my father's being challenged for maintaining that John was a more considerable artist than Orpen. Presently I was aware of him as the most successful painter in England, and as one esteemed by many as the best. In those days his success seemed both glittering and firmly based. There were the Rolls-Royces waiting beyond the paved forecourt of his magnificent studio in South Bolton Gardens, and there was the adulation of critics. But there was also the admiration, or at least the respect, of his fellow artists. If voices were raised in criticism of the forced lighting and obvious interpretations of character that marred certain of his portraits, these could be silenced by an allusion to one of his classic portraits, or, if that did not suffice, to some prodigy of drawing of his student days, or to the triumphant *Play Scene in 'Hamlet'* (Plate 28). To this impression of success built upon rocklike foundations the personality of the artist also contributed. His industry was prodigious; and in my own home I was able to apply the severest standard of comparison. There was always a sitter, or, in case the sitter should fail to arrive, a self-portrait in progress. His pretensions – within my hearing always – were of the most modest: to be a good craftsman, to paint what was in front of him, not blindly accepting its appearance, but making the fullest use of his knowledge. And whether in his high white studio, or the small house, long since demolished, in Royal Hospital Road, Chelsea, in which the little rooms resembled, in their subdued light and the polished high-lit quality of their furnishings, his own early 'interiors', there were always drawings – late as well as early – of which any artist might be proud, and which seemed to proclaim the fundamental soundness of his art.

Now, twenty years after his death, hardly anything remains of that vast reputation. Orpen is a fading 'period' memory. When his name is mentioned it is, more often than not, as a symbol of the hard, glossy portraiture patronized by successful public men in the second and third decades of the century.

Orpen was born on 27 November 1878 at Oriel, Stillorgan, County Dublin, the fourth son of Arthur Herbert Orpen, a Dublin solicitor, and christened William Newenham Montague. The Orpens are a respectable Protestant family, who claim descent from a Robert Orpen, who came to Ireland from Norfolk in the seventeenth

century. William Orpen's mother was the eldest daughter of
Charles Caulfield, Bishop of Nassau.

Membership of an Anglo-Irish family, the exceptional happiness
of his childhood, lack of any formal education, and attendance at an
art school as a full-time student while still a boy were four circumstances which, in their particular combination, chiefly determined
his character.

From his Anglo-Irish inheritance and upbringing he derived those
divided loyalties which always set him a little apart from his fellow
citizens, whether Irish or English. His Protestantism, his English
descent, and his residence in England during virtually the whole of
his adult life made him an unquestioning member of the British as
distinct from the Irish social system, yet he had a strong sense of
being an Irishman, and although without the most cursory interest
in politics, he regarded several of the Irish leaders with an affection
and veneration such as he never accorded to any public figure in
England – with the exception, towards the end of his life, of Lord
Derby. In a letter to my father he wrote: 'Larkin is the greatest man
I ever met.' I remember how particularly his three daughters, my
first cousins, maintained as children that they were 'Irish', even
though born in England of a mother with no traceable strain of any
blood but English. Until the First World War, he often took holidays in Ireland, taught occasionally at the Dublin Municipal School
of Art, and retained touch with fellow countrymen, notably Hugh
Lane, but also George Moore and others. It would be true, I think,
to say that Orpen's Irish life bore the sort of relation to his English
life as the unconscious does to the conscious. Had he received more
than the most elementary education, or intellectual discipline of any
kind, he might have reconciled his sentimental love for his native
country – for her most ardent aspirations he had no trace of
reasoned sympathy – with his effective identification with his
adopted one, but he left school at twelve, and never formed any habit
of reading great or even serious literature, and therefore grew into a
man, in the deeper sense, without a country. The early possession
of extraordinary dexterity as a draughtsman, and a consuming
ambition to develop it to the utmost, seem to have disposed him to
discontinue, with his departure from school, an education that may
hardly be said to have begun, which issued in lifelong intellectual

dyspepsia. Finally, his exceptionally happy childhood combined with this want of education to give him a kind of resentment against 'growing up', an instinctive sense of identification with the irresponsible spontaneous child as against the pompous adult.

At the age of seventeen he entered the Slade School, where he remained for four years, leaving in 1899. He was fortunate in that during his time there the School was at the climax of a period of extraordinary brilliance: the result of fierce and continuous competition between contending talents of a high order. Among his contemporaries were Wyndham Lewis, McEvoy, Edna Waugh and Augustus John. If on his arrival his drawing, although distinctly above the average and remarkable for a boy of his age, was not phenomenal, nothing that impassioned ambition could do to transform capability into brilliance was left undone. He drew, and shortly afterwards painted, with an intense and disciplined industry, and every moment he could spare from these labours he applied to the study (not like McEvoy, of the methods, but of the style) of the old masters. He was discovered at three o'clock one morning at work upon a Sketch Club composition by a fellow student, who afterwards observed: 'I have little doubt that he was punctually in his place at the School the same morning.' Whether he was looking at a model or at the work of an old master, he assiduously cultivated his exceptional powers of observation.

This combination of talent and industry did not have long to wait for its reward. Orpen shortly became one of the most accomplished draughtsmen in what was at the time probably the leading academy of drawing. By the staff – Brown, Steer and Tonks – he was enthusiastically acclaimed as the prodigy he was, and the attitude of many of his fellow students was accurately reflected in the opinion of one of them, who wrote not long after Orpen had left: 'When I was at the Slade, it was a one-man show; that man was Orpen.'[1]

However that may have been, there is no doubt that at the Slade Orpen made drawing after drawing of extraordinary brilliance. In my opinion, Orpen in his student years was within the first dozen draughtsmen that these islands have produced. Others have drawn with deeper insight and loftier imagination and greater originality,

[1] 'The Artist', August 1901.

but only very few have possessed so full and easy a command of the full possibilities of drawing. By many such an opinion will be dismissed – especially by my younger contemporaries – as fantastic, but I should be surprised if a comprehensive exhibition of British drawing did not confirm it. But Orpen did not only excel at drawing at the Slade: he painted one picture which seems to me, in a curious way, to be a masterpiece. This is *The Play Scene in 'Hamlet'*,[1] the 'Summer Composition' which won him the £40 Slade Prize in 1899. *Hamlet* was the subject set, but Orpen understood that the play scene alone offered scope for his exuberant whimsicality. It may be regarded, his biographers tell us, as 'an undisguised avowal of the sources from which he took nourishment'. It would be truer to say that it was a distillation of all his arduous and well-memorized studies. The lighting, at once dramatic and unifying, was derived from Rembrandt (of whose works there had been a great exhibition at Burlington House the previous winter), and the nude figure in the foreground was an ingenious theft from the same source, but the fruits of this young student's intense scrutiny of Goya, Daumier, Hogarth, Watteau, Rowlandson, Velazquez, Hals, Conder, Augustus John and a dozen others – most, in fact, of the romantic-realist masters of Northern Europe and of Spain – are easy to discern.

The notebooks which he filled during these years with detailed copies of every conceivable manifestation of art and craftsmanship to be found in the art galleries and museums of London and, to a lesser degree, of Paris and Dublin – Renaissance jewels, Gothic fan-vaulting, Assyrian reliefs, mediaeval works – testify to a fanatical determination to master the elements of style of all periods and races, and, most positively of all, of the great European draughtsmen, Rembrandt, Rubens, Michelangelo, Watteau and Hogarth for preference. But to take note of the huge extent of Orpen's debt is by no means to suggest that the picture lacks originality. On the contrary, it is highly original. The saying current in Oxford that to copy from one book is plagiarism, but to copy from several is research, has a certain applicability to this strange, precocious little masterpiece. There is an odd sentence in an essay on Orpen[2] published a few years after the picture was painted which conveys something of

[1] Privately owned.   [2] 'The Slade, 1893–1897', 1907.

the quality of the picture's strangeness. 'The workmanship', wrote a
fellow student, 'is so vigorously unhealthy as to appear to prove that
refined morbidity is the only road to rude health.' *The Play Scene in
'Hamlet'*, organized and executed with extraordinary skill and informed with a spirit in which irrepressible wit blends harmoniously
with mysterious grandeur, holds the spectator's attention, even now,
as few pictures of the time can hold it. It is an astonishing achievement for a twenty-one-year-old student: it was also the culmination
of Orpen's career as a painter. From this point the history of his life
as an artist is the history of decline. The 'Summer Composition'
picture raised his already brilliant reputation among artists to one of
eminence. It was agreed that a new star had risen; no one suspected
that it had already reached its zenith. There seemed no occasion for
the slightest misgivings; in fact, the three principal paintings which
he exhibited at the New English Art Club the following year set at
rest the doubts of those few disposed to discount his *Hamlet* as a
happy accident and won him a place among the leading painters of
the day. These paintings were a romantic *Portrait of Augustus John*,[1]
of that year, frankly based on Whistler's *Carlyle*; *A Mere Fracture*,[2]
of 1900, an admirable conversation-piece, inspired, I think, by my
father's domestic interiors (one of which, *The Browning Readers*,[3] of
1900, shows my mother with her sister, Grace, whom Orpen
married in 1901), and *The Mirror*,[4] also of 1900.

It was this last work that was decisive in the establishment of
Orpen's reputation. I know nothing about the particular circumstances in which it was painted, but it seems to me to mark a change
in Orpen's outlook as decisively as it did to his contemporaries at
the time. To them it marked the settling down to a steady mastery
of a brilliant but wayward student, but in retrospect it seems to mark
rather the rejection by a precocious master of precisely the qualities
that gave significance to his vision, of the exuberant but slightly
sinister humour, of the vivid if not yet steadily focused sense of
satire, and, notwithstanding his innumerable quotations – and long,
familiar quotations they often are – from the works of the old
masters, of the capacity to see life from a queer, unexpected angle.
The Mirror marks the rejection of all this, and more than this, in

[1] Whereabouts unknown.   [2] Privately owned.
[3] The City Art Gallery, Bradford.   [4] The Tate Gallery, London.

favour of a mastery that was a mastery without compelling purpose. Orpen's biographers exaggerate no more than pardonably when they write of it as being 'painted with the minute precision of a Terborch or a Metsu',[1] for it is beyond question a highly accomplished display of painting, though, compared with that of the two Dutchmen, the handling is cold and brittle. I have referred to this picture, notwithstanding the entirely unassuming character of the subject – a model named Emily Scobel seated beside a circular, convex mirror in which the artist is reflected at his easel with a woman looking over his shoulder – as a 'display' of painting, for it is no more than a brilliant essay in a style perfected centuries before. Orpen has not taken Dutch seventeenth-century subject and style as, for instance, Delacroix the style and subjects of Rubens, or even Haydon the Elgin Marbles, as incitements or as points of departure, but simply as a convenient and popular means of exercising his conspicuous skill.

The culmination of his biographers' eulogy of *The Mirror* is their claim that it is 'a picture that would have gained the whole-hearted applause of an Academy jury'. The claim is but too well founded, for it is one of the ablest manifestations of the moribund and therefore aimless academism of our times.

The Mirror is a melancholy portent, for the greater part of Orpen's subsequent endeavour was given to unreflective representations of aspects of the real world – representations which, with the passage of the years, first grew commonplace and at last on occasion shamelessly vulgar. But this did not exhaust his energies, for there was a part of him which so commonplace an activity did not satisfy, and which clamoured for expression as long as he was able to hold pencil or brush. *The Play Scene in 'Hamlet'* expressed the whole of Orpen: in this painting his skill, his memory, his observation are the faithful and wonderfully efficient servants of a personality full of wit and fantasy and the sense of mystery. But after the dedication of his talents to commonplace purposes the imaginative elements in his nature were without adequate means of expression. As he became ever more preoccupied with painting portraits of fashionable and highly placed persons, these elements were apt to obtrude themselves ineptly, even absurdly, in the products of the few working hours he

---

[1] 'William Orpen : Artist and Man', by P. G. Konody and Sidney Dark, 1932.

spared from the execution of his innumerable commissions, in such pointless whimsies as *Myself and Venus*,[1] of 1910, *On the Irish Shore: Fairy Ring*,[2] of 1911, and *Leading the Life in the West*,[3] of 1914. By this last year it seemed as though the submerged imaginative side of his nature had sufficiently atrophied to need no stronger expression than whimsies of this kind, but the First World War stirred it into violent animation. All through the war he continued to record, with all his customary industry and skill, if with little of his former distinction, the faces of generals and statesmen. The urge to comment upon life as well as to record it, the urge to satirize, to protest, to laugh, to mourn surged up irresistibly. What moved him most deeply and most continuously (as it moved the other war painters and poets) was the contrast between the men at the Front, who were torn and burnt, blinded and crazed, and who suffered these things and the fearful prospect of them with such stoicism and even cheerfulness, and the people at home – above all, those in authority and those who in some way profited by the war – who accepted with complacency and even with cynicism sacrifices beyond description. This contrast, though he himself was in certain respects a hard man, caused him an anguish which at the Peace Conference, where he was the principal British painter, in daily contact with the peace-makers, became an obsession. The only occasion when I can recall his speaking with vehemence upon a serious theme was one night in 1920 when we were sitting alone after dinner at his house. He talked, more than he habitually talked, incoherently and faster, about the sickening impact of the callousness and the petty self-interest of the peace-makers in Paris, above all of their forgetfulness of the millions of mangled, rotting corpses in the Flanders slime. He took out of his pocket a copy of Maurice Baring's poem 'In Memoriam' to his friend, Lord Lucas, which he read out, his jerky diction obscuring its qualities as a poem, but giving an enhanced intensity to its meaning.

'This poem', he declared, 'is the greatest work of art that's come out of this whole war. I got Maurice Baring to copy it out for me. Maurice Baring said to me: "I'm mad, but nobody's noticed it yet." That's true of us all: the whole world's mad.'

[1] The Carnegie Institute, Pittsburgh.   [2] The Johannesburg Art Gallery.
[3] The Metropolitan Museum, New York.

These words, spoken at that particular time by any one else, I might easily have forgotten. Spoken by Orpen, who had, his biographers justly note, 'few prejudices and no opinions', and whom 'any sort of serious talk bored', they were memorable. It is necessary to insist upon the earnestness of his obsession because this earnestness is not convincingly manifest in the pictures that he painted under its spell. Of these the chief was *To the Unknown British Soldier in France*. It was arranged that he should paint a group of the victorious Allied politicians, generals and admirals in one of the great rooms in the Palace of Versailles.

> I painted the room [he said at the time] and then I grouped the whole thirty-nine, or whatever the number was, in the room. It took me nine months' incessant painting; hard work. And then, you know, I couldn't go on. It all seemed so unimportant, somehow. In spite of all these eminent men, I kept thinking of the soldiers who remain in France for ever . . . so I rubbed all the statesmen and commanders out and painted the picture as you see it – the unknown soldier guarded by his dead comrades.[1]

The picture as originally painted showed the flag-draped catafalque standing at the entrance to the room, shown in significant darkness, where the Peace Treaty had been signed; on either side stood the two guardian figures based closely upon a study, *Blown up – mad*, done during the war. The arty pose of the legs (feet in the 'fifth position') and the length of classic drapery, calculated a shade too precisely to answer the requirements of modesty, gave these figures an air of utter incongruity with the grimness of the tableau in which they play the leading parts. The air of incongruity struck by these two wan, artificial figures was transformed into one almost of mockery by the presence above their heads of two frolicsome little Cupids on the wing. The exhibition of the picture at Burlington House in 1923 provoked a public outcry, which led to its rejection by the Imperial War Museum, for which it had been destined.[2]

It may perhaps be asked why I should dwell at some length upon one of the failures of an artist who painted other pictures of exceptional merit. I would answer that the weaknesses that made *To the*

[1] 'William Orpen: Artist and Man', p. 254.

[2] The Imperial War Museum finally accepted it after the artist had deleted the guardian Tommies and the winged Cupids.

31. MATTHEW SMITH. *Apples on a Dish* (1919).
Oil, 18×21½ in. The Tate Gallery, London.

32. MATTHEW SMITH. *Model à la Rose.* (1928).
Oil, $35\frac{7}{16} \times 25\frac{1}{2}$ in. Privately owned.

Unknown British Soldier in France so conspicuous a failure are just the weaknesses that betrayed the extraordinary combination of talent and industry which at first seemed so surely destined for triumphant achievement. The defects of this picture are the defects of his achievement as a whole writ large.

In writing of Orpen's early life, I noted a combination of four circumstances which, as it seems to me, were the principal agents in the formation of his character. I noted how the divided loyalties to which the Anglo-Irish are liable made Orpen sentimentally an Irishman and practically an Englishman: a man who put down no deep roots anywhere; his removal from school at an age so early that his innate intellectual incuriosity never had to meet the challenge of education, his total dedication to drawing and painting when he had scarcely emerged from childhood, which increased beyond the possibility of redress his predilection for manual skill as opposed to a developed mind; and the happy childhood, with which in the course of his journey through life he unconsciously compared the disappointing present, thereby feeding his antipathy to the operations of the intellect as activities distinctively adult.

These four circumstances combined to make him, and to an extraordinary degree, a man wanting in settled principles or convictions; a man wanting, above all, in the means whereby settled principles and convictions could be forged – namely, an enquiring and a disciplined mind.

I have seldom known any man, and never a man of superior talents, with so little intellectual curiosity and so feeble an intellectual grasp, or with so contemptuous an attitude towards the life of the mind as Orpen. 'He had nothing but scorn', say his biographers, 'for the lesser intelligentzia', but the truth is that his attitude towards those whom they would perhaps have called the greater intelligentzia was not very different. It is true that he revered Maurice Baring and entertained an affectionate regard for George Moore, but it was the personalities of these two, I fancy, rather than their intellects which appealed to him. His biographers note that he was unable to read Ruskin. He used to say, with a touch of pride, that he was brought up on the Irish Question, but what it was he had no idea. Yet this ignorance precluded the slightest rational sympathy for the aspirations of a people with whom, upon a certain level of consciousness, he felt intimate ties. Except for the occasion I have referred to, I never heard him speak at length upon any serious subject. He could not, of course, avoid allusions to serious subjects, but they were in general of the nature of epigrams, staccato but ambiguous, and an instant later the disjointed, machine-gun talk had rambled far away. Games – lawn tennis, table tennis and billiards for preference – were the subjects about which he talked most consecutively, and now and then he evoked a vivid image. For instance, W. M. Hughes, the Australian Prime Minister, coming sullen and reluctant to a sitting, reading 'The Times' throughout the grudgingly conceded hour, then at its conclusion folding the paper up and walking out without having spoken a word. My own experience of his aversion to serious discussion, of his total intellectual incuriosity, is paralleled by the experience of others who knew him better. But what, I shall impatiently be asked, has intellectual curiosity to do with the creative faculties? Little or nothing, according to the opinion which strongly prevails today. Art with an intellectual basis is contemptuously condemned in Academic circles as an 'art of "-isms"' (so runs the current cliché), while in avant-garde circles it is often quite deliberately rejected; Picasso, for instance, has declared in an interview with Christian Zervos,

I don't know in advance what I am going to put on the canvas, any more than I decide in advance what colours to use. While I work, I take no stock of what I am painting on the canvas. Everytime I begin a picture, I feel as though I were throwing myself into the void. I never know if I shall fall on my feet again.[1]

And the influence of such opinions is clearly reflected in an aggressive preference shown by the avant-garde for the art of children, primitives, the insane over that of rational men, and by the contemptuous belittlement of the most intellectual of all the great periods of art, that of the Italian Renaissance.

So long as Orpen was content to make the 'straightforward' representation of the human face and figure his principal concern, his dismissal of intellectual preoccupations as mere pretentiousness had no conspicuous consequences for his art. Even such accomplished

[1] Cahiers d'Art, nos. 3-5, 1932.

paintings as *The Mirror* and *Charles Wertheimer*,[1] of 1908 (an expertly
Sargentesque portrait of the well-known art dealer, the first picture
he sent to Burlington House), involved little intellectual exertion.
A year later, in 1909, Orpen painted a conversation-piece so admirable in its complex design and distinguished by such penetrating
insight into character as to suggest that even then he might, by a
great effort of will, have recognized upon what a broad and down-
ward road *The Mirror* and *Charles Wertheimer* were signposts and
have returned to the other and narrower way that he had left
after *Hamlet*. This picture was *Hommage à Manet*[2] (in fact, homage to
his friend, Sir Hugh Lane), in which George Moore, Steer, MacColl,
Sickert, Lane and his own master, Tonks, are gathered round a tea-
table beneath Manet's *Portrait of Eva Gonzales* at the house in South
Bolton Gardens which then belonged to Lane and which Orpen
afterwards acquired and used as a studio until his death. This (Plate 29)
seems to me beyond question his best picture after *Hamlet*, and
among the best conversation-pieces of the time. But evidently the
day for the retracing of steps was past, and *Hommage à Manet* proved
to be his Ave atque Vale to his own most exacting standards as a
painter, and to his old friends of the New English circle. Already
commissions for portraits, attracted by the *Charles Wertheimer* and
others, were pouring in. By 1910 Orpen was the most successful
portrait-painter of the age. There was no time for reflection; it
was the golden treadmill for him.

When I said just now that Orpen's failure to recognize the
potential contribution of the intellect to the creation of a work of
art had no conspicuous consequences for his portrait-painting, I did
not mean that it had none. On the contrary, it declared itself in an
increasing obviousness in his interpretation of character. There were
splendid exceptions. In particular, the Moore in *Hommage à Manet*.
There are a number of others sufficiently well known, and a retrospective exhibition would no doubt bring yet more to light. But
it can hardly be denied that, as the years passed, Orpen's magnates
became more obviously magnates personified, his aristocrats more

[1] Whereabouts unknown. Its exhibition the same year at Burlington House led
to Orpen's election as an Associate of the Royal Academy in 1910 and as a full
Member in 1919. Before 1908 he had shown his principal work at the New English
Art Club, of which he became a member in 1900.

[2] The City Art Gallery, Manchester.

obviously aristocrats, in the sense that heroes were quite simply heroes and villains were villains in Victorian popular drama. The effects of this increasing reluctance to meditate, to probe, and his increasing willingness to accept the most superficial aspect of a sitter and approximate it to that of some stock type, he made the more conspicuous by fierce and obviously artificial high-lighting and the virtual suppression of backgrounds. How rapid was the change may be seen by comparing the 'Moore' painted with such intimate satire, such comprehending affection, and the *Lord Spencer*[1] of seven years later, the personification of stagy hauteur, spot-lit. Neither the superficiality of interpretation, nor the forced and arbitrary lighting, nor the arbitrary sundering of heads from their backgrounds can obscure, however, the extraordinary sureness and vigour with which the best – even, perhaps, the majority – of Orpen's portraits were painted.

It was when he was under the necessity of representing not something material that could be observed but an intellectual perception that the consequences of his neglect of the intellectual values were shockingly apparent. The contrast between the heroism that animated the soldiers at the Front and the selfish complacency that prevailed at home, which stirred in Orpen such depths of indignation and pity, was a contrast grasped by the mind. To give it convincing visible form called for the exercise of intellectual powers far beyond his resources. His indignation and pity therefore did not move him to scathing utterance, but to incoherence. It is not surprising that the man who was brought up on the Irish Question, but who had no notion as to what it was, proved incapable of understanding or disentangling the complex question of the comparative conduct of those at the Front and those at home. To Orpen there was on the one hand 'the simple soldier man', than whom (I quote from his poem, 'Myself, Hate and Love'[2])

> No man did more
> Before.
> No love has been
> By this world seen
> Like his, since Christ
> Ascended.

[1] Privately owned.   [2] 'William Orpen: Artist and Man', p. 86.

On the other there was the petty, bickering, profiteering, and callous 'frock'. The fact that the men at the Front and the others elsewhere, however different their conduct may have been, were parts of a single whole, inextricably bound up together, entirely escaped him. He forgot that those at home were the fathers and mothers and brothers and sisters and children of those who served, and that returned soldiers could be profiteers, that even profiteers in khaki were sometimes heroes.

Orpen in the grip of a sympathy at once generous and bitter for the ardours and endurances of the inarticulate serving soldier – the most deeply felt emotion, I believe, of his entire life – is a subject tragic to contemplate. He possessed the emotional force, above all the capacity for indignation, the satiric spirit, a singular gift of incisive, expressive draughtsmanship and high competence as a painter – almost all the qualities needful to produce memorable works upon this theme. Yet with these almost superabundant talents he was able to accomplish scarcely anything, because he was unable to understand the nature of the events which so deeply moved him. It was inevitable that he should fail to express what he could not understand. Instead of memorable works, his indignation and pity spent themselves – except, of course, when he was recording what was before him – on tasteless incoherencies, such as *To the Unknown British Soldier in France*, *The Thinker on the Butte de Warlencourt*[1] and *Adam and Eve at Péronne*[2] – on these and in ludicrous verse.

During the epoch of peace-making in Paris, the small, whimsical, prodigiously gifted figure who, though he moved familiarly among the great statesmen of the day, was well known to hold them and their doings in small esteem, became a legend. When the satirical panorama of the feverish and glittering scene he had observed so closely and which was so expectantly awaited failed to take shape, his reputation waned.

Failure to express what he had felt most deeply caused him to respond with a growing apathy to the unending succession of sitters who presented themselves at South Bolton Gardens. But if he could no longer be moved, he determined to give everything that he had it in him to give. Driven by bitter conscientiousness, he harnessed all his energies, all his will to the single end of securing perfect

[1] The Imperial War Museum, London.   [2] The Imperial War Museum, London.

P

'likeness' of face and figure. What he produced was something akin to what we may expect of the mechanical brain when it is adjusted to paint portraits. Of these post-war mechanical marvels, *The Surgeon: Ivor Back*[1] may stand as an example.

The succession of portraits of this character hardened the scepticism about his stature engendered by his inability to exploit the possibilities offered by Versailles to his satiric talents and his angry mood, and at his death his reputation, which was once so solidly based, looked imposing only to those who took little notice of professional opinion, or else were ignorant of it. Coming out of St. James's Church, Piccadilly, after the memorial service, I remember the florid Chairman of the Walker Art Gallery in Liverpool exclaiming, 'We have lost the greatest artist England ever had', and I remember the unresponsive faces of Orpen's painter friends. Yet abilities so ample, matched by a sense of life so vivid and personal as Orpen's – even though, for want of a lucid and enquiring mind, incapable of that 'fundamental brain-work' which Rossetti postulated as necessary for the artist – resulted in work of more merit than current opinion is disposed to allow. The best of his painting is likely to be valued more highly than it is to-day, and his drawing more highly still. He continued to draw well long after his painting was in decline. Certain of his war drawings I would place not far below his best work at the Slade, and the pen-and-ink sketches with which he used to illustrate his letters are often brilliant revelations of a wit and imagination absent from all but his earliest painting.

Orpen died on 29 September 1931. I have tried to suggest something of the spiritual barrenness which he experienced as a consequence of harbouring deep emotions to which, as an artist, he was unable to give coherent expression. During the years between his return from Paris after the signature of the Peace of Versailles and his own death his malady showed itself in an almost desperate reluctance to speak of, or even to hear, anything that was not trivial, as though it might turn his thoughts towards the aridness within. It declared itself, in the presence of the slightest threat to triviality, in outbursts of horseplay (to which he had earlier been more moderately addicted). He would get down from the dinner table to bark at a dog, or he would bring out a mechanical toy. But it declared

[1] Privately owned.

itself most plainly in the trivial relations which he cultivated with those with whom he came in contact, a symptom of which was his habit of speaking of himself, in the third person, as 'little Orps' or even as 'Orpsie boy'. It would be difficult to imagine a more effective protection against intimacy. Whether such a reading of the inner life of his last years would find favour with his friends at the Arts Club, where he used to take me to lunch, or the Savile Club, where we often met, I am inclined to doubt, for in these places his total freedom from pretentiousness, innumerable small acts of kindness, and above all his staccato yet rambling conversation, half inaudible yet strangely vivid, won him an aura of popularity that masked the sterility within.

A few days after his death I saw on the easel in his studio a recent version of *Lord George Hell*, a picture he had painted years before as an illustration to Max Beerbohm's *Happy Hypocrite*. This he painted when, forbidden to work, he escaped to his studio from time to time from the nursing-home where he spent the last months of his life. His biographers assert that his 'last pictures do not mark a final step in his artistic evolution . . . and without hesitation may be eliminated from the sum-total of his achievement'. This judgement can hardly be questioned, but this picture testifies that the last act of the dying man, amid the failure of his mental and physical powers, was an attempt, however feeble, to recapture the imaginative qualities of his earliest years.

MATTHEW SMITH
1879—1957

THERE are certain artists whose work is an extension, direct and obvious, of their personalities. No friend of Rubens or of Byron would have been surprised by the painting of the one or the poetry of the other. There are others whose work is the expression of a part, sometimes a hidden part, of their personality. Shakespeare, for instance, does not appear to have impressed his contemporaries as a great man as distinct from a great dramatist. The painting of Rossetti and of Whistler respectively, while not incongruous with their personalities, discloses nothing of Rossetti's robust sense of humour or of his robuster tastes and appetites, nor of the combative arrogance that was Whistler's most conspicuous characteristic. Then there are the artists whose work is in entire contradiction to all that they seem personally to be: men and women whose art represents, in the psychological jargon of to-day, a 'compensation', an ideal which they cannot realize in their lives. Nothing could have been more incongruous with Pater, the fusty don, the zealous follower of the fortunes of his College on river and playing-field, than Pater the author of 'Marius'. It is in this last category that we must place Matthew Smith.

How completely the painter seems to differ from the man will emerge in the course of this brief study: a study in which I shall attempt to give something more than biographical landmarks. If facts about the man are of any value, as in my opinion they are, in the study of his art, facts concerning a man who appears to differ from his art are evidently of more value than those which relate to a man of whom his art is an unmistakable projection of himself. Furthermore, very little is known about Matthew Smith. He constitutes the outstanding example of the paucity of writing about English painters to which I have earlier referred. At the present moment Matthew Smith is probably the most admired painter in England, more especially among his fellow artists, yet, so far as I am aware, the elementary facts concerning him have never been put down. Even the admirably informed and highly patriotic 'Yorkshire Post', the leading newspaper of his native county, once published the statement that he was born in Manchester.

Matthew Arnold Bracy Smith was born at Elm View, Halifax, on 22 October 1879, in the West Riding of Yorkshire, the third of the five children of Frederic Smith, a wire manufacturer, and his wife Frances, born Holroyd, who came from Edgbaston, Birmingham. Frederic Smith was a cultivated man and an amateur of the arts. He wrote occasional verse, a collection of which, 'A Chest of Viols', was published in 1896; he collected pictures of the kind then in vogue with northern manufacturers, representing monks fishing or carousing and similar subjects, by Dendy Sadler and other painters of popular genre. The principal interest of his leisure hours was violins, of which he seems to have been an impassioned and discerning collector. He possessed two or three by Stradivarius, and his house became a place of pilgrimage for those who shared his interests. A memorial of his preoccupation with pictures and violins survives in the form of a painting, *Stradivarius in His Studio*, which he commissioned Seymour Lucas to make and which was shown at Burlington House a few years before the First World War.

At about the age of ten, Matthew Smith began to show a vague interest in painting. He collected invitation cards when they bore reproductions of drawings on them and stuck them into a book, and he copied elaborately a portrait of Lord Leighton out of 'The Pall Mall Gazette'. But he took no interest at all in the paintings by the popular academic artists that hung on the walls of his father's large, gloomy house. His preoccupation with painting grew in intensity, but it brought with it no definite aspirations, but only a growing sense of isolation. He yearned to speak to someone about painting. One day a successful painter named Prescott Davis called to see his father. As he was about to leave, the shy boy formed the desperate resolution of showing him his sketch-book, but the drawer in which it reposed stuck fast. After this humiliating, although unwitnessed defeat, his sense of isolation reached a pitch where he could hardly endure it. Believing that a business-man ought to have intelligent interests to occupy his leisure, his father at first encouraged his predilection for painting, but so soon as it threatened to exclude all other interests, he began to regard it with hostile apprehension. Presently, by means

of an occasional reproduction, news of the Impressionist painters
found its way into the grim twilight of the West Riding. At once it
filled Matthew Smith with an unfamiliar agitation which his father
recognized as subversive of what he himself believed. From that
time relations between father and son were strained. If he suffered
from a sense of isolation at home, his school life, at Halifax Grammar
School, at Hilderthorpe, Scarborough, and, worst of all, at Giggleswick, was one of misery unredeemed.

The unhappiness of his early years was no doubt aggravated by
want of sympathy at home with his vague aspirations towards
painting and by the conditions which prevailed at the schools he
attended, but it would be unjust to his parents at least to conceal the
fact that he was a neurasthenic child, and his ailment heightened an
extreme natural sensibility. At the age of seven he had the mis-
fortune to see another boy suffer from a fit in a Halifax Street, and
for years the memory of the struggling figure at the foot of a lamp-
post, his contorted face picked out from the surrounding darkness
by the yellow gaslight, was one he was unable to suppress.

After he left Giggleswick, about the age of seventeen, he was sent
to Bradford to work in the firm of Empsall and Firth, and although
then he showed no aptitude for business his father took him into
the family concern. When he was about twenty the family moved to
Bowden in Cheshire. His by now constant preoccupation with the
arts and his manifest incapacity for business brought about some
modification in the attitude of his father, who agreed to his entering
the Manchester School of Art, but only for the purpose of learning
industrial design. The four years he spent there were wholly wasted
except for a short period towards the end, when he managed to
insinuate himself into the life-class. By this time it was evident to his
father that he was no more fitted to become an industrial designer
than a business-man; he resigned himself, but without a vestige of
confidence, to his son's attending the Slade, where he remained for
two years. Tonks shared the opinion of his father respecting his
talents, and took every opportunity of giving it humiliating expression. On one occasion, in front of the whole school, he said to him,
'What in the world made *you* think of taking up painting? I give
you six months to see what you can do.' The fear aroused by the
threat to expel him, to proclaim his failure to his family, brought

about the complete breakdown of his health. He had to leave the Slade for a doctor's care. When he had partially recovered, he secured his father's consent to his studying abroad, on condition that he did not go to Paris. A London friend had often talked to him of Brittany, and the knowledge that Gauguin had worked there quickened his interest. To Brittany therefore he went in 1908 and settled in Pont Aven, where Gauguin had lived. 'Here', he once said to me, 'my life began; my mind began to open out.' At Pont Aven he made two friends, Guy Maynard, an American painter and the most interesting personality it had yet been his fortune to meet, who thought much as he did, only more maturely and in the light of a wider experience, and Madame Julia, the proprietress of the Hôtel Julia, where he lodged, who enjoyed doing kindnesses to the young man in whose face and bearing she discerned perhaps something of his bleak and troubled life. He remained at Pont Aven from September 1908 until June the following year, when he migrated to Etaples, which, besides a change in landscape, possessed for him the yet stronger attraction of relative proximity to Paris. It was at Etaples that he painted a *Self-Portrait*,[1] one of the few surviving examples of his work of this period, and the earliest known to me. It represents a shy, friendly young face, with blinking eyes that peer out at you with an expression of mild surprise. When Matthew Smith first showed me this picture in the winter of 1949, I was at once reminded of another, not only curiously similar in character, but which occupies a similar position in the œuvre of a painter as dissimilar as possible from him. A few months previously, in Léger's studio in Paris, I had noticed a portrait of an elderly man,[2] painted throughout with the same short strokes with brushes heavily loaded with the same drab colours. It expressed, too, the same diffident honesty. When I asked Léger what it was, he said: 'But that's where I started from.'

On 10 January 1910, having sold his bicycle in order to be able to pay the fare, Matthew Smith went at last to Paris. Here he attended Matisse's school in the Boulevard des Invalides, but his

[1] Privately owned.

[2] Privately owned. This picture was included (No. 1) under the title of *Portrait of the Artist's Uncle* in the Léger exhibition arranged by the Arts Council at the Tate Gallery in 1950.

pupillage was of brief duration, for the school closed after he had been there for a month. Matisse himself went round on Saturday mornings, and any student who wished for criticism might leave out his work, but Matthew Smith was too shy to invite this ordeal. It has sometimes been stated that he was closely associated with Matisse, but this is not the case. He attended none of the 'open Sundays' that Matisse held for students and others; he saw him, in fact, only on the three occasions when he visited the school. On one of his visits, Matisse put up a copy of a drawing of four figures by Signorelli and analysed its structure with an acuteness which delighted his diffident English student. 'Voici l'architecture', he concluded, and walked out. For the rest Matthew Smith worked by himself in a small, impossible studio in the Avenue du Maine (steel tramlines were hammered into shape on the floor below), existing on the £6 a month that his father allowed him. For the first time, life assumed for him an aspect at once benign and settled: his own work and his studies in the Louvre (where he made an elaborate copy of Ingres' *Madame Rivière*) and at the galleries where contemporary art was to be seen were giving him the beginnings of confidence in his powers and clarity to his ideas. In February 1912 he took a step which seems to have had the effect of bringing this tranquil period to an end. That is to say, he married Gwen Salmond, one of the ablest Slade students of her time, whom he had met the previous year at a holiday painting class at Whitby. They moved from place to place, living successively in Fontainebleau, Grez-sur-Loing (where he formed a lasting friendship with Delius) and finally London, in a flat at Grenville Place, Kensington.

When the First World War broke out he was rejected as unfit by the Artists' Rifles and the Honourable Artillery Company. In 1916 he was called up and joined the Inns of Court Officers' Training Corps, with which he spent a desolate winter training at Berkhamsted. The first morning he arrived on parade with the evidence showing too clearly in his face and bearing of the party (attended by members of 19 Fitzroy Street) at which he had spent the previous night. When his commanding officer told him to 'fall out', he dropped his rifle. The misery of his situation kindled in the mind of this pacific and almost pathologically shy young man the determination to become an officer. He applied for a commission. When asked if he had any experience in the control of men he answered, 'Yes'. 'What sort of men?' the interviewing officer enquired. 'Yorkshiremen', said Matthew Smith. He was promptly gazetted second lieutenant. Although harassed by his military duties and other difficulties, he managed, at irregular intervals, to paint. In 1913 he had taken a room in Percy Street, but he soon settled at 2 Fitzroy Street in an attic room that he retained, and occupied whenever he was able, until the end of the First World War.

In these, the least propitious circumstances he had ever known, the art of Matthew Smith underwent an extraordinary transformation. This art, that had been as tentative and diffident as the painter himself, suddenly attained an aggressive maturity first noticeable in the fine *Lilies*,[1] of about 1914, but which was resoundingly manifest in two big nudes, both seated in chairs, which he called after the room where they were painted – *Fitzroy Street I*[2] (Plate 30) and *Fitzroy Street II*.[3] Both were painted in 1916 direct and from the same model in the same pose. Both are painted with a startling violence of colour derived immediately from Fauvisme. These two nudes, especially considering the hesitancy of the artist's long apprenticeship, are astonishing productions: astonishing in their strident boldness and in their powerful draughtsmanship. They are among the most vivid and the strongest of all his paintings, yet they are hardly, in the full sense of the term, paintings at all: they are powerful drawings, coloured with a harsh, disciplined violence. For a moment it seemed as though the artist were concerned primarily with problems of form. Both paintings were rejected by the London Group, at that time closely controlled by Fry. But work of such exceptional power could not remain unknown. They made an impression upon several artists who happened to see them. The girl who sat for these two pictures introduced the painter to Sickert, who called at the attic room. 'You paint', he said, 'like a painter and you draw like a draughtsman.' For a time a close friendship subsisted between them. Sickert encouraged Matthew Smith, who found him wonderful company and 'full', he told me, 'of uncommon sense'.

In 1919 Matthew Smith was demobilized and his health collapsed. The immediate occasion of his breakdown may have been the sudden

---

[1] The City Art Gallery, Leeds.   [2] The Tate Gallery, London.
[3] The British Council.

relaxation of the wartime tension that had given temporary cohesion to temperaments, coalitions and organisms of many kinds. Whatever the immediate occasion, the cause was the unhappiness of his childhood, deepened, in the years that followed it, by the obstructions placed in his way to becoming an artist. It was as though the effort to become an artist was so exacting that, having achieved his purpose and having, with the two *Fitzroy Street* nudes, triumphantly proclaimed it, the tax upon his overstrained mind was greater than it could endure. He used to remain shut up for days together at 2 Fitzroy Street, making copies from reproductions of paintings by Delacroix and Ingres, unable to face without apprehension contacts with the world outside. About this time he painted several still-lifes of fruit. One of these, *Apples on a Dish*,[1] of 1919 (Plate 31), is as fine, I think, as any of the numerous paintings of similar subjects that he has made since. It too often happens that contemporary artists represent 'simple' subjects because elaborate ones would be beyond their powers, but in this still-life Matthew Smith has followed the injunction of the dying Crome to his son to dignify whatever he painted, and his apples have an almost breathtaking nobility of form, and, fused with it, colour that is both audacious and delicately astringent.

Early in 1920 he left London and spent half the year at St. Columb Major in Cornwall. At first he could accomplish nothing; he remained there alone after his wife and sons had left, and eventually became absorbed by landscape. This was a fruitful time, in which he produced a group of small landscapes, low and rich in tone, which express a sombre, sometimes even an almost anguished joy in the dour Cornish countryside. In these pictures, although they are built up upon a basis of firm drawing, which in certain cases the artist has not attempted to disguise, he showed, in his representation of atmosphere by the use of a wider range of colours and tones and by the closer fusion of colour and form, that he had begun to see as a painter rather than a draughtsman. I have called his stay in Cornwall a fruitful one because he made, for the first time, a group of pictures in which he painted, in fact, like a painter (for the first half of Sickert's compliment was simple flattery). These Cornish landscapes are still regarded as among his best paintings. But, like

1 The Tate Gallery, London.

certain paintings of Constable's later life, stormy canvases such as
Hadleigh Castle or *Stonehenge*, whose sombre and troubled splendour
reflected the artist's distress of spirit, the Cornish landscapes of
Matthew Smith, with their black oppressive skies and trance-livid
fields, roads and trees, were the products of a darkening mind, a mind
engaged in a losing struggle to maintain its equilibrium. He went to
Brittany, where he collapsed into a distracted melancholy in which
he wandered from Grez to Paris, from Paris to Lausanne, from
Lausanne to Lyons, in search of a doctor who could cure him.
Whether it was that his infirmity had run its mysterious course, or
whether the specialist at Lyons was more skilful than those many
others who had passed him, pessimistically, from one to another, at
Lyons, in 1922, he began to emerge from the shadowy limbo in
which he had lived for about two years. He was able to work: he
made a copy of the El Greco in the Lyons Museum. The next year
he was back in London, where he remained for about two years in
a room at 115 Charlotte Street. The two following years he spent
mostly in Paris, in a studio at 6 bis Villa Brune.

Between 1922 and 1926, Matthew Smith evolved in all essentials
both the way of seeing and the highly individual method appropriate to its expression that he has developed consistently ever since.
For all their violence, the *Fitzroy Street* nudes seem to express a
vision intellectual, constructive, and, as already noted, a draughtsman's. His later paintings, mostly still-lifes and nudes – that is to say,
by far the larger and most important part of his life's work – have
expressed a vision in every respect the precise opposite of all this,
an attitude in which passion and intuition play the dominant parts,
and in which the operations of the intellect count for little; the
vision of an impassioned painter and an indifferent draughtsman.

At the Mayor Gallery in Sackville Street from 7–28 April 1926,
Matthew Smith held his first one-man exhibition. During these
four years his work had come to be regarded with a respectful
interest by his fellow artists and by discerning critics, but this
exhibition placed him in the front rank of the younger English
painters.

The most important sign of recognition was an article by Roger
Fry that appeared on 1 May in 'The Nation'. This article was the first
attempt at a considered estimate of the work of Matthew Smith,

and, slight though it is, it remains one of the best.[1] How just a notion he had formed of what Matthew Smith was about is plain from the two following passages:

> It is evident [wrote Fry] even from the first that his intention is neither to achieve dramatic expressiveness, although a certain almost melo-dramatic mood seems at times to result as an accidental by-product, nor to create decorative harmonies. He is clearly after some more intimate and significant interpretation of vision. . . . And one sees that it is upon colour that he lays the task of situating his planes in the spatial and plastic construction. Upon colour, too, he relies to achieve the suggestions of chiaroscuro. In all this he is pushing to the furthest limits the essentially modern view of the functional as opposed to the ornamental role played by colour in pictorial design.

Although generous in his praise, Fry did not overlook one of the painter's besetting weaknesses: 'I mean', he observed in gentle admonition, 'his tendency to define his volumes with too uniformly rounded, too insensitive a contour.'

In December the year following he held a second one-man exhibition at the Gallery of Alex. Reid and Lefevre in King Street. On this occasion he was treated not as a promising beginner but as a painter with an established position. The position he had gained after so long and painful a struggle was reflected as clearly in the prices which his pictures commanded as in the respectful attitude of the critics. *The Girl with a Rose*[2] (Plate 32), painted in 1925 (to my thinking one of those works in which his finest qualities are fully realized), priced in the 1926 catalogue at £30, reappeared as *Femme à la Rose* at £150. Ever since 1926 his reputation has grown steadily until, at the time when I write these words, there is probably no English painter so widely admired among those who care for the plastic arts. It is interesting to recall that Mr. Churchill once publicly reproached the Royal Academy for its failure to exhibit his work.[3] But the highest tribute he has yet received came some six years earlier, from the pen of his admirer and close friend, Augustus John.

[1] As originally published, it formed part of a review entitled 'The Mayor and Claridge Galleries', and it was later incorporated in a longer essay, 'Plastic Colour', and published in 'Transformations', 1926.

[2] Now known as *Model à la Rose*.

[3] 'The Daily Mail', 16 May 1934.

With a cataract of emotional sensibility [he wrote], he casts upon the canvas a pageant of grandiose and voluptuous form and sumptuous colour, which are none the less controlled by an ordered design and a thoroughly learned command of technique. This makes him one of the most brilliant and individual figures in modern English painting.[1]

The decisive growth in self-knowledge during the early twenties which allowed him to develop, at long last, so personal and so consistent a vision of things was partly instinctive and partly deliberate.

Matthew Smith was very much aware that the *Fitzroy Street* nudes and the Cornish landscapes represented an immense stride forward, and even that they were, in their way, formidable productions, but the more he considered them the more he was convinced that, whatever their qualities, they were not true reflections of his own innermost intuitions. He became convinced, on the contrary, that by his close study, his sedulous imitation even, of Post-Impressionists, of Fauves, of Cézanne above all, he had built himself what he described to me as a spiritual prison. His dissatisfaction at last became unbearable. Certain that his earlier works were the products of this prison, and false, he determined at no matter what cost to cultivate a sensibility entirely his own and to search for the means of giving it appropriate expression. Under the stress of his dissatisfaction, he actually called upon himself aloud to be himself. The consequent renunciation of the firm, constructive way of painting, the strident or gloomy colouring he had evolved during the first five years or so of his maturity, was no easy gesture. Until his middle thirties he had struggled and groped, an unconsidered failure. Then, in four years, he seemed to be justified, was sought out and praised by Sickert and others, and, far more important, he had seemed at last to have earned the right to be confident in himself. It was bitter to have to discount all this as, at best, a false dawn. Deeply despondent, he started to roll up his stone again. But he was rewarded with a strange promptitude. Having by a sustained effort of will expelled the fruits of years' intensive study of other painters, he made the exhilarating discovery that he was able to paint, whether from the model or from flowers, with a fluency he had never known, and, what was of greater consequence, that when he painted with

[1] 'Vogue', 5 October 1928.

mind, as it were, swept and garnished, he could express what he exultingly recognized as uniquely his own.

His natural approach to things was not intellectual; he was not deeply preoccupied with the problems of their structure, and, released from the necessity of concern with what did not really interest him, he became with extraordinary ease what he fundamentally must always have been, a man moved by passion, guided by intuition rather than by the operations of the intellect. By 1926 all this was fully apparent, and during the quarter of a century since, his work has undergone extraordinarily little change. This gain in self-confidence, which brought with it the release of his creative faculties, although it led with a surprising promptitude to the formation of a relatively unvarying style, has never been accompanied by a vestige of complacency. The discontent of Matthew Smith with his own work is acute and continuous. And not without reason, for an art so reckless, pursued in an age that does not possess a tradition, cannot be otherwise than uneven. It distresses him that after painting a picture resonant and beautifully expressive in colour and with a noble largeness of form, he is liable to find himself struggling with what obstinately remains no more than so much paint, with forms that no less obstinately remain insensitive, monotonous and confused. Matthew Smith is well aware of the relative facility of his orchestration of colour and the precariousness of his grasp of form and composition. Upon these he lavishes endless care, and suffers depression that lifts only when, through some providential alchemy, colour, form and composition fuse into a masterpiece.

This exasperated discontent with his own work – not so much with his drawings and preliminary studies as with the results of sustained effort – is one by which the serious artist is peculiarly afflicted. Ethel Walker is the only painter treated of in these pages to take a frank delight in her own work, and even her habit of self-praise may have sprung from a determination that others should admire it. There are modest minor artists and Sunday painters, but they are, I think, more liable, if not to the sin of pride, at any rate to the disabling error of complacency. Of this last I recall an extreme yet not uncharacteristic example. When I was Director, in the middle nineteen-thirties of the City Art Galleries in Sheffield, the members of the art club of a neighbouring city came to see, under the guidance of their President, an exhibition of contemporary painting. The President, a locally well-known Sunday painter of garish, rigid figures who fixed one with an epileptic stare, stopped in front of one of the most masterly of Steer's Cotswold landscapes. 'All I can say about this', he observed to his expectant disciples, 'is, it's not *my* method.'

Matthew Smith's prestige with critics and collectors and his hardly won fluency brought him personal difficulties and disillusions of a kind he had not earlier encountered. As a failure, he had met much neglect, but also much kindness. As a success, he inspired professional jealousy and interested friendship.

The two men to whom, perhaps, he owed most – Sickert for his encouragement, and Fry for his advocacy – were conspicuous among those whom he had to count among his enemies. The first time they met after the publication of Fry's article, Sickert was unable to conceal his resentment. The following year Matthew Smith said to Sickert: 'I've sent you a card for my show. But you needn't go; it's only complimentary.' 'You may be sure', answered Sickert, 'that my visit won't be complimentary.' After this encounter they rarely met again.

It was believed by some artists that one of the constant objects of Fry's continuous intrigues was the exaltation of Duncan Grant. In earlier days Matthew Smith had shared with certain other artists the impression that in the interests of Duncan Grant their reputations were 'played down' by Fry; then, to his surprise, there appeared the article in 'The Nation'. This was followed by an invitation on the part of Fry to join the London Artists' Association. The gratitude that Matthew Smith felt for Fry did not eradicate his earlier impression that he was a crafty politician who issued, whenever he returned from Paris, new orders, fresh variants on the party line; and he therefore declined the invitation. Fry's response was to cut him in the street.

In the meanwhile his restless habit of moving from place to place had become an established feature of his way of life. After his departure from Paris in 1926, he paid a long visit to Dieppe; in 1927 and 1928 he was in Fitzroy Street again. In 1929 – the year of his retrospective exhibition at Tooth's Gallery from 16 October to

16 November – he moved to the Grove End Road, St. John's Wood, and spent some time at Arles. From 1930 until 1932 he was in Paris, living in the Passage Noirot. During 1931, 1932 and 1933 he also lived partly in Cagnes. In 1934 he settled in Aix-en-Provence, where he remained until 1940. At Aix he was happier, and as a consequence less restless than at any time in his life. He visited Paris in 1936, living at the Villa Seurat, and in 1939 he spent Christmas in London, the first Christmas of the Second World War. From Aix he was finally driven by the ominous events of the spring of the following year that culminated at Dunkirk. He flew from Marseilles to Paris, where he found himself for the time being trapped. In Paris no telephones worked, but bad news travelled, it seemed, the faster. Eventually, on 8 June, the British Embassy was able to arrange for him to be flown to London. In England, he continued to move, with accelerated speed, from place to place. The Cumberland and the Royal Court Hotels, studios in Regent's Park and Maida Vale followed in quick succession. It was during this, for him, more than usually restless period that I first came to know him.

We used to meet, after the manner of bees who return to hover about a ruined hive, in the hideously transformed brasserie of the Café Royal, attracted by the prospect of seeing others who similarly hovered about the ochre-and-scarlet room in the raw glare of the art nouveau hanging lanterns. To me, as to most of them, the historic and oddly beautiful earlier room walled with mirrors set in slim gilt pilasters, the painted ceiling supported by ornate gilt columns, in which everything but the glass was toned by generations of tobacco smoke to the colour of a meerschaum pipe, was no more than a boy-hood memory, yet its ghost retained vestiges of magnetic power still.

I was at first surprised to observe how often Matthew Smith dined alone, and the more so when, after I had the privilege of dining with him, I discovered that this illustrious and affection-ately regarded man was often lonely. But this caused me less wonder than the effect of his society upon myself. After our first dinner together, as I walked home exhilarated by the awareness of having spent one of the most enjoyable of evenings, I tried to recollect precisely what it was that had afforded me so much pleasure. But I scrutinized the evening's impressions without reaching an adequate conclusion. The clearest impression was of a melancholy man of about sixty, very pale, wearing a grey check suit of rather formal cut, who read the menu from very near through thick-lensed spectacles, who spoke in an even voice so quiet that it seemed to come from far away, who repeated sentences to which he wished to give emphasis twice over, in precisely similar tones. The principal subject of our conversation, if my memory serves, was the problem – acute for everyone in those bomb-ravaging times, but, as I was later to discover, a constant preoccupation with Matthew Smith – of living and working accommodation. He occupied at that time a room in a large, dilapidated and not entirely reputable boarding-house in Piccadilly and a studio with a leaking roof in Maida Vale, for both of which he had formed a gnawing aversion. The studio I never visited, but one day as we were leaving his room in the house in Piccadilly there emerged like a great bat from the murk of the corridor, into which she noiselessly disappeared again, the Countess Casati wearing a triple cloak, leopard-skin gloves and a hat that framed a face in which I could discern no features but the huge dark eyes. 'Oh, hullo, hullo', whispered Matthew Smith mildly into the unresponding gloom.

'But there was a studio in Dieppe', he said with feeling, 'on which I had an option, but I gave it up to somebody else, a friend, you know, who didn't really want it, but the owner wouldn't give me another chance. I was terribly disappointed over that studio. I could have worked there. I could see my future pictures stacked there in rows. Stacked there in rows, you know.'

Often the conversation ranged more widely, but whatever its subject, I have never left Matthew Smith without the same sense of exhilaration as I experienced that first night, although later intensified with gratitude for the privilege of his friendship. The charm of his presence arises, I think, from the fact that almost any subject of conversation, or even silence, suffices to reveal the qualities of the man, the courage of a nature constitutionally timid and without a vestige of an aggressive impulse, and the active but masked benevolence, but a benevolence that does not compromise his candour. I never remember his saying a gratuitously cruel thing, nor

Q

failing to express himself with perfect frankness when occasion required it. His conversation reveals, too, another of his qualities: an extreme but entirely unassertive love of independence. He avoids all commitments which would restrict his freedom to live and to paint in accordance with the dictates of his own nature, and he would, I think, accept no honours or distinctions liable to compromise this freedom. The conduct of life, he finds, I fancy, sufficiently complicated in itself to make him wary of all needless entanglements. Earlier on I referred to my surprise at finding how often, in spite of being liable to loneliness, he dined alone. Many men, as they advance in their professions, form the habit, whether from preference or a sense of obligation, to associate with successful confrères and successful or at least established persons in general. In this they are moved by a vague sense of the appropriateness of such associations, of their value, above all, to the consolidation of their positions. From all such considerations Matthew Smith is entirely free. But he has positive reasons for avoiding associations of this kind: for he takes a spontaneous delight in eccentric characters and persons of wit and talent – above all, perhaps, in beautiful women – whatever their position or occupation. In consequence, he is bored as readily as a child by those whose 'importance' is their chief recommendation, as well as by casual companions who do not arouse his interest. He has no ambition, I think, to be the focus of attention, but I have seen him taking as much pleasure in a party at three in the morning, as he would if he were a very young man who had never been to one before. It is not surprising that he inspires the same degree of friendship as a man as he does admiration as a painter.

I have written nothing about his development since he formed his highly personal language of painting in the early nineteen-twenties, because in essentials it has varied extraordinarily little. In a detailed study there would be fluctuations of style to be recorded, and periods when nudes, faces, flowers, fruit or landscapes monopolized his interest. There is also discoverable an increasing emphasis upon bold and emphatic linear rhythms, but this emphasis is already pronounced by 1925, in, for instance, *La Femme du Cirque*.[1] If we compare, for example, *Flowers*,[2] of about 1920, the earliest example

[1] Privately owned.   [2] Temple Newsam, Leeds.
[2] The City Art Gallery, Leeds.

of his mature style known to me, with his *Blue Jug*,[1] of 1937, or his *Peaches*,[2] of about 1940, this change is evident, but it is by similarities rather than differences that we are impressed. Nor, since he evolved his mature style so slowly and in the face of so much difficulty, has he altered his technical procedure. Almost invariably he paints direct from his subject, only very rarely making use of preliminary studies. First he draws in his composition on a blank canvas in thin paint (well diluted with oil) so that it may easily be washed off. Deeply imbued with the classical idea that design is more important than colour, and aware that he has a natural sense of colour, but a sense of design cultivated by the sweat of his brow, he labours upon his composition until it satisfies him. Often he spends an anguished morning or, if need be, a whole day getting his composition right, but once he has succeeded he is able to work at great speed and the picture is soon finished.

'A picture', he explained to me, 'should be "finished" from the start. In painting the gravest immorality is to try to finish what isn't well begun. But a picture that is well begun may be left off at any point. Look at Cézanne's water-colours. . . .'

Matthew Smith does not begin a picture until he sees it in his mind's eye in its completeness.

He has not the advantage of working, like Poussin, for example, in an age in which the practice of painting is ordered by certain generally accepted rules. That nothing of importance can be achieved by the mere observance of rules, however sound, scarcely needs saying, but what is widely forgotten to-day is that by wise observance errors may be avoided. Every original work of art must be a perilous adventure, but in such anarchic times as our own it is a leap in the dark. Matthew Smith is a passionate and an instinctive painter, naturally impatient of rules and suspicious of them as tend-ing to compromise individuality; and, as already noted, his grasp of structure is fluctuating. ('His linear drawings', Paul Nash once observed, 'hardly suggest the consummate painter he is.') It is not therefore surprising that he should be the most uneven of living painters of his stature.

'He does not often hit the nail on the head', wrote an anonymous

---

[1] Privately owned.

[2] The Tate Gallery, London.

critic, 'but you should just see the wood all round' – but, I hastily add, he *does* sometimes hit it, and then you should just see. . . !

These words were written many years ago, but true though they are, the sum of the nails hit on the head with resounding blows is now considerable. These paintings, reckless and rhetorical hymns of praise to the colour and warmth and ripeness in the world, give him an assured place among the major English painters of the age.

BIOGRAPHIES

GILMAN, HAROLD, 1876–1919
Painter of interiors, portraits and landscapes. Harold John Wilder Gilman
was born on 11 February 1876, at Rode, Somerset, the second son of the
Rev. John Gilman, Rector of Snargate with Snave, Romney Marsh,
Kent, and his wife Emily Purcell, born Gulliver. They had three sons and
three daughters. After attending schools at Abingdon, Rochester and
Tonbridge he went up to Brasenose College, Oxford in 1894 where he
remained, owing to ill health, for only one year. In 1895 he went as
tutor to a family living in Odessa. A year later, having decided to become
a painter he spent 1896 at the Hastings Art School and 1897–1901 at the
Slade School where he met Spencer Gore, with the rest of whose short
life he was closely identified. Visited Spain in 1903 where he studied
Velazquez and Goya; in Spain he met an American, Grace Canedy, whom
he married. For four years they lived in England and the United States.
She, declining to settle in England and wishing him to abandon painting
for her father's business, left him, taking with her their two children.
The marriage was dissolved. Towards the end of 1906 he became an
active member of Sickert's circle in Fitzroy Street. 1910 was a crucial
year. 'Manet and the Post-Impressionists' exhibition which moved him
deeply was followed by a visit with Ginner, under whose informed and
discerning guidance he saw the room at Bernheim's entirely decorated by
Van Goghs, Péllerins, Cézannes, Durand—Ruel's Impressionists, as well
as works by Douanier Rousseau, Vuillard, Picasso and others. Visited
Norway and Sweden in 1912–13. With Gore and Ginner he formed the
'hard core' of the Camden Town Group and in 1913 was elected the first
president of the London Group. In 1914 he exhibited with Gore at the
Carfax Gallery, and the following year with Ginner (who contributed an
article to the catalogue) at the Goupil. In 1915, with Ginner and others he
showed at exhibitions organized by their friend Robert Bevan in his
rooms overlooking Cumberland Market. They became known as the
Cumberland Market Group. Gilman was unfit for military service and in
1915 taught at the Westminster School of Art. In 1917 he married Sylvia
Hardy, a former Slade student, who bore him a son. Commissioned by
the Canadian Government to make a large painting 'Halifax Harbour
after the Explosion', he accordingly went to Nova Scotia in 1918 to make
the preliminary studies. In 1919 Gilman moved to Hampstead from his
rooms at 47 Maple Street – where he had been looked after by Mrs.
Mounter, the subject of several of his finest paintings and drawings –
which Ginner took over. Ginner caught influenza, an epidemic of which
was raging over Europe, and Gilman returned to look after him. Both
caught pneumonia, of which Gilman died on 12 February, the day after
his forty-third birthday.

Memorial and retrospective exhibitions were held at the Leicester Galleries in 1919; the Tate Gallery, organized by the Arts Council, in 1955; Paintings and Drawings by Harold Gilman, with a catalogue introduction by J. Wood Palmer, was held at the Reid Gallery in 1964.

Harold Gilman: an appreciation by Wyndham Lewis and Louis J. Ferguson, was published in 1919.

GINNER, CHARLES, 1878–1952
Painter mainly of landscape, both urban and rural and occasional interiors with figures. Born 4 March 1878 in Cannes, the second surviving son of the four children of Isaac Benjamin Ginner and his wife Adeline, born Wightman. Ginner was christened Isaac Charles, but disliking Isaac he first relegated it to his second name and eventually ceased to use it. (The character of the family's names was due to his grandfather's passion for the great figures of the Old Testament.) His father, an amateur painter, established the Pharmacie Ginner. Charles attended Stanislas College; after leaving, his family being opposed to his becoming an artist, he worked briefly in an engineer's office in Cannes. When he came of age in 1899, he worked for four years in an architect's office. With the help of a relative of his mother's he entered the Académie Vitti, but owing to his teacher's dislike of him, left for the École des Beaux-Arts, but when this particular teacher retired he returned to Vitti's and was taught by the Catalan Anglada y Camarasa, whose contempt for Van Gogh, Cézanne and Gauguin, the three modern painters whom Ginner most admired, made him hardly a less unsympathetic teacher. He left Vitti's in 1908. In 1909 he joined the Allied Artists' Association and sent some paintings to their enormous exhibition at the Albert Hall, which were admired by Spencer Gore. In April he visited Buenos Aires, where he held a one-man exhibition at the Salon Costa, and sold two paintings. Ginner returned to Paris. The Allied Artists' Association was preparing to hold its third exhibition and instead of a jury, members were invited to serve on the hanging committee in alphabetical order. In 1910 it was the turn of the 'Gs' and he came over specially from Paris to serve, and on the committee were two other 'Gs', destined to be intimates and close associates. From that time onwards he made London his home, living first briefly in Chelsea before moving to Camden Town. Ginner regularly attended the meetings of the Fitzroy Street Group, took part in the formation of the Camden Town Group and was a founder member of the London Group. In 1916 he was called up, joining the Royal Ordnance Corps as a private, but in view of his perfect French he was transferred to Intelligence and stationed for a time at Marseilles. Later he worked as an artist for Canadian War Records, with the honorary rank of lieutenant. For a short time in 1919 he shared, without success, a teaching studio in Soho with Gilman. Early in 1919 Ginner caught influenza and Gilman looked after him; both developed pneumonia and were taken to the French Hospital and occu-

pied beds side by side. Gilman died but Ginner made a quick recovery. He took studios in the Camden Road and at 51 High Street, Hampstead (living in the latter from 1919–38), also living above the Étoile Restaurant and at Gilman's rooms at 47 Maple Street, Gilman having moved to Hampstead. In 1920 he became a member of the New English Art Club and an Associate of the Royal Academy in 1942. In 1950 he was awarded the C.B.E. He held an exhibition with Gilman at the Goupil Gallery in 1914 in the catalogue of which was republished his essay *Neo-Realism* which had originally appeared in *The New Age* in January of that year; he also held a one-man exhibition at the Godfrey Phillips Galleries in 1929. Ginner died on 6 January 1952, at 66 Claverton Street, Pimlico, where he had lived since 1938.

A memorial exhibition was toured by the Arts Council in 1953, and shown at the Tate Gallery in 1954, the catalogue was prefaced by an essay by Hubert Wellington, originally published in *The Listener* in January 1952, and an extract from *Neo Realism* was also republished. An exhibition of his paintings and drawings was held at the Piccadilly Gallery in 1969. Considering how ardently admired Ginner has been, extraordinarily little has been written about him. A highly informative account accompanies *Paintings and Drawings by Harold Gilman and Charles Ginner in the collection of Edward le Bas* by Fairfax Hall, 1965, but this was limited to 105 copies and priced at fifty guineas. (I tried vainly to persuade Ginner, as the only major survivor among the leaders of the Camden Town Group, to write a book about it, but after much argument he only consented to write an article for *The Studio* (November 1945). This was republished in Fairfax Hall's splendid portfolio.)

GORE, SPENCER FREDERICK, 1878–1914
Painter of music-hall scenes, landscapes, interiors with figures, still-life and occasional portraits. Born 26 May 1878 at Epsom, the third of the four children (two boys and two girls) of Spencer Walter Gore and his wife Amy, born Smith. With his brother he went to Harrow; studied at the Slade from 1896–99 under Frederick Brown, where his life-long friend Gilman was a fellow-student, as well as Augustus John, Wyndham Lewis and Albert Rutherston. Visited Madrid with Lewis in 1902 and in 1904 Dieppe with Walter Russell and Rutherston, who introduced him to Sickert. (There is a painting by Russell of Gore and Rutherston playing billiards.) In 1904 his father, a highly successful business man who had run into financial difficulties, deserted his family. Spencer Gore's uncle Bishop Gore, tried to persuade him to abandon painting and take up some profession that would enable him to maintain his mother and sisters. Gore refused, and after borrowing a modest sum from an aunt he was able to live by his art and help his family. In 1911 he married Mollie Kerr, Sickert being best man. The charm that concealed a firm purposefulness made him an active and influential figure in the London art world: from

1906 he joined Sickert, Pissarro, Gilman and Ginner; he was closely associated with the foundation of The Allied Artists' Association in 1908; a member of the New English Art Club from 1909; a founder and first president of the Camden Town Group in 1911, in which year he began to teach at The Technical Institute, Westminster and a member of the London Group in 1913. He contributed an article to *The Art News* in 1910, on 'The Third London Salon of the Allied Artists' Association'. Little of his work before 1905 survives, but the direction of his painting was from an Impressionist concentration on colour towards emphasis on construction that he shared with the Post-Impressionists. His music-hall paintings were made at the Alhambra from about 1905–1911. During the summers of 1907, 1908 and 1909 he painted at his mother's home, Garth House, Hertingfordbury; in London – in Mornington Crescent, Rowlandson House, 141 Hampstead Road (where Sickert ran his school) and 2 Houghton Place and in Richmond, where he died on 27 March 1914. An obituary tribute in *Blast* by Wyndham Lewis put Gore's paintings of the theatre above those of Degas: 'Gore gets everything that Degas with his hard and rather paltry science apparently did not see'.

Memorial exhibitions were held at the Carfax Gallery in 1916 with a catalogue introduction by Sickert, and 1918; the Paterson and Carfax Gallery in 1920; the Leicester Galleries in 1928 and an Arts Council retrospective exhibition in 1955. Others have been held at the Minories, Colchester, also shown at the Ashmolean Museum, Oxford and the Graves Art Gallery, Sheffield in 1970 and at the d'Offay Gallery in 1974, with a catalogue introduction and a memoir by John Woodeson and the artist's son Frederick Gore, respectively.

HODGKINS, FRANCES, 1869–1947
Painter chiefly of landscape, still-life and figures; for two years designer of textiles. Frances Mary Hodgkins was born on 28 April 1869 in Dunedin, New Zealand, the second daughter and third child of William Mathew Hodgkins, and his wife Rachel Owen, born Parker. Received instruction in watercolour painting from her father, a barrister and enthusiastic amateur painter who helped to found the Dunedin Art Gallery; she also attended classes at the Dunedin School of Art. From 1890 she exhibited with the Otago Art Society and elsewhere. Determined to go to Europe she raised the necessary funds by teaching the piano, selling watercolours and contributing illustrations to *The Otago Witness*. Sailed for Europe in 1901, travelling for nearly three years in England, France and Italy, as well as Morocco. On her return to Wellington, New Zealand she attempted, without success, to re-establish herself and in 1906 again left for Europe. Held her first one-woman exhibition in 1907 in London at W. B. Patterson's Gallery; settled in Paris in 1908, teaching for a year at the Atelier Colarossi, later running a small school of her own. In 1912 she visited New Zealand and Australia, holding several exhibitions. She spent

the war years in England, mainly in St. Ives, Cornwall, at 7 Porthmeor
Studios. About 1915 she made her first oil painting – having worked
previously in only watercolour or gouache – *Loveday and Ann: Two
Women with a Basket of Flowers*. From 1919 she travelled in England,
France and Spain. For two years (1925–7) she worked in Manchester as
a designer for calico printers. Painted frequently in the south of France and
Spain, also in various parts of England, including the Constable country,
staying for several months at Flatford Mill, which she also painted, together with several other Constable subjects, such as Willy Lott's Cottage.
She held a one-man exhibition at the Claridge Gallery in 1928, at the
St. George's Gallery in 1930 and a retrospective at the Lefevre Gallery in
1946. Member of the 7-and-5 Society 1929–34. Spent her last years mainly
at Corfe Castle, Dorset; she died at Dorchester on 13 May 1947.

Memorial exhibitions were held by the Isle of Purbeck Arts Club in
1948; the St. George's Gallery in 1949; at the Tate Gallery (with Ethel
Walker and Gwen John) in 1952, which was sent on a provincial tour by
the Arts Council, and a Centenary Exhibition by the Queen Elizabeth II
Arts Council of New Zealand, which was brought to the Commonwealth
Institute, London, in 1970. She has been the subject of four monographs, *Frances Hodgkins* by Myfanwy Evans, 1948; *Frances Hodgkins, Four
Vital Years* by Arthur R. Howell, 1951; *The Works of Frances Hodgkins in
New Zealand* and *The Expatriate* both by E. H. McCormick, 1954; and
of a commemorative issue of *Ascent: A Journal of the Arts of New Zealand*,
1969, published in association with the Queen Elizabeth II Arts Council,
and *The Origins of Frances Hodgkins* by the Hocken Library, University
of Otago, 1969.

JOHN, AUGUSTUS EDWIN, 1878–1961
Painter mainly of portraits but also of large figure compositions, landscapes and flowers, draughtsman and etcher. Often indebted to the Old
Masters, most notably Rembrandt and El Greco; from about 1910 he was
influenced for a few years by the bright colours and simplified forms of
the Post-Impressionists. Born 4 January 1878 at Belgrave House, Tenby,
Pembrokeshire, the third of the four children of Edwin William John, a
solicitor, and his wife Augusta, born Smith, of a Brighton family. Studied
at the Slade School 1894–98, where his rare ability as a draughtsman
attracted widespread admiration; won a Scholarship in 1896 and the
Summer Composition Prize in 1898. First visited Paris in 1900, and
exhibited at the New English Art Club of which he became a member in
1903, where he also held his first one-man exhibition at the Carfax
Gallery. Professor of Painting, Liverpool University 1901–1904. Painted
much in Ireland, also in Wales where he camped with gypsies; several of
his visits in 1911–14 were made with J. D. Innes and Derwent Lees.
Travelled widely in Europe and paid several visits to Jamaica. His work
was frequently exhibited; retrospective exhibitions included one consist-

ing of his drawings at the National Gallery in 1940; of paintings and drawings at Temple Newsam, Leeds in 1946; the Leicester Galleries in 1948; Welsh National Eisteddfod and Welsh and English Tour (organized by the Arts Council) in 1948–49; Scott & Fowles, New York in 1949; Royal Academy in 1954; Graves Art Gallery, Sheffield in 1956. Associate of the Royal Academy 1921; Academician 1928; resigned 1938; re-elected 1940. Trustee of the Tate Gallery 1933–40. President of the Gypsy Lore Society 1937. Awarded the Order of Merit 1942. *Chiaroscuro, Fragments of Autobiography* was published in 1952, and *Fifty-Two Drawings* with a note by the artist and an Introduction by Lord David Cecil, in 1957. Died 31 October 1961 at his home in Fordingbridge, Hampshire.

A Memorial exhibition was organized by the Dalhousie Art Gallery for the extension services of the National Gallery of Canada, 1973–74. Two retrospective exhibitions were to be held at the National Portrait Gallery in 1975. A second part of his autobiography *Finishing Touches* edited by Daniel George, was published in 1964. A number of books about him have been published including: *Augustus John* by A(nthony) B(ertram), 1923; *Augustus John* by T. W. Earp, undated, c. 1931; *Augustus John: Drawings* edited by Lillian Browse, with a 'note on drawing' by the artist and a preface by T. W. Earp, 1941; *Augustus John* by John Rothenstein, 1944; *Portraits of the Artist's Family* by Malcolm Easton, 1970; *Augustus John I: Years of Innocence*, 1974 and *Augustus John II: Years of Experience* (with a bibliography) by Michael Holroyd, 1975; *The Art of Augustus John* (with a chronology and lists of works exhibited at the New English & Royal Academy) by Malcolm Easton and Michael Holroyd, 1974.

JOHN, GWEN, 1876–1939

Painter, chiefly of portraits, studies of single figures of women, children and, occasionally, cats. Gwendolen Mary John was born on 22 June 1876 at 7 Victoria Terrace, Haverfordwest, Pembrokeshire, the second of the four children of Edwin William John, a solicitor, and his wife Augusta, born Smith, of a Brighton family. The family later moved to Tenby, living for a time at 5 Lexden Terrace, where she and her brother Augustus used to draw and paint in an attic. Studied at the Slade School 1894–7 and with Whistler in Paris where she made her home, though paying occasional visits to England. From about 1906 she became an intimate friend of Rodin, settling, in about 1914, at Meudon. Among other close friends were Rainer Maria Rilke and Jacques Maritain. Received into the Catholic Church in 1913. Exhibited at the New English Art Club from 1913; with Augustus John at the Carfax Gallery in 1903; at the Goupil Gallery and the Société des Artistes Français in 1920; held her first one-woman exhibition at the Chenil Gallery in 1926. Died in Dieppe 13 September 1939.

Her work remained little known until the Memorial Exhibition in 1946 at the Matthiesen Gallery – with an introduction to the catalogue by her brother Augustus – where a second was held in 1961. A memorial exhibition with Ethel Walker and Frances Hodgkins was held at the Tate Gallery in 1952. A retrospective exhibition, organized by the Arts Council, was shown in London, Sheffield and The National Museum of Wales in 1968, by Davis and Long, New York, in 1970 and by Anthony d'Offay in 1976.

McEVOY, AMBROSE, 1878–1927

Painter of portraits, interiors with figures and landscapes Arthur Ambrose McEvoy was born on 12 August 1878 at Crudwell, Wiltshire, the elder son (the younger was the playwright Charles) of Captain Charles Ambrose McEvoy and his wife Jane Mary. Captain McEvoy was believed to have been a West Countryman of Irish heritage, who was in North America when the War between the States broke out, served with the Army of the Confederacy and was wounded at the Battle of Bull Run, then becoming an authority on submarine construction. Dr. Whistler, brother of the artist, tended his wound and the two families became friends. Captain McEvoy returned to Britain, settling in Crudwell but moving, in 1879, to London. Both his father and James McNeill Whistler encouraged Ambrose to become a painter and at the age of fifteen he went to the Slade School, where he studied under Fred Brown for three years. Among his fellow students was Augustus John with whom he used to spend painting holidays in Wales. In 1901 he married Mary Spencer Edwards who had been a fellow student at the Slade. They had a son and daughter. He made copies of paintings by Titian, Velazquez, Rembrandt, Hogarth and Gainsborough, spending a week on each; he later worked with Sickert in Neuville in 1909 and studied etching with him the following year in London. He began to achieve success in about 1914, his *Madame* (Mrs McEvoy) being widely admired and bought for the Luxembourg. Served for three months as a War Artist on the western front before being attached to The Royal Naval Division 1916–18, mainly with the Fleet in the North Sea, making portraits of Naval officers which are now in the Imperial War Museum. A member of the New English Art Club in 1902; and held one-man exhibitions at the Carfax Gallery in 1907, at the Duveen Gallerie, New York in 1926, of watercolours at the Leicester Galleries in 1927; he also exhibited at the Grosvenor and Grafton Galleries. *Anna* (his daughter) painted in 1926 was his last work. He died from pneumonia on 4 January 1927 in his house at 107 Grosvenor Road, which had been his home since 1906.

A memorial exhibition of his work (with that of Orpen and Ricketts) was held in Manchester in 1933; others were held at the Ulster Museum, Belfast in 1968 which was toured by the Arts Council, at the Chelsea Arts Club in 1971 and a retrospective at Morley College, London in 1971. Claude Johnson edited *The Works of Ambrose McEvoy from 1900 to May 1919*, 1919 and *Ambrose McEvoy* by R(eginald)G(leadowe), was published in 1924.

NICHOLSON, Sir William, 1872–1949
Painter of still-life, landscape and portraits, engraver and designer for the theatre. William Newzam Prior Nicholson was born on 5 February 1872 at Newark-on-Trent, the youngest child of William Newzam Nicholson, and engineer and later M.P. for Newark, and his wife Annie Elizabeth, born Prior. Attended the Magnus School, Newark, where his drawing-master had been a pupil of Sir William Beechey. Studied art at Herko-mer's School at Bushey 1888–89 – where among the fellow students whom he came to know were Mabel Pryde, destined to become his wife and James, her brother, for some years his partner – and at the Academie Julian, Paris 1889–90; also in London and Newark. Academic instruction, however, helped him little in comparison with his intensive study of Velazquez; he also learnt much from Manet and Whistler. In 1893 he married Mabel Pryde and at about the same time with James Pryde, designed posters, under the pseudonym 'J. & W. Beggarstaff' until 1899. Encouraged by Whistler, who in 1896 recommended him to Heinemann the publisher, for whom he made woodcut illustrations in colour for books, including *An Alphabet; An Almanac of Twelve Sports*; *London Types*, all in 1898; *Characters of Romance*, 1900; *Clever Bill*, 1926; *The Pirate Twins*, 1929; *The Book of Blokes*, 1930 and a book of the buildings of Oxford. For the first two, Rudyard Kipling and W. E. Henley, respec-tively, wrote verses. For his woodcuts he was awarded a gold medal at the Paris Exposition Universelle in 1900. At the invitation of James Barrie he designed, in 1904, the costumes for the first production of *Peter Pan* and later for several other plays. By the beginning of the new century, again with the encouragement of Whistler, Nicholson resumed painting, which for several years he had practised little, showing at the International Society in 1898 an oil painted in collaboration with Pryde; in 1899 two oils of his own and in 1901, five. Visited the United States in 1901 and 1921, India in 1915–16 and South Africa in 1931. Married Edith, daughter of Sir Lionel Phillips in 1919. Held his first one-man exhibition at the W. B. Patterson Gallery in 1906 and others regularly at various other galleries, including the retrospectives, at the Museum and Art Gallery, Nottingham, the Beaux-Arts Gallery, London in 1933; the City Museum and Art Gallery, Belfast in 1934; the National Gallery (with Jack Yeats) in 1942. Knighted 1936. A trustee of the Tate Gallery 1934–39. Died 16 May 1949 at Blewbury, Berkshire.

He is the subject of four books, *William Nicholson* by S. K(ennedy) N(orth), 1923; *William Nicholson* by Marguerite Steen, 1943; *William Nicholson* by Robert Nichols, 1948 and *William Nicholson* by Lillian Browse, 1956.

ORPEN, Sir William, 1878–1931
Painter of portraits and genre. Born 27 November 1878 at Stillorgan, County Dublin, William Newenham Montague Orpen was the fourth

and youngest son of Arthur Herbert Orpen, a Dublin solicitor and Anne, eldest daughter of Charles Caulfield, Bishop of Nassau. At the pheno-menal age of eleven – such was his precocious talent as a draughtsman – he entered the Metropolitan School of Art, Dublin, going on six years, later, to the Slade, where he remained from 1897–9, winning the Summer Prize with his *Play Scene from Hamlet*, one of his finest paintings. Briefly ran a teaching studio in Chelsea with Augustus John. In 1901 he married Grace, the third daughter and youngest of the four children of Walter John Knewstub, painter, friend and assistant to Rossetti. Member of the New English Art Club 1900; Associate of the Royal Hibernian Academy 1904; Member 1908–15; Associate, Royal Academy 1910; Member 1919, and of other art societies. Held a one-man exhibition of drawings at the Goupil Gallery in 1912. Although he had settled in London in 1897, he retained his affection for Ireland and visited Dublin to take life-classes at the Metropolitan Art School. From 1917–19 he served as an Official War Artist in France, as a Major in The Royal Army Service Corps and at the Peace Conference at Versailles. After showing his war pictures at Agnew's in 1918 he presented them to the nation; they were allocated to the Imperial War Museum. Knighted 1918. Wrote *An Onlooker in France 1917–19*, 1921; *Stories of Old Ireland and Myself*, 1924; edited *The Outline of Art*, 1923 – a work in which, I understand he played little part. He suffered a serious illness during the war at Amiens in 1918, which permanently affected his health. He died on 29 September 1931 in London.

Memorial Exhibitions were held at the Royal Academy (late Members), Birmingham, and with McEvoy and Ricketts in Manchester, all in 1933, and Paintings, Watercolours and Drawings, at the Rye Art Gallery in 1968. He is the subject of two monographs, *Sir William Orpen* by R. P(ickle), 1923 and *Sir William Orpen Artist and Man* (with a chronological list of paintings) by P. G. Konody and Sidney Dark, 1952.

PISSARRO, LUCIEN, 1863–1944
Landscape painter, wood engraver, designer and printer of fine books; an important link between French Impressionism and British painting. Born 20 February 1863 in Paris, the eldest of the seven children of Jacob, known as Camille, Pissarro and Julie Vellay; father of the painter Orovida Pissarro (1893–1968). Studied under his father; also influenced by Seurat. Exhibited at the last Impressionist Exhibition 1886, and at the Salon des Independants 1886–94. Attended Van Gogh's funeral in 1890. Commis-sioned to make woodcut illustrations for *La Revue Illustrée* 1886. Visited England in 1870 and 1883–84, settling in London in 1890, becoming a British subject in 1916; but he used to call himself a 'Channel painter', continuing to visit the south of France from 1922. Introduced by the poet John Gray to Ricketts and Shannon shortly after his establishment in London, he contributed to *The Dial* – an occasional magazine which

they produced – and published in 1890 a portfolio of twelve of his woodcuts. Moved to Epping in 1893, following his marriage to Esther L. Bensusan the previous year. In 1896 he established, with Esther, the Eragny Press (named after his former home near Gisors) and two years afterwards they began to print books with his own illustrations, some sixteen in all; the earlier were printed in Ricketts' 'Vale' type until 1904 when the Vale Press was closed; the later were in his own 'Brook' type (named after 'the Brook', Stamford Brook, Hammersmith, where he moved in 1902 from 62 Bath Road, Chiswick), in which he published a further sixteen books before the Eragny Press closed in 1914. Exhibited with the New English Art Club from 1904; associated with the Fitzroy Street group, whose members, notably Gore, learnt much from Pissarro's expositions of the theories of his father and of Seurat, especially in relation to the use of pure colour. He was widely travelled in both England and France. Was a founder member of the Camden Town Group 1911. He held his first one-man exhibition at the Carfax Gallery in 1913; retrospective exhibitions at the Hampstead Art Gallery in 1920; at the City Art Galleries, Manchester and Blackpool in 1935; represented in 'Three Generations of Pissarro' at Miller's, Lewes in 1943. Died 10 July 1944 at Heywood, Chard, Somerset, where he had lived since 1940.

A centenary exhibition of paintings, watercolours, drawings and graphic work was organized by the Arts Council and toured in 1963, and 'Three Generations of the Pissarro Family' was held at the Leicester Galleries in 1973.

Pissarro's *Notes on the Eragny Press* edited by Alan Fern, was privately printed in 1957, and a biography, *Lucien Pissarro, un coeur simple* by W. S. Meadmore, with an introduction by John Rewald, was published in 1962.

PRYDE, JAMES, 1866–1941
Painter of architectural fantasies and interiors; also lithographer and designer of posters. James Ferrier Pryde was born 30 March 1866 in Edinburgh at 23 London Street, the family moving in 1870 first to 10 then to 22 Fettes Row. He was the only son among the six children of David Pryde, headmaster of Edinburgh Ladies' College, and his wife Barbara, born Lander. From her he no doubt inherited his artistic sense, she being the niece of the painters R. S. and J. E. Lauder, and from his father, a historian, his response to the sombre, romantic aura of old Edinburgh, characterized by the houses in Fettes Row – tall, dimly lit, high ceilinged; also by nearby Holyrood. With both parents he shared a lasting interest in the theatre. After leaving George Watson's Boys' College he studied at the Royal Scottish Academy School 1886–7. At the age of twenty-one he moved into a studio at 4 Charlotte Place, and studied for three months in Paris under Bouguereau at the Académie Julian. After a brief visit to his native city he settled, in 1890, permanently in London where he led a bohemian life. Shared lodgings with his sister Mabel, with whom he

attended Herkomer's school at Bushey; William Nicholson (whom she married in 1893) was a fellow student, with whom Pryde produced, 1894–99, posters under the pseudonym 'J. & W. Beggarstaff' at Nicholson's home at Denham. Pryde also made, without much effect, occasional appearances on the stage, touring Scotland acting small parts with Gordon Craign. In 1899 he married Marian, daughter of George Symons, of Silverton, Devon. They separated in 1914, after having a daughter who died young. Made a number of lithographs, including a series entitled *Celebrated Criminals*. It was not until around 1905 that Pryde began to express the emotions generated by his early impressions of the sombre yet shabby grandeur of the architecture of the part of Edinburgh in which he was brought up, exemplified by *The Doctor* 1908, at the Tate Gallery, and *The Slum* 1910, at the Musée National d'Art Moderne, Paris. *The Doctor* is the first of a series entitled *The Human Comedy* which occupied a large part of Pryde's working life: like *The Doctor* the others are dominated by his early memories of the four-poster bed of Mary Queen of Scots at Holyrood. The last of the series, *The Grave* No. 9, c. 1924, is also his last major work. It is also at the Tate. From 1912 he carried out several large decorative paintings at Dunecht, Aberdeenshire, for Viscountess Cowdray, an important patron. From about 1925 his creative energies languished and his production, never large, declined both in quality and quantity, and during the last decade of his life he produced very little. In 1930, however, he designed the scenery and costumes for Paul Robeson's *Othello*. From 1914 he worked in a studio lent to him by another important patron, Sir Edmund Davis (who from 1910 to 1913 owned *The Doctor*), in Lansdowne House, Holland Park. Pryde's first one-man exhibition was held at the Baillie Gallery, Edinburgh. From 1901 he was an Associate of the International Society, becoming its Vice-president in 1910. A retrospective exhibition was held at the Leicester Galleries in 1933. He died on 24 February 1941 in St. Mary Abbott's Hospital, Kensington.

The Arts Council held a memorial exhibition in 1949, which was shown in Edinburgh, Brighton and at the Tate Gallery. A biography, *James Pryde* by Derek Hudson, was published in 1949; this contains an autobiographical fragment.

ROTHENSTEIN, SIR WILLIAM, 1872–1945
Painter, portrait draughtsman, writer and teacher. In his paintings he 'sought to combine austerity of design and unflinching research into drawing with radiance of tone': Allan Gwynne-Jones, *Portrait Painters* 1950, p. 33. Born 29 January 1872 in Bradford, Yorkshire, the second son and fifth of the six children of Moritz Rothenstein and his wife Bertha, born Dux. After leaving Bradford Grammar School he studied at the Slade under Legros 1888 and 1889–93 and the Académie Julian, Paris, under Doucet and Lefebvre. In 1891 he held with Conder his first exhibition, arranged by Toulouse-Lautrec, at the Galerie Thomas;

encouraged by Degas and Pissarro. Friendship with Whistler; exhibited at
Salon du Champ de Mars 1892. Visited Spain (as a result writing the
first English book on Goya) and Morocco; went to Oxford to begin the
first of his thirteen books of reproductions of portraits:*Oxford Characters*,
1893–1896. Settled, in 1893, in Chelsea; Member of the New English
Art Club 1894; contributed to *The Yellow Book* (volume I) 1894. In 1899
he married Alice Mary, the eldest daughter of Walter John Knewstub,
pupil and assistant of Rossetti's. First of a number of one-man exhibitions
was held at the Carfax Gallery, 1900; others at the Venice Biennale, 1930
and a retrospective at the Leicester Galleries, 1938. Visited Italy 1905;
India 1910; the United States 1912, holding exhibitions in New York,
Boston and Chicago; settled in Gloucestershire 1912. Official artist to
British and Canadian Armies in France and on the Rhine 1917-18.
Principal of the Royal College of Art 1920-35. Painted *The Arrival of
Sir Thomas Roe in India* in St. Stephen's Hall, Houses of Parliament
1926-28. Knighted 1931. Hon. D.Lit., Oxford 1934. Attached to R.A.F.
1939–41. Died at Far Oakridge, Gloucestersire on 14 February 1945.

A memorial exhibition was held at the Tate Gallery in 1950, the
catalogue included an Appreciation by Augustus John and Biographical
and Critical Notes by John Piper; a retrospective at the City Art Gallery,
Gloucester in 1966, and a centenary exhibition at the City Art Gallery,
Bradford in 1972, the catalogue with a chronology, a list of publications
by the artist and selected critical opinions.

Among Rothenstein's various publications are *Men and Memories*,
1931–1932 and *Since Fifty*, 1939. A monograph was included in *Contemporary British Artists* by H(ubert) W(ellington), 1923 and a biography
by Robert Speaight was published in 1969. *Imperfect Encounter: Letters
of William Rothenstein and Rabindranath Tagore* 1911–1941, published in
1972 and *Max and Will: Max Beerbohm and William Rothenstein, Their
Friendship and Letters*, 1893–1945, published in 1975, were both edited by
Mary M. Lago and Karl Beckson.

SICKERT, WALTER RICHARD, 1860–1942

Painter of figure compositions, urban landscapes, etcher and teacher.
Born in Munich on 31 May 1860, the eldest of the six children of Oswald
Adalbert Sickert, painter and illustrator of Danish descent, and Elinor,
daughter of Richard Sheepshanks, the astronomer, who had married in
Harrow in 1859. They returned to Munich but in 1868 the family settled
in England. Walter attended a boarding school at Reading, University
College School c. 1870–1, Bayswater Collegiate School and in 1875 went
to King's College School. Worked as an actor under the pseudonym Mr
Nemo 1877–81. Met Whistler in 1879 and paid the first of his many
visits to Dieppe. Studied painting at the Slade School 1881–2, leaving to
become Whistler's pupil and assistant. Entrusted by Whistler to take his
Portrait of my Mother to Paris for exhibition at the Salon, with intro-

ductions to Degas and Manet; the former became a friend and predominant influence, the latter was too ill to see him. In 1885 he married Ellen Millicent Cobden (by whom he was divorced in 1899), daughter of Richard Cobden M.P. The following year he held his first one-man exhibitions at Dowdeswell's Gallery. Joined the New English Art Club in 1888, from which he resigned finally in 1917. Contributed to *The Yellow Book* 1894–95. Between 1894 and 1905 (when he returned permanently to London) he lived mainly in Dieppe and Venice. One-man exhibitions at Durand-Ruél, Paris, 1900 and 1904, and at Bernheim-Jeune, Paris, 1904, 1907 and 1909. In the former year he joined the Fitzroy Street Group, an informal association with frequently changing membership. Walter Russell, Harold Gilman, William and Albert Rothenstein and Sickert himself were the original members. In 1908 he supported the foundation and exhibited with the Allied Artists' Association; likewise, in 1911, the Camden Town Group, which consisted of a number of the male frequenters of the Fitzroy Street gatherings, including Gore, Ginner and Gilman, which held its first exhibition at the Carfax Gallery. In the same year he married Christine Angus who died in 1920. Joined the London Group in 1916 showing with it from time to time until 1934, resigning in 1936; Associate of the Royal Academy in 1924, Academician 1934 resigning the following year. In 1926 he married Therese Lessore. Between 1893 and 1927 he held private classes from time to time, and c. 1908–18 at the Westminster Technical Institute. During the war he took studios at Red Lion Square, first at 24, then at 26. Awarded an Hon. LL.D by Manchester University in 1932 and a D.Litt from the University of Reading in 1938. Of his many exhibitions the last and most representative, consisting of 132 paintings and drawings, was held at the National Gallery in 1941. In 1934 settled in Hautville, St. Peter's in Thanet, Kent, moving in 1938 to St. George's Hill House, Bathampton, near Bath, where he died on 22 January 1942, his wife surviving him for three years.

Since his death some twenty-eight exhibitions of his work have been held: in the United States, Australia and France as well as, of course, in Britain. the first was in 1942 at Temple Newsam, Leeds; the most wideranging was that organized by the Arts Council in 1960 and shown at the Tate Gallery, at Southampton and Bradford; the most recent was at the Fine Art Society in 1973 in London and Edinburgh, with an exceptionally useful catalogue.

The literature about Sickert is considerable. Among the monographs entitled to special mention are two by Lillian Browse, 1943 and 1960; *The Life and Opinions of Walter Richard Sickert* by Robert Emmons, 1941; A handbook to the Sickertiana in the Islington Public Libraries, edited by C. A. Elliott; *A Free House: or The Artist as Craftsman being the Writings of Walter Richard Sickert* edited by Osbert Sitwell, 1947, and *Sickert* by Wendy Baron, a highly informative work, including a list of exhibitions and an extensive bibliography, 1973.

SMITH, Sir Matthew, 1879–1957
Painter of nudes, still-life and landscape. The sharp oppositions of colour
in his early manner gave place to richer, more varied harmonies, while the
forms became freer and more opulent. Matthew Arnold Bracy Smith was
born in Halifax, Yorkshire on 22 October 1879, second of the three sons
of Frederic Smith, a steel wire manufacturer who was a strict Non-
conformist attending chapel twice every Sunday, and his wife Frances,
born Holroyd. Attended a private school, Halifax Grammar School and
Giggleswick School. After leaving Giggleswick he was put to work in a
woollen firm in Bradford, and briefly, after the family moved to Manchester, in the copper wire factory that his father had established there.
In both he proved himself a failure. After a struggle of wills with his father
he was allowed, in 1900, to attend the Manchester School of Art, where
however, his father insisted that he should study only applied design and
gave instructions to the principal that Matthew should not be allowed near
any classroom where women were posing in the nude. After four years
study in Manchester he spent two years, 1905–7, at the Slade School.
Owing primarily to his unhappiness at both schools he became ill. When
his doctor recommended a holiday abroad, it was agreed that he should
visit France provided he kept away from Paris. In 1908 he settled in Pont-
Aven, Britanny. In 1909 he went to Dieppe, and on to Etaples, and at·
last, in 1910, to the forbidden city. There he remained for two years,
attending Matisse's school just before it closed. In 1911 and 1912 he
exhibited at the Salon des Indépendants. In 1912, when he returned to
England, he married Gwen Salmond (daughter of General Sir W.
Salmond) whom he had known at the Slade where she, Ida Nettleship
and Gwen John – the first shortly to be married to Augustus John, the
second his sister – were the school's three outstanding women students.
Matthew and Gwen spent much time in France during the first two years
of their marriage, returning to England in 1914, he taking an attic studio
at 2 Fitzroy Street where he painted Lilies, his first work to be exhibited in
England – at the London Group in 1916. In the meanwhile he enlisted in
the Artists' Rifles, serving in the Army from 1916 until 1919, being wounded in 1918. Lived 1920–38 mainly in Aix-en-Provence, also working in
Cornwall, London and briefly in Scotland. A member of the London
Group in 1920; he held his first one-man exhibition at the Mayor Gallery
in 1926 and a retrospective at Arthur Tooth's in 1929. In 1946 he revisited
Aix, but the larger part of his later years were spent in London, where he
frequently changed studios. Exhibitions of his work were held at the
Venice Biennale in 1938 and 1960, at Temple Newsam, Leeds in 1942 and
at the Tate Gallery in 1953. Awarded a C.B.E. in 1953, a knighthood in
1954 and in 1956 an Hon. D.Lit, by the University of London. He died
in London on 29 September 1957. A memorial exhibition at the Royal
Academy was held in 1960; Matthew Smith, arranged by the Welsh
Committee of the Arts Council, toured in Wales, in 1966; Matthew

Smith: a loan exhibition Paintings from 1920–1950 was held at the Waddington Galleries in 1968; a touring exhibition of Paintings from the Artist's studio was organized by the Arts Council in 1972.

He is the subject of four monographs: *Matthew Smith* by Philip Hendy, in 1944; *Matthew Smith* by Philip Hendy, Francis Halliday and John Russell and *Matthew Smith* by John Rothenstein, both in 1962.

STEER, PHILIP WILSON, 1860–1942
Painter of landscape, figures and occasionally of portraits; a leading figure in the English Impressionist movement. Born at 39 Grange Mount, Birkenhead on 28 December 1860, the second son and third child of Philip Steer, portrait and landscape painter and teacher, and his wife Emma, daughter of the Rev. William Harrison, Perpetual Curate of Woore, Shropshire. In 1864 the family moved to The Grange (later renamed Apsley House) at Whitchurch, Shropshire. Steer was educated at home, later attending a preparatory school at Whitchurch and Hereford Cathedral School 1875–7, then under a private tutor. Although he always drew and painted he took a course in 1878 to prepare him for entry to the British Museum, but finding it tedious he attended instead the Gloucester School of Art, studying under John Kemp 1878–80. After an unsuccessful application to enter the Royal Academy School he went to Paris and studied at The Académie Julian under Bouguereau 1882–3 and at the École des Beaux-Arts under Cabanel, 1883–4. Influenced first by Whistler, briefly by the French Impressionists, but by the turn of the century he had evolved a style which placed him in the English tradition – a successor of Gainsborough, Turner but most conspicuously of Constable. In summer he painted in the west country – the Severn Valley and its environs was a region in which he particularly delighted – in Yorkshire, on the east and south coasts, Dorset, and elsewhere, e.g. Walberswick, Richmond (Yorkshire and Surrey), Knaresborough, Ludlow, Dover, Malden, Bridgnorth, and in 1907 he made an expedition to France painting in Montreuil and visiting Paris. In 1886 he became a foundation member of the New English Art Club, where he continued to exhibit regularly. In winter, disliking cold, he painted indoors – interiors, figures and a few portraits. During the last fifteen years of his working life he turned largely to watercolours. He lived almost all his adult life in Chelsea, first in Manresa Road, then after an interlude in Addison Road he moved, in 1898, to 109 Cheyne Walk, where he lived for the rest of his life. He held his first one-man exhibition at the Goupil Gallery in 1894; others were held at the Carfax Gallery, in 1902, 1909 and 1924; at Barbizon House in 1934, 1935, 1937 and 1939, and a retrospective at the Tate Gallery in 1929. Taught painting once a week at the Slade School c. 1893–1930. After 1935, as a result of failing sight he was scarcely able to work, apart from making a few watercolours between 1935 and 1938. Awarded O.M. 1931. Died of bronchitis at his house in Chelsea on 21 March 1942.

Memorial exhibitions were held at the National Gallery (organized by the Tate Gallery) in 1943; Temple Newsam, Leeds, in 1944; the Birkenhead Art Gallery in 1951; the Tate Gallery (organized by the Arts Council) in 1960 and the Fine Art Society in 1968.

Three informative books have been published: *Wilson Steer* by Robin Ironside, in 1943; *Philip Wilson Steer: Life, Work and Setting* by D. S. MacColl, in 1945, and *Philip Wilson Steer 1860–1942* (with a chronological list of paintings and an extensive bibliography) by Bruce Laughton, in 1971. There are forty-seven of his sketchbooks (forty-five presented in 1945 by his legatees) in the Victoria and Albert Museum.

TONKS, Henry, 1862–1937

Draughtsman and painter of figure subjects, often interiors, caricatures; teacher. Born 9 April 1862 at Solihull, Warwickshire, the second son and fifth of the eleven children of Edmund Tonks, brass-founder, and his wife Julia, born Johnson, After leaving Clifton College he studied medicine at the Royal Sussex County Hospital, Brighton in 1880 and at the London Hospital in 1881; F.R.C.S. 1888; he was later Senior Medical Officer, Royal Free Hospital. By about 1890 his interest in art had become dominant and he studied at the Westminster School of Art under Fred Brown. Finally gave up medicine when, in 1893, Brown became Slade Professor and Tonks accepted his invitation to be his assistant teacher. On Brown's retirement in 1917 he succeeded him, remaining Slade Professor until 1930. A teacher of outstanding talent, though of militantly traditional opinions, violently opposed to Cubism, Futurism, Abstraction and other emerging movements. A member of the New English Art Club from 1895. Practised plastic surgery during 1914–18 war and in 1919 he visited Archangel as an official war artist. An exhibition of his work was held at the Tate Gallery in 1936. Died 8 January 1937.

The Life of Henry Tonks by Joseph Hone, was published in 1939.

WALKER, Ethel, 1861–1951

Painter of portraits – mostly of women and girls – flower-pieces, sea-pieces, decorative compositions and occasional sculptor. Influenced by Valazquez, Impressionism, Puvis de Chavannes, Gauguin and Oriental art. Born in Edinburgh, 9 June 1861, daughter of Arthur Abney Walker and his second wife Isabella, born Robertson. Arthur Walker, a Yorkshireman, was a member of the firm of iron founders who built Southwark Bridge. Around 1870 the family settled in Wimbledon, where Ethel attended a private school. Showed no interest in art until her late twenties when she attended the Ridley School of Art and, about 1893, the Putney School of Art. Visited Madrid in 1884 and copied Velazquez, who, she used to say, 'made me a painter'. On her way back through Paris she saw the Manet exhibition held that year, and met George Moore, who showed her the Impressionists. Ethel Walker·and her travelling companion Claire Christian figure in his *Hail and Farewell* as 'Florence' and 'Stella'. She was widely read and deeply interested in theosophy and the religious doctrines of Swedenborg and the East, which she believed affected her big visionary decorations such as *The Zone of Love* and *The Zone of Hate* (of c. 1914–15 and 1930–2, which she presented to the Tate Gallery in 1946). Studied for three months under Fred Brown at the Westminster School of Art and followed him to the Slade School when, in 1892, he succeeded Legros as Professor. After two years there she attended Sickert's and other evening classes, but resumed her studies at the Slade 1912–13, 1916–19 and 1921–2, in the meanwhile studying sculpture under James Havard Thomas. Exhibited at the Royal Academy from 1898; a member of the New English Art Club 1900 and of the 7-and-5 in 1929. First one-woman exhibition at the Redfern Gallery 1927; others were held at Wildenstein's in 1936, at The Lefevre Galleries in 1939 and 1942 and at Agnews in 1947. C.B.E. 1938; D.B.E. 1948. Worked mainly in London and Robin Hood's Bay, Yorkshire, where she owned a fisherman's cottage, The White Gate, overlooking the sea. Some time before her death – on 2 March 1951, at her studio at 127 Cheyne Walk, Chelsea – she had ceased to paint and had given away her brushes.

A memorial exhibition of her work, together with that of Gwen John and Frances Hodgkins, was held at the Tate Gallery in 1952 and toured by the Arts Council; the section on Ethel Walker, which had a catalogue with an Introduction by T. W. Earp, was toured separately. An exhibition was held at the Courtauld Institute Galleries in 1973, and in 1974, at Roland, Browse and Delbanco: 'Distinguished British Paintings 1875–1950 an Accent on Ethel Walker'.

INDEX

Page references in bold type refer to the sections of the book dealing with that particular artist.